# THE ARAB–ISRAELI CONFLICT

## THIRD EDITION

# STUDIES IN CONTEMPORARY HISTORY

Series Editors: T. G. Fraser and J. O. Springhall

PUBLISHED

THE ARAB–ISRAELI CONFLICT (third edition)
*T. G. Fraser*

AMERICA AND THE WORLD SINCE 1945
*T. G. Fraser and Donette Murray*

THE ULSTER QUESTION SINCE 1945 (second edition)
*James Loughlin*

GERMANY SINCE 1945
*Pól O'Dochartaigh*

THE RISE AND FALL OF THE SOVIET EMPIRE
(second edition)
*Raymond Pearson*

THE CIVIL RIGHTS MOVEMENT: Struggle and Resistance
(second edition)
*William T. Martin Riches*

THE UNITED NATIONS AND INTERNATIONAL POLITICS
*Stephen Ryan*

JAPAN SINCE 1945
*Dennis B. Smith*

DECOLONIZATION SINCE 1945
*John Springhall*

---

**Studies in Contemporary History**
**Series Standing Order**
**ISBN 0–333–71706–6 hardback**
**ISBN 0–333–69351–5 paperback**
(*outside North America only*)

You can receive future titles in this series as they are published by placing a standing order. Please contact your bookseller or, in the case of difficulty, write to us at the address below with your name and address, the title of the series and an ISBN quoted above.

Customer Services Department, Macmillan Distribution Ltd
Houndmills, Basingstoke, Hampshire RG21 6XS, England

---

# The Arab–Israeli Conflict

## Third edition

T. G. Fraser

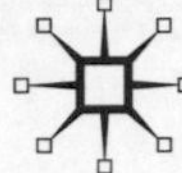



First edition 1995
Second edition 2004
Third edition 2008

Published by
PALGRAVE MACMILLAN
Houndmills, Basingstoke, Hampshire RG21 6XS and
175 Fifth Avenue, New York, NY 10010
Companies and representatives throughout the world

PALGRAVE MACMILLAN is the global academic imprint of the Palgrave Macmillan division of St. Martin's Press, LLC and of Palgrave Macmillan Ltd. Macmillan® is a registered trademark in the United States, United Kingdom and other countries. Palgrave is a registered trademark in the European Union and other countries.

ISBN-13: 978–0–230–00468–9 hardback
ISBN-10: 0–230–00468–7 hardback
ISBN-13: 978–0–230–00469–6 paperback
ISBN-10: 0–230–00469–5 paperback

This book is printed on paper suitable for recycling and made from fully managed and sustained forest sources. Logging, pulping and manufacturing processes are expected to conform to the environmental regulations of the country of origin.

A catalogue record for this book is available from the British Library.

A catalog record for this book is available from the Library of Congress .

10 9 8 7 6 5 4 3 2 1
17 16 15 14 13 12 11 10 09 08

Printed and bound in China

For Grace

# Contents

# SERIES EDITORS' PREFACE

There are those, politicians among them, who feel that historians should not teach or write about contemporary events and people – many of whom are still living – because of the difficulty of treating such matters with historical perspective, that it is right to draw some distinction between the study of history and the study of current affairs. Proponents of this view seem to be unaware of the concept of contemporary history to which this series is devoted, that the history of the recent past can and should be written with a degree of objectivity. As memories of the Second World War recede, it is surely time to place in perspective the postwar history that has shaped all our lives, whether we were born in the 1940s or the 1970s.

Many countries – Britain, the United States and Germany among them – allow access to their public records under a thirty-year rule, opening up much of the post-war period to archival research. For more recent events, diaries, memoirs and the investigations of newspapers and television confirm the view of the famous historian Sir Lewis Namier that all secrets are in print provided you know where to look for them. Contemporary historians also have the opportunity, denied to historians of earlier periods, of interviewing participants in the events they are analysing. The problem facing the contemporary historian is, if anything, the embarrassment of riches.

In any case, the nature and extent of world changes since the late 1980s have clearly signalled the need for concise discussion of major themes in post-1945 history. For many of us the difficult thing to grasp is how dramatically the world has changed over recent years: the end of the Cold War and of Soviet hegemony over eastern Europe; the collapse of the Soviet Union and Russian Communism; the unification of Germany; the pace of integration in the European Union; the disintegration of Yugoslavia; political and economic turbulence in South East Asia; Communist China's reconciliation with consumer capitalism; the faltering economic progress of Japan. Writing in a structured and cogent way about these seismic changes is what makes contemporary history so challenging and we hope that the end result will convey some of this excitement and interest to our readers.

The general objective of this series is to offer concise and up-to-date treatments of post-war themes considered of historical and political significance and to stimulate critical thought about the theoretical assumptions and conceptual apparatus underlying interpretations of the topics under discussion. The series should bring some of the central themes and problems confronting students and teachers of recent history, politics and international affairs into sharper focus than the textbook writer alone could provide. The blend required to write contemporary history which is both readable and easily understood but also accurate and scholarly is not easy to achieve, but we hope that this series will prove worthwhile for both students and teachers interested in world affairs since 1945.

*University of Ulster*

T. G. FRASER
J. O. SPRINGHALL

# Acknowledgements

I acknowledge the permission of the Controller of Her Majesty's Stationery Office for permission to quote Crown Copyright material. I am also grateful to the United Nations Organization, the Israel Ministry of Foreign Affairs and the Knesset for permission to use material.

My thanks are due to Paul Lalor, Donette Murray and Leonie Murray for their incisive and stimulating comments on parts of my manuscript. I cannot thank them enough for sharing their expertise and insights into Middle-Eastern politics and contemporary American foreign policy. My sincere thanks must also go to Israeli and Palestinian friends and colleagues who painstakingly showed me the situation on the ground, and debated issues, in the course of my visits to Israel and the Palestinian Authority. Over many years studying this subject, I have derived enormous benefit from the insights of a number of American and British figures whose lives touched the topic; in particular, Sir Harold Beeley, Sir Francis Evans, the Honorable Loy W. Henderson, Sir John Martin, former Secretary of State Dean Rusk, and Professor L. F. Rushbrook Williams, CBE, CIE. My friend Keith Kyle, who commented on earlier drafts of this book and with whom I enjoyed many conversations on the topic when he was Visiting Professor of History at the University of Ulster, died just days before I completed this third edition. I cannot thank him enough for his kindness and generosity. Responsibility for the interpretation of events is my own. I must also thank Janet Farren and Simon Fraser for their invaluable assistance with the typescript. My colleague and fellow historian Alan Sharp, Provost of the Coleraine campus at the University of Ulster, was an unfailing source of support at a time when it was most needed, as were Keith Jeffery and Sally Visick.

*Magee Campus, University of Ulster* T. G. F.

# Glossary

**Aliyah** term for immigration (technically 'ascent') of Jews into the Land of Israel

**A'yan** Arab 'notables' of Palestine, e.g. the Husseinis

**Diaspora** term for the 'Dispersion' of the Jews

**Fatah** 'Movement for the Liberation of Palestine', Palestinian group, founded by Yasser Arafat

**Gush Emunim** 'Block of the Faithful', a movement in the 1970s and 1980s to settle Jews in the Occupied Territories

**Haganah** 'Defence', the official defence force of the Jewish Agency, which formed the basis of the Israeli army

**Hamas** 'Islamic Resistance Movement', founded in 1987

**Hizbollah** 'Party of God', Lebanese Shi'ite militia and political party, formed in 1982

**Hibbat Zion** 'The Love of Zion', movement to settle Russian Jews in Palestine in the 1880s

**Intifada** 'Uprising', used for the revolt in the Occupied Territories which began in 1987, and again in 2000

**Irgun Zvai Leumi** 'National Military Organisation', right-wing underground army led by Menahem Begin

**Kadima** 'Forward', political party founded by Ariel Sharon in 2005

**Knesset** name for the Israeli parliament or assembly

**Leh'i** 'Fighters for the Freedom of Israel', right-wing underground group sometimes known as the Stern Gang after its founder Avraham Stern

**Likud** 'Union', right-wing political coalition led by Menahem Begin, and subsequently by Yitzhak Shamir, Binyamin Netanyahu and Ariel Sharon

**Mapai** 'The Workers' United Party'
**Musha'** system of landholding in Palestine
**Al-Nakba** 'the catastrophe or disaster', term used from 1948 for the fate of the Palestinians
**Yishuv** term for the Jewish community in Palestine before 1948

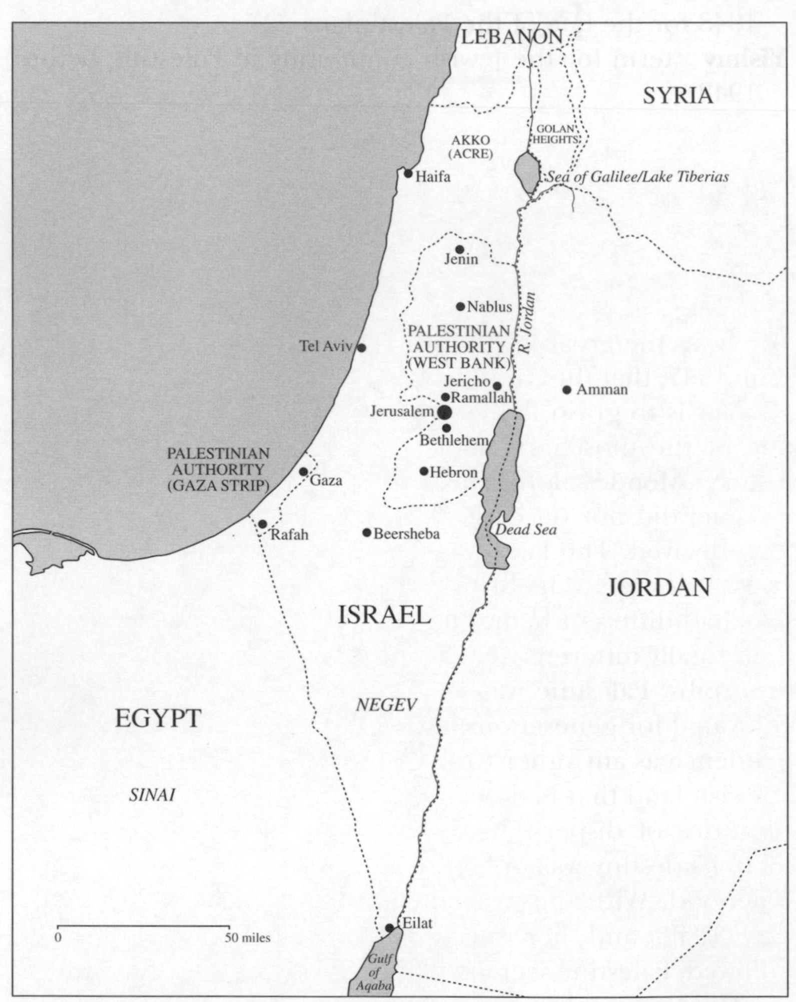


Israel, the Palestinian Authority* and their Arab Neighbours

* Under the 1998 Wye Agreement, the Palestinian Authority assumed control for some 40 per cent of the West Bank.

# Introduction

To say, as the great Jewish philosopher Martin Buber did in June 1947, that the Arab–Israeli conflict is over a land of two peoples is to grasp the essence of a problem that has been one of the most intractable, and tragic, in contemporary history (Mendes-Flohr, 1983). When Buber spoke, the State of Israel did not yet exist, though its coming was not to be long delayed. The land was then Filastin to its Arab inhabitants, Palestine to its British rulers. The fact that Arabs and Jews had different names for the land they shared reflected their totally different views of its past, present and future. To the Arabs, Palestine was an Arab land whose soil they had cultivated for generations; as such, it was as entitled to independence as any other Arab country. To the Jews, Israel was a Jewish land that had been their inspiration throughout 18 centuries of dispersion, dispossession and persecution; as such, its destiny was to be the fulfillment of their dreams of statehood. With the proclamation of the State of Israel in May 1948, and her successful defence in the war that followed, Palestine seemed to have vanished from the map of the Middle East, but the Palestinians did not disappear and the quarrel remained, gaining intensity over the following decades. Five subsequent wars, and two Intifadas, merely confirmed that the intensity of the Arab–Israeli conflict was undiminished. Peace moves between Israel and the Palestinians in 1993 seemed to point to the possibility of an accommodation between them, though even this proved to be premature. Years of complex negotiation, false starts, diplomatic stalemates, violence and reprisal reinforced the view that the Arab–Israeli conflict held no easy solutions.

## The Origins of the Arab–Israeli Conflict

In the 1880s, neither Palestine nor Israel existed. The area that came to embrace the Arab–Israeli conflict had not yet emerged as a political entity; instead, it consisted of parts of two administrative districts of the Ottoman (Turkish) Empire, the Sanjak of Jerusalem and the Vilayet of Beirut. Since the Turks did not conduct a census, the exact population may only be guessed at, but it is assumed to be just over 600,000, the vast majority of them Arabs, mostly of the Sunni Muslim religion but with a significant minority of Christians. Certain towns and cities had well-established economic functions, Jerusalem and Nablus in the interior, and Acre, Jaffa and Gaza on the coast, but the predominant way of life was agricultural, some 64 per cent of the population being dependent on farming according to the 1931 (British) census. Broadly speaking, Arab cultivators were divided into the semi-nomadic bedouin of the Negev Desert and parts of Galilee, and the much more numerous fellahin, who farmed set areas of land. Passionately attached to the land though the latter were, their actual titles were often less than secure. Much of the land was held by landlords and in half the villages land was held in common through the musha' system, which parcelled out portions to individuals for two- or three-year periods. These practices were to leave the fellahin terribly vulnerable. Leadership lay with the a'yan or 'notables', an urban elite often with extensive landholdings. Prominent among them were the Husseinis, Nashashibis, Khalidis and Nusseibehs, who were to provide the political elite for much of the period. These Arab families exerted influence through a kind of mutual interdependence with the Turks. Few, it seems, were attracted by the idea of full Arab independence from Constantinople, but many would have preferred some kind of increased autonomy within the empire. In that sense the Arabs were little different to the various nationalities within the Habsburg Empire in Europe. European comparisons mislead, however, for this was a deeply rooted Arab society comfortable in the culture and way of life of the Middle East.

From 1517 the Arab lands of the eastern Mediterranean and Egypt were part of the Ottoman Empire ruled from Constantinople. As an empire which at its height took in almost all of the Arab Middle East, North Africa and much of the Balkans, it had to accommodate diverse communities and religious minorities, such as the Jews and various forms of Christianity. For the most part it did so with subtlety and sophistication, the empire providing the region with stability and cohesion. But after the siege of Vienna in 1683 it was an empire in retreat, first by the resurgent Habsburgs, then by the stirring nationalities of the Balkans, and finally by the expansionism of Britain and France. For much of the nineteenth century the fate of the empire, the so-called 'Eastern Question', seemed to dominate the chancelleries of Europe. That Arab intellectuals would catch something of the spirit of nationalism affecting so much of Europe at that time was almost certain, though before the twentieth century nothing much seems to have stirred beyond small groups of interested, educated Arabs in Beirut and Damascus. By general consent, the starting-point for Arab nationalism was the Turkish revolution of 1908, which resulted in the coming to power of the 'Young Turks' whose policy was to assert the Turkish character of the empire, pulling it away from what had become a partnership with Arab elites. From that point certain Arabs began looking for more autonomy for their parts of the empire. It was this sentiment that the British tried to tap once war broke out in 1914, though it must be borne in mind that Arab nationalism was still a very tender growth in the early part of the century.

What could ultimately fuel Arab nationalism was a sense of the glory of their past before the Turkish conquest. For most Arabs that past was associated above all with the life and teachings of Muhammad and the power of his message, embodied in the Qur'an and expressed through the Arabic language. The Muslim faith gave the Arab Middle East, North Africa and Iberia a civilisation of depth and sophistication. Eleventh-century Baghdad, Cairo and Cordoba far surpassed their counterparts in Christian Europe in the size of their populations and the range of their civic amenities. It was the Arabs who preserved much of the teachings and philosophy of classical Greece. Arab scholars developed mathematics, medicine and science, passing the words 'algebra' and 'alchemy' into European languages. Compared with the largely manufactured cultures of many nineteenth- and twentieth-century European nationalisms, Arab nationalism could draw strength and inspiration from centuries when the Middle East was at the centre of world civilisation.

In the 1880s, Arab society in Ottoman Palestine was forced to confront the unanticipated challenge of Jews anxious to recreate their own way of life in their ancestral homeland. From the time of the Jewish Diaspora ('Dispersion') at the hands of the Romans, Jews – whether in Europe or the Middle East – had never forgotten the source of their faith. Their religious longing had been symbolised by the Western Wall, the one fragment of their Temple that the Romans had allowed to stand as a reminder of what had been lost. Some struggled to sustain a Jewish presence, such as the pious Jews who prayed and studied over the centuries in the holy cities of Jerusalem, Safed, Tiberias and Hebron. Overwhelmingly, however, the focus of Jewish life moved to Europe where, like Christianity, it developed with, and out of the ruins of, the Roman Empire. A minority in medieval Europe, Jews often led an unenviable existence, shunted into unpopular occupations, restricted to certain areas, and castigated as the killers of Christ. Throughout the centuries, when they were pushed to the margins of European life, they found strength and solace in their religious faith, central to which was a longing for Zion or Jerusalem. It was not until the French Revolution spread new ideas of tolerance across Europe that their position seemed set to improve. As new opportunities beckoned, men such as Benjamin Disraeli in Britain, Jacques Offenbach in France, and Felix Mendelssohn and Heinrich Heine in Germany contributed their talents to the general advance of European civilisation. In western and central Europe the signs seemed hopeful. Jewish banks and department stores helped generate economic progress and raise the standard of life. Jewish doctors and scientists fought disease. In towns and cities across Europe Jewish artisans sought a modest living. In return, Jews hoped that their services would be valued by their fellow citizens, that they would be liked and respected. But new doctrines of nationalism and racialism were arising in late nineteenth-century Europe which were to confound these hopes, and lead to the greatest tragedy in Jewish history.

The largest numbers of Jews did not by then live in western and central Europe but in the Russian Empire, where they were confined to the Pale of Settlement, restricted in their access to education and entry into the professions. After the murder of Tsar Alexander II by Russian revolutionaries in 1881, popular sentiment was whipped up against the Jews; the 'pogroms' which followed introduced a new word into English. Moreover, the 'May Laws' of 1882 subjected the Jews to a more official form of discrimination, expelling them from towns and villages where they had been allowed to settle. Out of these persecutions, which continued down to 1914, came the great mass Jewish migration to the United States which, within two generations, saw them transformed from the 'huddled masses' immortalised on the Statue of Liberty into one of the most vigorous groups in the country. For others the source of inspiration lay elsewhere, in the land of their ancestors. Out of this came the movement known as Hibbat

Zion ('The Love of Zion'), which in the 1880s began to channel small groups of idealists to settle in Palestine. Among these early Jewish settlements were Rishon l'Zion, Petah Tikvah and Rehovoth, near Jaffa, and Rosh Pinna in Galilee, their survival owing much to the generosity of Baron Edmond de Rothschild (Laqueur, 1989).

These settlements of the First Aliyah marked the beginning of the modern Jewish return to Palestine, but the origins of political Zionism are to be found in events in Paris and, more especially, Vienna. No city in Europe was more intellectually alive at the end of the nineteenth century and beginning of the twentieth than Vienna, with Jews like Gustav Mahler in music, Arthur Schnitzler in literature and Sigmund Freud in psychoanalysis well to the fore. Prominent in its journalistic life was Theodor Herzl who seemed to have erased his Jewish origins in order to identify with the city's German–Austrian culture. But the city had its troubles, and these surfaced in 1895 when the Christian Socialist Dr Karl Lueger was elected mayor on an openly anti-Semitic platform. The winter of 1894–95 also saw Herzl in Paris for the trial and degradation of the Jewish army officer, Alfred Dreyfus, convicted, falsely as it turned out, of betraying military secrets to Germany. Appalled by the degree of anti-Semitism thus exposed in these two cities, Herzl's thoughts turned to the Jewish future, the results being published in 1896 in his little book, *Der Judenstaat* ('The Jewish State' or, more correctly, 'The Jew State'). The book's thesis was contained in its title; namely, that as the Jews were a people who had not been allowed to assimilate into European life, they would have to unite in a state of their own. The following year, the first Zionist Congress was held under Herzl's leadership at Basle in Switzerland, proclaiming as its goal the creation of a 'home' for the Jews in Palestine (Bein, 1941; Herzl, 1972). Although Herzl died in 1904, the Zionist movement spent the next decade expanding its base amongst the Jews of the Diaspora and building new settlements in Palestine, even though it remained a minority movement in world Jewry, not least amongst the highly assimilated Jews of Germany and Austria–Hungary.

## The Impact of the First World War

Turkey's entry into the First World War on the side of Germany and Austria–Hungary in November 1914 brought into focus the fate of the Ottoman Empire. In order to embarrass the Turks, Britain was prepared to court the Arabs through the Sharif of Mecca, Husayn, head of the Hashemite family. In the course of 1915 Husayn negotiated with the British High Commissioner in Cairo, Sir Henry McMahon, who gave what the Arabs believed to be important pledges on their future independence in return for their help against the Turks. These pledges contained a specific, if ultimately controversial, exclusion: namely, that parts of Syria to the west of the districts of Damascus, Homs, Hama and Aleppo were excluded.

While the Arabs assumed that this referred to portions of what became Syria and Lebanon, the British later claimed that the excluded area was Palestine, despite the fact that neither 'Palestine' nor 'Jerusalem' appeared in any of the documents (Cmd. 5957; Fraser, 1980; Fromkin, 1989). It was to become a bitter source of controversy between them, the salient feature being what the Arabs believed the British had promised them. It was enough to bring Husayn on to the British side.

By the summer of 1917, the British government had begun to look to the Zionist movement as another possible ally in a war which seemed to be going badly for the Allies on all fronts. The British Zionists were supremely fortunate in having a diplomat of genius who was positioned to influence the views of key politicians. This was Dr Chaim Weizmann, a Russian-born chemist teaching at Manchester University. In pre-war Manchester he had come into contact with a number of leading Liberal and Conservative politicians, including former Prime Minister Arthur Balfour. During the war his work on the production of acetone, needed for the making of cordite, brought him into close contact with the Minister of Munitions, David Lloyd George. By 1917, Lloyd George and Balfour, now Prime Minister and Foreign Secretary, were searching for anything that might help lift the war effort. The Zionists, it was felt, might be useful in two respects: in helping to sustain the Russian front, which was in danger of collapsing altogether after the February Revolution, and in trying to galvanise the American war effort. Both were illusions, for Russian and most American Jews were too poor to have any influence, but the British government was desperate enough to grasp at anything. Weizmann proved the ideal conduit. The result, on 2 November 1917, was the Balfour Declaration which assured the British Zionist Federation that:

> His Majesty's Government view with favour the establishment in Palestine of a national home for the Jewish people, and will use their best endeavours to facilitate the achievement of this object, it being clearly understood that nothing shall be done which may prejudice the civil and religious rights of existing non Jewish communities in Palestine, or the rights and political status enjoyed by Jews in any other country.
>
> (Cmd. 5479; Stein, 1961)

Just over a month later the British army entered Jerusalem.

## The British Mandate over Palestine

Victory over Turkey left Britain in control of Palestine for the next 30 years, not as a colony but as a Mandate from the newly established League of Nations. From the start British rule was handicapped by the incompatibility of the promises made during the war. These were apparent in the terms of the Mandate, which were approved by the League in July 1922. Britain was to be:

> responsible for placing the country under such political, administrative, and economic conditions as will secure the establishment of the Jewish national home, as laid down in the preamble, and the development of self-governing institutions, and also for safeguarding the civil and religious rights of all the inhabitants of Palestine, irrespective of race and religion.

The problems associated with such a policy had already surfaced in the form of serious Arab disturbances in 1920 and 1921, directed both at British rule and Jewish settlement. Faced with the extent of discontent, the British sought to reassure the Arabs in a memorandum issued in 1922 by the Colonial Secretary, Winston Churchill, in which significant qualifications were put on the term 'national home', which now became 'a centre in which the Jewish people as a whole may take, on grounds of religion and race, an interest and a pride' (Cmd. 1700; Fraser, 1980; Fromkin, 1989). This fell far short of how the Zionists had hoped the national home would develop, particularly since Churchill also confined Palestine to west of the River Jordan. To the east was created Transjordan, to be ruled by the Hashemite Abdullah.

During the 1920s the national home did expand, though not dramatically: in 1922 Jews accounted for 83,790 of a total population of 752,048; by 1929 they were 156,481 in a population of 992,559 (Anon., 1939). More significant than their numbers were the institutions that the terms of the Mandate allowed the Jews to build up. Jewish sympathy in the Diaspora was mustered through the World Zionist Organization in which Dr Weizmann commanded immense prestige. This was in close contact with the Jewish Agency for Palestine set up under the Mandate, which rapidly established itself as a government for the Jews of Palestine, buying land and building schools and hospitals. Of immense symbolism for the revival of Jewish life in Palestine was the foundation in 1925 of the Hebrew University on Jerusalem's Mount Scopus. The Agency's dominant figure by the mid-1930s, David Ben-Gurion, stood in stark contrast to the intellectual and cosmopolitan Weizmann. Born David Gryn in Plonsk near Warsaw in 1886, at the age of 19 Ben-Gurion came to Palestine to work on the land, almost dying of malaria. A strong socialist, he was instrumental in founding and directing the Histadrut, which sought to organise Jewish workers on social democratic lines, and the Mapai ('The Workers' United Party'), which became the dominant political voice in Jewish Palestine. A hard-driving man of robust intelligence, Ben-Gurion was to give matchless service to Zionism, even though he was less decisive in practice than the image he liked to portray. The philosophy of Ben-Gurion and his colleagues was that they were 'building Zion', forging a Jewish nation through manual work, something which had been denied the Jews of the Diaspora. It was a vision that took little account of the Arab majority (Sachar, 1976).

Arab institutions could not match those being developed by the Jews. The Arab Executive proved a feeble vehicle for their aspirations, beset by feuds between followers of the Husseinis and Nashashibis. In 1921 the principal office of Arab Palestine, Mufti of Jerusalem, was given to Haj Amin al-Husseini, a former officer in the Ottoman army who had joined Husayn's revolt, and who had declared himself willing to work with the British. A strong nationalist, Haj Amin began to worry the British authorities by the late 1920s, and by the mid-1930s he rapidly assumed the role of arch-villain. In practice, though his dedication to the Palestinian cause was absolute, he was to prove unequal to the task of leadership, in some respects disastrously so (Mattar, 1988; Rogan and Shlaim, 2001).

Palestine was largely quiet between 1922 and 1928, when violence returned in the form of disturbances between Arabs and Jews at the Western Wall in Jerusalem. More serious confrontations there in August 1929 resulted in a wave of violence in which 133 Jews and 116 Arabs were killed. Particularly worrying for the Jews were attacks on the long-established Orthodox communities of Hebron, where 60 were killed, and Safed, where 45 were killed and wounded. The events of 1929 cruelly exposed the fault-line in mandatory Palestine. Two British Commissions, under Sir Walter Shaw and Sir John Hope-Simpson, then attempted to redefine Britain's policy in Palestine, identifying Arab fear of Jewish immigration and land purchase at the root of the difficulties. Hope-Simpson's recommendation that the nature of the land would only allow for a further 20,000 Jewish immigrants provoked inevitable Zionist fury. When Weizmann was joined by leading Conservatives in denouncing the proposals, the government found it necessary to retreat. In February 1931, the British Prime Minister, Ramsay MacDonald, wrote telling Weizmann that the government had no intention of prohibiting Jewish immigration. For the time being, it seemed, the Palestine situation had stabilised.

It was not to remain so for very long, for forces were at work in Europe that were permanently to change the nature of the Arab–Jewish conflict. On 30 January 1933, Adolf Hitler became German Chancellor, and by March had secured his dictatorship. The systematic exclusion of Jews from German national life soon followed. As a young man in Vienna before the First World War, Hitler had absorbed the anti-Semitism which had brought Karl Lueger to power. As a front-line German soldier in the war, he had only been able to come to terms with defeat by blaming Jews and revolutionaries for undermining the country's war effort. The reasons for Hitler's obsessive anti-Semitism may never be known for certain, but it was deadly enough. Faced with Hitler's regime, and anti-Semitism in Poland and Romania, Jews began to leave Europe in large numbers. Restrictions on immigration into the United States left Palestine as the only option. By 1936, the Jewish population had grown to 370,483 in a total Palestinian population of 1,336,518 (Anon., 1939).

This new Jewish population differed from previous migrations both in extent and character, for the new immigrants were overwhelmingly attracted by the urban lifestyles of Tel Aviv, Haifa and Jerusalem.

An Arab reaction against what they saw as the unwelcome transformation of their country was unavoidable, particularly as the events of 1931 had apparently confirmed the Zionists' ability to intervene in London. A clear sign of the temper of the Arabs of Palestine came in November 1935 with the operations in the Galilee hills of a small group led by Sheikh Izz al-Din al-Qassam. Although he was killed by the police the following month, his funeral in Haifa proved to be the occasion for a great demonstration of Arab emotion. Moreover, he was to prove an inspiring figure for later generation of Palestinians (Cmd. 5479, 1937; Marlowe, 1959). The 'Arab Revolt' began on 15 April 1936 with the murder of a Jew near Nablus. It was followed by the formation of the Arab Higher Committee with Haj Amin as its leading figure. The scale of the uprising led to a large-scale deployment of British forces, but also official goodwill towards the Haganah, the underground defence force of the Jewish Agency. The Revolt ate into British military resources at a time of increasing international tension in Europe and the Mediterranean, making it necessary to attempt once again a political solution. The Palestine Royal Commission under Lord Peel was charged with investigating the underlying causes of the disturbances and recommending how to deal with the 'legitimate grievances' of Arabs and Jews. Its most articulate member, Professor Reginald Coupland of Oxford University, soon came to the conclusion that there were two civilisations in Palestine, an Arab one which was Asian and a Jewish one which was European. As two such contrasting peoples could never develop a sense of service to a single state, Coupland's proposed solution was partition. Not only did he succeed in converting his fellow-members to this novel idea, but he also convinced Weizmann, who became a consistent supporter of partition. Not all Zionists were convinced and the Arabs were implacably opposed; nevertheless, the British Government did flirt with the idea in the summer of 1937 once the Commission had published its recommendation. Coupland's work was important, for it provided the intellectual basis for the partition of Palestine which came ten years later (Fraser, 1984).

By the end of 1937, the British had come to regret their brief support for partition, for the force of Arab opposition had to be taken into account at a time when the international situation was growing so dangerous. A second Commission, under Sir John Woodhead, was sent to Palestine, ostensibly to draw up the details of partition, but with confidential instructions to kill it off. By the time it reported in September 1938, the Munich Crisis was signalling the likelihood of war. It was now more than ever necessary to secure Arab goodwill, not just because Palestine was tying down troops but because Britain needed to secure the oil of the Middle East as well as communications to India, Australia and the East. A new statement of policy was prepared by the Colonial Secretary, Malcolm MacDonald, which clearly signalled the end of Britain's commitment to the Jews. Published weeks before the outbreak of war, it conceded that Palestine would become independent in ten years' time as a united country. Jewish migration would be limited to 75,000, thus confirming their minority status, at which point Britain would consider its obligation to foster the national home to be at an end (Bethell, 1979). Haj Amin, by this time in exile, was not attracted by MacDonald's offer, despite the fact that other Palestinian leaders realised how far it went in their direction. Making his way to Germany, his well-publicised meeting with Hitler, and efforts to recruit Bosnian Muslims into the SS, were to do the Palestinian cause incalculable harm, associating it with a genocidal regime (Rogan and Shlaim, 2001). Britain's principal Arab allies, however, Abdullah of Transjordan and Ibn Saud of Saudi Arabia, were able to use the new policy to great effect in keeping the Middle East quiet in the Allied interest.

Generals Wavell, Auchinleck and Montgomery were able to fight their battles; and in time the region became the launching pad for the invasion of southern Europe, through which supplies could reach the Soviet Union, and, above all, the oil reserves of the Middle East, which were an essential element in any Allied victory.

## The Holocaust

For the Jews, MacDonald's policy was an act of the deepest betrayal at the time of their greatest peril. In November 1938, the *Reichskristallnacht*, when the Nazis unleashed the full terror of the state against the Jews, had revealed the true nature of the German Reich. As Jews began to leave Germany in increasing numbers, Hitler made a speech on 30 January 1939, the sixth anniversary of his coming to power, in which he predicted the destruction of the Jews of Europe should war be 'forced' upon him. It was part of his preparation for the war he had decided to launch, and his chilling reference to the Jews was no accident.

This speech of Hitler's is one to which he often returned, both publicly and in private conversation, and there is little reason to doubt that it represented his true purpose. While the end result of Hitler's policies is not in question, Nazi policy towards the Jews went through various phases. Before the war their tactic was to encourage Jewish emigration. At the time of the fall of France in July 1940 the SS toyed with the idea of transporting Europe's Jews to Madagascar in the Indian Ocean, though this would have been nothing more than a large concentration camp. Britain's refusal to come to terms with Nazi Germany put an end to this scheme, if it ever had any substance. In the meantime, the SS were reorganising eastern Europe according to the racial policies of Hitler and the Nazi leadership. An extensive area of western Poland, renamed the Reichsgau Wartheland, was annexed to the Reich with a view to its ruthless 'Germanisation' at the expense of its Polish and Jewish inhabitants. The rump of Poland was designated the General Government. In both these areas the SS had control of some two million Jews who were systematically herded into sealed ghettos, notably Warsaw, Lodz and Crakow, over the first two years of the war. Although many acts of brutality were carried out against Jews in this period, the Nazis' ultimate purpose was as yet unclear. Some understanding of the lives endured in the ghettos may be had from the 'Chronicle' of the Lodz ghetto, a systematic record maintained from January 1941 until the eve of its liquidation in August 1944. The fears and false hopes, as well as the privations, of this sealed community make agonizing reading (Dobroszycki, 1984).

On 22 June 1941, the defining moment of Hitler's Third Reich arrived with the invasion of the Soviet Union. This was a war unlike those waged in Western Europe in 1940, for its purpose was both to create *Lebensraum* for Germany in the east and to destroy Bolshevism, long conflated in Hitler's mind as 'Judaeo-Marxism'. It was to be a pitiless struggle in which the terms of the Geneva Convention did not apply. The Wehrmacht's early victories left some four million Jews under German control. Mass killings occurred from the start, culminating in the massacre of some 34,000 Jews in Kiev at the end of September 1941 in retaliation for sabotage in the city. At the same time, hundreds of thousands of Soviet prisoners of war were being murdered or dying as the result of starvation and ill-treatment. The twentieth century had entered a new phase in which genocide was no longer a moral impossibility, certainly not by the SS leadership, which saw as its mission the 'racial purity' of the eastern lands and which had long since placed itself outside any legal, ethical or religious constraints. Moreover, a new sense of radicalism, even nihilism, had entered Nazi politics, marked by Hitler's reckless declaration of war on the United States, the world's most powerful economy, and by the reality of defeat outside Moscow. As Hitler's ill-prepared soldiers faced their first Russian winter, moves were under way to ensure that whatever the war might hold, the Jews would not survive it.

While no one knows for certain when the precise orders for the extermination of Europe's Jews were given, the key document appears to have been the directive issued on 31 July 1941 by Hermann Goering to Reinhard Heydrich, deputy head of the SS, charging him with a 'total solution of the Jewish question'. That the order was made with Hitler's knowledge and approval cannot be doubted, and it was put into effect over the winter of 1941–42. In the autumn of 1941 the remaining Jews of Germany were transported for 'resettlement' in the east. What this meant became brutally clear when the mass murder of Reich Jews took place in Kaunas and Riga in November 1941. Systematic killings of the indigenous Jewish population were taking place in Belorussia, the former Baltic states and other areas to the rear of the eastern front. It was in November, too, that the first gassing facilities were installed at Chelmno and Belzec. The reality behind Hitler's 1939 'prophecy' was fast becoming apparent (Browning, 2004).

It was probably to introduce some system into what was taking place piecemeal in the Wartheland and General Government that on 20 January 1942 Heydrich convened a conference of representatives of various government agencies at Wannsee outside Berlin. What Heydrich wanted to get across was that the 'final solution' for the Jews would be carried out across occupied Europe and that the principle was to be that Jews were to be divided into those fit for work and those judged unfit. The former would be worked to death in forced labour camps, the latter selected for extermination. Although this was framed in suitably euphemistic terms, it is, in fact, what happened on a systematic basis from then until the early months of 1945 (Roseman, 2002).

It is impossible to convey in clinical prose the true horror of what happened in the camps of eastern Europe during this period. Four camps, Chelmno, Belzec, Sobibor and Treblinka, existed for the sole purpose of extermination. But it is the vast Auschwitz–Birkenau complex, capable of holding over 100,000 prisoners, that has come to symbolise what came to be known as the Holocaust, for on arrival Jews were selected by SS doctors either for a quick, if terrifying, death in the gas chambers or a more prolonged one in the camp's chemical factories in appalling living conditions, subject to the whims of their SS guards. In what has been described as the industrialisation of mass murder, between 5,600,000 and 6,900,000 Jews were killed, a record etched for ever on the record of European civilisation (Reitlinger, 1953; Bullock, 1991). These events are fundamental to any understanding of the Arab–Israeli conflict. They led to what the American Department of State described as a 'cosmic' urge on the part of survivors to secure a Jewish state. They also meant that in the future Jewish leaders would think long and hard before embarking on any policy that might lead their people to another such tragedy. For Jews the Holocaust, coming as it did after centuries of European anti-Semitism, confirmed the need to secure their future in their own hands.

What compounded this tragedy for the Jews was the seeming indifference of the Allies to what was happening, not least Britain's continuing determination to bar Palestine to Jewish refugees. In December 1941, the SS *Struma* arrived at Istanbul with 769 Jewish refugees. Denied entry by the Turks and forbidden by the British to proceed to Palestine, the unseaworthy vessel was forced to leave harbour and sank with all its passengers. While Jews had no alternative but to fight or escape Nazism, such incidents confirmed the belief that ultimate protection could only come in a state where Jews controlled their own destiny. With this aim in mind, the Haganah began to collect arms. More ominous for the British were the activities of two other underground groups, the Irgun Zvai Leumi ('National Military Organisation') and Leh'i ('Fighters for the Freedom of Israel'), which represented a right-wing tradition within Zionism at odds with the Jewish Agency and the official movement. The Irgun was drawn from supporters of Vladimir Jabotinsky, whose Revisionists had seceded from the World Zionist Organization in 1935 to become the New Zionists. Central to Jabotinsky's vision was that the Jews had the right to their homeland on both banks of the Jordan, contrary to Churchill's 1922 decision (Fromkin, 1989; Shlaim, 2000). Detested by Ben-Gurion, Jabotinsky thus began the basic split which was to characterise both Zionism and the politics of the future State of Israel. In February 1944, the Irgun, led by a young Polish Jew, Menahem Begin, proclaimed that the British had betrayed the Jewish people, and declared war on the Mandate (Silver, 1984). The Leh'i was the creation of another Polish Jew, Avraham Stern, whose bitterness against the British had led him to make overtures to the Germans. Although Stern was killed by the police in 1942, the organisation survived under the leadership of Nathan Yellin-Mor. On 6 November 1944, its members assassinated Lord Moyne, the British minister in the Middle East. Although Leh'i was known to represent no more than the extremist tip of Zionism, the action symbolised the gulf between Britain and the Jews. It alienated Prime Minister Churchill, a close friend of Moyne, who had been planning to move quickly towards Jewish statehood after the war.

## American Jewish Support for Zionism

Although it was not immediately apparent, British intentions towards Palestine no longer mattered quite so much, for the decisive voice in world affairs was rapidly becoming that of the United States. Moreover, the unfolding tragedy in Europe was increasingly engaging the emotions of the American Jewish community. Since the American Jews were to become such an influential factor in the Arab–Israeli conflict after 1945, it is essential to sketch something of their origins and concerns. Jews had lived in North America since early colonial times, the first Dutch Jews arriving in

New Amsterdam in 1654. It was only in the mid-nineteenth century with the arrival of German Jews in the aftermath of the failed revolutions of 1848 that Jews started to become a significant element in the American population. But it really took the mass arrival from the 1880s of Jews fleeing poverty, persecution and general lack of opportunity in the Russian Empire to transform the community. Between 1881 and 1914, some 2,019,000 came to the United States. Overwhelmingly, they settled in New York, at first in the slums of Manhattan's Lower East Side, then, as prosperity grew, moving in large numbers to Brooklyn and the Bronx. In the free atmosphere of the United States they flourished in ways that would have been inconceivable in eastern Europe, though prejudice against them was certainly present. The 'German' Jews of the mid-nineteenth century had already made a name for themselves in publishing, journalism and retailing. The great department stores of New York – Macy's, Bloomingdale's and Gimbel's – were the products of such German Jewish enterprise, as was Chicago's mail-order empire, Sears Roebuck, whose catalogues brought nothing less than a social revolution to the lives of ordinary Americans. The achievements of the later immigrants from eastern Europe were no less remarkable. Perhaps their unique contribution to their new country was in popular culture and in music. Building on the vigorous musical tradition of east European Jewry, they established themselves in the world of the theatre and the rapidly evolving motion-picture industry. Seeing the potential of the cinema, and barred from following a variety of other professions, men such as the Warner Brothers, Samuel Goldwyn and Louis B. Mayer defined what was to become the mass art form of the twentieth century. Twentieth-century American musical life is studded with names like Aaron Copeland, Leonard Bernstein, George Gershwin, Al Jolson, Benny Goodman, Jascha Heifetz and Isaac Stern. One son of a Jewish immigrant contributed more to American popular music than any other single individual: Irving

Berlin, whose songs helped carry Americans through two world wars, and lift them through the gloom of the Great Depression.

It would be naïve to imagine that American Jews did not have to confront anti-Semitism. Although it was not part of state policy as it was in parts of Europe, groups and individuals like the Ku Klux Klan, the car manufacturer Henry Ford and the 'Radio Priest' Father Coughlin maintained a stream of crude, anti-Jewish propaganda between the two world wars, while more discreetly certain universities maintained quotas on Jewish students, and some clubs excluded Jews from membership. The new immigration laws of the early 1920s, which discriminated against eastern and southern Europeans, were a severe blow to Jews, with fatal results once Hitler's persecutions began. Zionism was present amongst American Jews almost from the start. Flags had flown at half mast in the Lower East Side in 1904 when news came of Theodor Herzl's death and a number of influential American Jews, for example the eminent jurists Felix Frankfurter and Louis D. Brandeis, became keen Zionists. Even so, only a minority of American Jews gave Zionism their active support before the late 1930s when Hitler's actions gave them cause to reconsider.

By then, Jews seemed well on their way to becoming firmly established in American life. Franklin D. Roosevelt's election as President in 1932 opened up new opportunities, for he had a number of prominent Jews as his advisers. But ultimately Roosevelt became a disappointment, for he did little to help Europe's Jews by easing immigration quotas. This was graphically illustrated in May 1939 when the *St Louis* was forced to return from Havana to Hamburg with almost 900 Jewish passengers who had believed they were about to become eligible for entry into the United States. Nor, once news of the Holocaust began to reach the United States in 1942, did American Jews feel that Roosevelt had done enough to stop the tragedy, though, in truth, he had no influence whatsoever over the Nazi leadership.

What they did hope to do was enlist Roosevelt's support over Palestine. At a conference in May 1942, convened at New York's Biltmore Hotel, the old Basle Programme of 1897 was significantly altered; Palestine was to become a Jewish Commonwealth, in short a state. Although Zionists had always assumed they would have a state in Palestine, this now came officially into the public domain, with American Jews well to the fore in pushing for its advancement. Their feelings were channelled through the American Zionist Emergency Council, headed by Rabbi Stephen Wise, a strong Democrat and Roosevelt supporter, and Rabbi Abba Hillel Silver, an equally committed Republican. These events demonstrated that the United States had become the main focus of Zionist activity, increasingly so as the destruction of the Jewish communities of Europe accelerated (Schneiderman and Fine, 1943).

Although the Zionists had high hopes of Roosevelt, not least because he had brought a number of Jews into important posts in his administration, his sympathies remained elusive. Only too aware of the importance of the Middle East, notably its oil, to the Allied war effort, he was anxious that this should not be endangered by overt support for Jewish claims in Palestine. Hence, in May 1943 he assured Ibn Saud of Saudi Arabia that nothing would be done to alter the status of Palestine 'without full consultation with both Arabs and Jews'. In 1944, he moved to ward off pro-Zionist resolutions in Congress. This was presidential election year, with Roosevelt set on securing an unprecedented fourth term which would allow him to carry out his pledge of winning the war and winning the peace that followed. His vice-presidential nominee was Senator Harry S. Truman, untried in foreign affairs but well-placed to ensure that Roosevelt's post-war plans would secure the necessary backing in Congress. Both the Democratic and Republican election platforms endorsed the Biltmore Program, though there was nothing surprising in political parties making the correct noises towards ethnic groups at election time. Even so, in October

1944 Roosevelt felt it necessary to assure a pro-Zionist senator that, if re-elected, he would help to bring about the 'establishment of Palestine as a free and independent Jewish commonwealth'.

Roosevelt was well aware that as both Arabs and Jews were laying claim to Palestine it was going to become a burning issue for the post-war world. Hence, in February 1945 he broke his return journey from the Yalta Conference to meet Ibn Saud in Egypt. The Saudi ruler seemingly convinced him that if restitution were to be made to the Jews for what they had suffered, then that should fall to the Axis countries and not the Arabs. Conscious of the strength of Arab opposition to Zionism, Roosevelt assured Ibn Saud that 'he would do nothing to assist the Jews against the Arabs and would make no move hostile to the Arab people' (Fraser, 1989). When Roosevelt died on 12 April, he had put the United States in the same position as Britain at the end of the previous war by leading both Arabs and Jews to believe that they had his support. Hitler's defeat and suicide shortly afterwards meant that the Arab–Jewish conflict over Palestine was going to be resolved in a world totally removed from that of 1939. If nothing else, Hitler had seen to that.

# 1

# THE PARTITION OF PALESTINE AND THE CREATION OF ISRAEL

## British and American Policies towards Palestine

With the end of the war came the 'Jewish Revolt', which drove the British out of Palestine and prepared the way for Jewish statehood. Despite the intense feeling of betrayal over the 1939 White Paper and continuing tensions between the Yishuv and the mandatory authorities during the war, the leaders of the Jewish Agency did not initially have the sense that conflict was inevitable, for in July 1945 Britain elected a new Labour government which was believed to be sympathetic to their aims. The British Labour Party had long professed a fellow-feeling with Zionism, which shared its social democratic ethos, and at its Blackpool conference in 1944 overwhelmingly endorsed the principle of a Jewish Palestine. But the initial enthusiasm with which Ben-Gurion and his colleagues greeted the election of their fellow socialists soon turned to incredulity and disillusion when it became clear that the 1939 White Paper policy still stood. Behind the Labour government's apparent volte-face was the formidable figure of Ernest Bevin, a former trade-union leader now Foreign Secretary. A hard, unsentimental man,

Bevin was not likely to be moved by his party's traditional sympathy with Zionism as much as by his view of Britain's needs in the immediate post-war world. It was an analysis created and sustained by permanent Foreign Office officials who had long since concluded that Britain's interests could only be served by a pro-Arab policy.

Principal spokesman for that view was Bevin's chief adviser on Palestine, Harold Beeley, who had been regarded with great suspicion by Zionists even before the war, and who was to become their bête noire as he increasingly seemed to be influencing his chief against them. But Bevin was not likely to be easily swayed against his better judgement, and he was not long in office before he came to share the Foreign Office's pro-Arab sympathies. At the heart of his concerns was Britain's need to retain access to the oilfields of the Middle East and the pipelines which crossed Arab territory to the terminal at Haifa. This was believed to be essential to the economic reconstruction of a Britain which had been crippled by the financial costs of six years of war. In short, the Labour Party's emotional and ideological sympathy with Zionism was shunted aside by the Labour government's hard-headed view of where Britain's interests lay in the Middle East. Under Bevin, Britain stood by the provisions of the 1939 White Paper (Louis, 1984).

Much of the Arab Middle East still lay under British influence or control, but its politics were febrile and its structures brittle and undeveloped. In addition to the Aden colony, Britain had extensive interests in the Gulf and retained two air bases in Iraq. Of the states bordering Palestine, Lebanon and Syria had been freed from the French Mandate, but only just, in 1943 and 1946. Egypt was still uneasily linked to Britain by the 1936 treaty, the powerful symbol of which was the British military presence in the Suez Canal Zone, its future already challenged by the Egyptians in June 1945. Transjordan became independent in 1946, but was still tightly bound to Britain. If Arab opinion smarted under these conditions, Palestine provided a particular focus for their frustrations. But at what was to prove the decisive moment in their history, the Palestinians lacked the political structures and leadership they needed. Haj Amin, an exile since 1937, made his way at the end of the war to Egypt and Lebanon, but his knowledge of conditions in Palestine was inevitably second hand, and not everyone trusted his judgement. An alternative leadership failed to emerge, however. The Palestinians faced the further problems that they had always lacked political structures to mirror those built up so carefully by the Jewish Agency, and that they had never really recovered from the British repression of their revolt in the years 1936–39. In short, the Arab world in general, and Arab Palestine in particular, was in poor condition to resist the determined challenge soon to be mounted by the Zionists (Kirk, 1954; Mattar, 1988; Rogan and Shlaim, 2001).

Bevin's view that the West's interests lay with the Arabs found a strong echo in Washington where key officials of the Department of State broadly shared the perceptions of their counterparts in the Foreign Office. The Department's leading Arabist was the experienced diplomat, now head of the Division of Near Eastern and African Affairs, Loy W. Henderson. A former specialist on the Soviet Union whose jaundiced views of Stalin became inconvenient during the war, in 1942 Henderson was posted off as ambassador to Baghdad. His travels in the Middle East taught him the degree of Arab opposition to Jewish claims in Palestine, from which he drew two lessons. The first was that Jewish statehood could only come about through violence. The second that, even if statehood could be attained, the unremitting nature of Arab hostility would leave the Jews in the unenviable position of replacing the ghettos of Europe for a larger one in the Middle East. A surer future, he felt, would be found by settling in the United States, Latin America and the British Commonwealth. Such arguments did not endear him to American Zionists and others in Washington who were advising the President that a Jewish state could be accomplished without war, but Henderson was never afraid to repeat them. His views became those of the Department, establishing a tradition of pro-Arab attitudes amongst foreign-policy professionals that proved extremely persistent.

But responsibility for the making of American foreign policy rests ultimately with the President. Harry S. Truman, who had succeeded on Roosevelt's death, was acutely conscious of that prerogative. His entire background had, in a sense, immunised him against the kind of advice coming from Henderson and his colleagues. Unlike his immediate predecessors as President, Truman had no college education, and his feisty sense of self-reliance made him suspect the professionals, the 'striped pants boys' as he liked to call them, with their apparent Ivy League condescension. Thus the tone of the Department's first approach to him on Palestine, only six days after taking up office, with the patronising advice that the matter was 'highly complex' and that he should only take action after seeking 'full and detailed advice', proved to be uniquely ill-chosen. Far from following the Department's position on Palestine, Truman's earlier career meant that he was likely to respond positively to the Jews. During his service in the First World War he had made friends with a Jewish sergeant called Eddie Jacobson. After the war the two men set up a haberdashery business in Kansas City, only to see their hopes ruined in the Depression. For years they battled their way back to solvency. When Truman went to Washington in the 1930s as Senator for Missouri, he was befriended by the great Jewish lawyer Louis Brandeis, who widened enormously Truman's cultural and social perspectives.

Truman's pivotal position made it certain that he would be lobbied by American Zionist groups, and pressure from them built up steadily between 1945 and 1948. While he accepted that such lobbying would go on, he disliked it, preferring instead to listen to the advice of trusted colleagues. Two in particular, Clark Clifford and David Niles, came to have a decisive influence on his actions over Palestine. Clifford's view that the Jews were entitled to their own country was reinforced by his key role in helping ensure Truman's re-election in 1948. Why should the President forfeit any political advantage to the Republicans? In the context of American politics it was a logical question with an inevitable answer and it has led to a lively controversy about the motives behind Truman's support for Jewish statehood. It is pointless to deny that political considerations were part of Truman's motivation, but they were not the whole story. Like any decent person, he was moved by what he learned of the fate of European Jews, and that sympathy was reinforced by David Niles. Ostensibly Truman's adviser on minority affairs, Niles was really his link with the Jewish community. Niles was born into a poor Jewish family in Boston, and had become a trusted official of the New Deal. There is little evidence of any involvement with Zionism in the 1930s, but by 1945 it is clear that Niles felt keenly the distress experienced by the Jewish survivors of the Holocaust in Europe. Niles's advice that something had to be done for them proved very important, for Truman trusted his judgement and his moderation, which contrasted favourably with the stridency of much of the lobbying campaign which was directed at him. Little in Truman's background made him sensitive to the Arab case over Palestine or responsive to the State Department's advocacy of it; but his friendships and emotions, combined with the political needs of his party, made him likely to respond positively to the Jews (Snetsinger, 1974; Ganin, 1979; Cohen, 1982; Louis, 1984; Fraser, 1989).

While Truman's later interventions were to prove critical for the establishment of Israel, his initial moves were of a different order, designed to offer some relief to the Jewish survivors in Europe. Indeed, he only turned to Palestine after the failure of attempts to persuade congressional leaders to permit large numbers of Jews to settle in the United States. This was followed by the dispatch to Europe of Earl G. Harrison, Dean of Law at the University of Pennsylvania, who was to report back on the conditions and desires of the Jewish 'Displaced Persons'. The policy of General Eisenhower's military administration was to persuade the Jews to return to their countries of origin; Harrison's report pointed firmly to Palestine. Shaken by what he saw of the condition of the 'Displaced Persons', Harrison readily adopted the suggestion of the Jewish Agency that 100,000 should be admitted into Palestine. It was exactly what Truman wanted. On 31 August, he formally requested that the British government issue 100,000 immigration certificates, pointing out that 'no other single matter is so important for those who have known the horrors of concentration camps'. The British response was both negative and, in the circumstances, callously insensitive, pointing out that the European camps held many victims of Hitler and that the Jews should not be put 'at the head of the queue'. The nature and tone of the British rejection showed just how far the government had travelled from the pro-Zionist sentiments of its 1944 Labour party conference, and the way was now clear for open resistance from the Jews of Palestine (Louis, 1984).

## The Jewish Revolt

Although the Irgun and Leh'i had not been afraid to strike at the British before the end of the war, the leaders of the Jewish Agency had too many long-standing connections to the British for open warfare to be undertaken lightly. Moreover, the Jewish Agency was a legal body whose position would be imperilled once the Haganah started operations. However reluctantly, Ben-Gurion and his colleagues knew it was a decision that had to be taken and on 1 October the Haganah was ordered to begin the armed revolt. First, however, it was necessary to reach a working arrangement with the other two armed groups. At a meeting convened by the Haganah leader Moshe Sneh, Menahem Begin of the Irgun and Leh'i's Nathan Yellin-Mor agreed to cooperate in a united Hebrew Resistance Movement. Although the unified command flourished through the winter of 1945–46, it was always an uneasy alliance of unequal groups under

Haganah primacy. But there could be no denying its effectiveness, backed as it was by the united resolve of the Yishuv and haunted by the fate of the Jews of Europe.

The striking power of the new alliance was demonstrated in a coordinated operation on the night of 31 October/1 November 1945 when the Haganah struck at the hated instruments of the British exclusion policy – police patrol boats – sinking two at Haifa and one at Jaffa. Simultaneously, Haganah forces disrupted the railway network with some 500 explosions, while the Irgun destroyed a locomotive and damaged six others at Lydda goods-yard. The operation also claimed its first victim when Leh'i member Moishele Bar Giora was killed in a premature explosion during an abortive attack on the Haifa oil storage tanks. Faced with this challenge, the British built up their troops and police to a total of 100,000, a burden their straitened economy could not long sustain. The virtually unanimous support of the Yishuv rendered the Hebrew Resistance impervious to penetration and memories of the German occupation in Europe were too close for the British security forces to resort to tough measures. Thus the winter of 1945–46 saw them consistently outwitted. On 25 February 1946, three airfields were attacked with the loss of 20 planes at an estimated cost of £2 million. Strikes against the communications system and installations continued, as did attacks on British personnel. On 25 April, seven paratroopers died in a Leh'i attack in Tel Aviv. The final symbol of British impotence came on the night of 16/17 June when a joint operation succeeded in destroying 10 of the 11 road and rail bridges into Palestine, temporarily isolating it from the rest of the Middle East (Bell, 1979).

### The Anglo-American Committee of Inquiry

While the British forces were being baffled by the Jewish underground groups, the winter of 1945–46 also saw a major attempt at a political settlement – the

Anglo–American Committee of Inquiry – whose origins lay in a British attempt to involve their American critics directly in the affairs of Palestine. Irritated by what he saw as the gratuitous nature of Truman's intervention over Palestine, Bevin invited the Americans to take part in a joint inquiry into the linked issues of Palestine and the Displaced Persons. As announced on 13 November 1945, the committee, six Americans and six British, was to examine the 'political, economic and social conditions in Palestine as they bear upon the problem of Jewish immigration and settlement therein and the well-being of the people now living therein'. Although the two governments were agreed that no one of Arab or Jewish origin would serve, Truman and Niles went to some length to ensure that three of the Americans, Frank W. Buxton, James G. McDonald and Bartley C. Crum, sympathised with the Zionist position. Crum, in particular, maintained direct links with Niles during the committee's work. The 12 men approached their task with great seriousness, hearing evidence in Washington and London before visiting camps in Germany, Austria, Czechoslovakia and Poland. After travelling to various parts of the Middle East, they had extensive hearings in Palestine with the Mandatory government, the Arab Higher Committee and the Jewish Agency.

When the committee reported in May 1946, it was clear that the Jewish Agency had secured one major concession: 100,000 Jews from the European camps were to be allowed into Palestine. But the Jews could take much less comfort from the recommendations on the country's political future, for only two members, McDonald and Crum, were prepared to see Jewish statehood come about through the mechanism of partition. Their colleagues believed that this would only make the situation worse. Instead, they were prepared to identify Palestine as the Holy Land, setting it 'completely apart from other lands' and dedicating it 'to the precepts and practices of the brotherhood of man, not of narrow nationalism'. Hence, Palestine was to be 'neither a Jewish state nor an Arab state', and was to be governed under a continuing system of trusteeship. Before these conclusions are too hastily dismissed, two things ought to be clearly noted: the rejection of partition as an unworkable device, and the unwillingness to concede either Arab or Jewish statehood. The responses of the Arab Higher Committee and the Jewish Agency were equally bitter (Nachmani, 1987).

In the summer of 1946 two events conspired to throw the British Mandate into its final crisis. On the diplomatic front the conclusions of the Anglo–American Committee failed to attract the support of either government in Washington or London, let alone the Arabs and Jews. This was despite an initial welcome from Truman who seems to have been ready to grasp at any viable proposal, especially one that gave him the 100,000 immigration certificates to which he had publicly committed himself. Bevin was not prepared to let him off so lightly. The British government's response to the report was to ask the Americans to provide two divisions of troops which they believed would be necessary to cope with the Arab disturbances that the extra 100,000 Jews would provoke. When the Joint Chiefs of Staff in Washington told Truman that there were no troops available for such a mission, the committee's conclusions were clearly in serious trouble. The President was, in any case, coming under very severe pressure from the American Zionists who were incensed at the committee's failure to endorse Jewish statehood. A further attempt at progress in July met with no greater success. Truman sent Henry F. Grady to London in an attempt to secure some movement on the 100,000 certificates. The plan that Grady agreed with the British minister Herbert Morrison, the so-called 'Morrison–Grady Plan', would have created autonomous Arab and Jewish provinces under a continued form of trusteeship. But this still fell far short of Jewish hopes and, after a stormy series of meetings with pro-Zionist congressional leaders, Truman telegraphed his rejection of the proposals to London on 7 August.

## The King David Hotel Attack and its Consequences

During this period of ill-fated attempts at Anglo-American cooperation in the summer of 1946, the situation in Palestine worsened alarmingly from the British point of view. After the dramatically successful attack on the bridges into the country on the night of 16–17 June, the British decided on tough measures to try to regain the security initiative by striking at the heart of the Jewish Agency. 'Operation Agatha' sealed off Tel Aviv and the main Jewish areas of Jerusalem and Haifa in pre-dawn raids, which concentration camp survivors found all too reminiscent of recent events in Europe. Jewish Agency leaders were seized and detained, though not key figures like Ben-Gurion who was in Paris, or Sneh who went underground, or the elder statesman Weizmann who was not disturbed. Few arms were found. The response planned by Sneh and his colleagues in the Hebrew Resistance was to be threefold. The Haganah was to attack the arsenal at Bat Galim, and Leh'i the Palestine Information Office in Jerusalem. Begin and the Irgun were set as their target the government headquarters in Jerusalem's King David Hotel, an operation the organisation had been contemplating for some time. Then the remaining Jewish Agency leaders drew back, not least at the urging of Weizmann with his stubborn faith in British intentions. Although the decision was taken to call off the joint operation, Sneh, anxious to keep the Irgun a full part of the resistance, merely asked Begin to postpone his part of the plan. But Begin went ahead. On 22 July, bombs exploded in the King David Hotel: an entire wing of the building collapsed and 91 people were killed. It was by far the most dramatic blow delivered at the British and it had far-reaching consequences. Sneh resigned as head of the Haganah and the organisation suspended its operations against the British, leaving the Irgun and Leh'i alone in their campaign (Clarke, 1981). The Jewish Agency's denunciations of the attack stung Begin and his organisation, contributing to a legacy of bitterness between the two wings of the movement that was to continue for decades after statehood had been achieved. More immediately, the attack convinced the British that they needed to resume the search for a political settlement.

The Palestine Conference that convened in London in September proved to be yet another exercise in futility, but at least it brought into sharp focus the strong possibility that the country's future would be decided on the basis of partition. The Arabs, led by Jamal Husseini, continued to reject the idea, as they had done consistently from the time of its first appearance in 1937, and they were strongly supported by Bevin. Since 1937, Zionist policy towards the prospect of partition had not been consistent, some seeing it as the only realistic way forward, others dismissing it as a betrayal of the Zionist dream. These hesitations could still be seen at a meeting of the executive of the Jewish Agency in Paris in August when, by divided vote, it was decided to break with the Biltmore Program and work instead for partition on the basis of 'the establishment of a viable Jewish State in an adequate area of Palestine'. This significant shift in policy was soon matched in Washington. Throughout the summer of 1946, Truman had been subjected to intensive lobbying by the American Zionists who had become increasingly alarmed at the nature of the proposals coming forward. With senatorial and gubernatorial elections due to be held in November, it was inevitable that there would be no lessening of their campaign, especially as Truman was vulnerable over his apparent inability to deliver the 100,000 immigration certificates. The result, on 4 October, was his 'Yom Kippur Statement', announcing America's support for partition as the best way forward. The United States had now committed itself to Jewish statehood, and to partition as the means of achieving it (Fraser, 1989).

Despite Arab opposition, the British were now under pressure to bring partition to the top of the agenda and there were those, notably in the Colonial Office, who believed that it was the only way of reconciling the various pledges Britain had made over the years. But Ben-Gurion, perhaps too conscious of the divided views of his supporters, would not be drawn into detailed discussions, with the result that the common ground was not seized. It was clear enough, however, that Ben-Gurion and the British were far apart in their thinking as to what might constitute an 'adequate' area for the Jewish state. Palestine was now only one of a number of problems pressing on a country enduring a miserable and impoverished winter. On 7 February 1947, the cabinet decided to present final proposals to the two sides which would involve a transition to independence over five years with considerable autonomy for Arab and Jewish areas. When these were rejected a week later, the problem was referred to the United Nations, without, it would appear, much thought being given as to the possible outcome.

## The UNSCOP Report

If the British imagined that in doing this they were allowing themselves something of a respite and that the United Nations would prove too inchoate for anything of substance to emerge, then they were soon to be confounded, for there were strong feelings elsewhere that this new international body must be seen to work effectively. A special session of the General Assembly was convened in May. It was notable for an early declaration by the Soviet Union in favour of Jewish statehood. Its main result was the establishment of the United Nations Special Committee on Palestine (UNSCOP), charged with reporting back to the General Assembly by 1 September with its conclusions on the country's future. Its membership was to avoid the major powers and the Arab countries, whose sympathies were felt to be too engaged, and, with these exceptions, to reflect the nature of the membership: thus, Peru, Uruguay, Guatemala, Sweden, the Netherlands, Czechoslovakia, Yugoslavia, Canada, Australia, India and Iran were selected.

In retrospect, it is clear that UNSCOP's conclusions were always likely to have a decisive effect upon Palestine's future, but at the time this was something the Palestinian Arabs failed to grasp, with disastrous results. Believing that the committee was unfairly weighted against them, the Arab Higher Committee decided to boycott it. It was possibly the single most disastrous decision made by the Arab leadership. The Jews made no such mistake, offering full cooperation both in the public sessions and by attaching to the committee two able liaison officers, David Horowitz and Abba Eban, whose brief was to remind its members of the Zionist case. The Jewish purpose was twofold: they had to convince the committee of the futility of pursuing any kind of continuing British trusteeship, and then persuade it to recommend partition. The first was brought about by the ruthlessness of the Irgun and an act of considerable daring and sophistication by the Haganah. In July, the Irgun hanged two British sergeants in retaliation for the execution of three of its members. It was an action that attracted widespread publicity, not least because the bodies were left boobytrapped. Anti-Semitic incidents in a number of British cities, with the prospect of a revival of the pre-war Fascist movement, helped convince leading opinion in Britain that the Palestine Mandate was not really worth the struggle. Much more significant was the brilliant propaganda exercise conducted by the Haganah in mounting a spectacular challenge to the British during UNSCOP's time in Palestine. Chartering an elderly American ferry, the *President Warfield*, which they renamed *Exodus 1947*, the organisation sailed 4500 Jewish Displaced Persons from Sète in southern France towards the coast of Palestine where ships of the Royal Navy were waiting. After a violent confrontation, filmed for use by the American newsreels, the ship was brought into Haifa where its passengers were disembarked under the eyes of three UNSCOP members. The episode confirmed, as it was intended to, the longing of the Jews for Palestine and the bankruptcy of the British regime. As if to drive home that lesson, Bevin insisted that the passengers be returned to refugee camps in Germany. It was hardly surprising that UNSCOP was unanimous in recommending the end of the Mandate.

Partition was less obvious, not least because the Jews themselves were still not united behind it. In presenting the Jewish Agency's case before UNSCOP in Jerusalem, Ben-Gurion still had to press for acceptance of the Biltmore Program, but this was a formality. Weizmann then put forward, ostensibly unofficially, the case for partition, which Ben-Gurion confirmed he would consider. In reality, from the start Horowitz and Eban had been instructed to work for this outcome and Ben-Gurion privately assured UNSCOP's members that it was partition he wanted. Belatedly, the Arabs realised that the ground was threatening to slip from under them. A hastily arranged visit to Beirut allowed Arab foreign ministers to argue against partition, but it was all too little and far too late. By the time the committee retired to Geneva to consider its findings, a majority had been convinced that partition offered the only way forward.

The basic principle underlying the UNSCOP plan was that the claims to Palestine of the Arabs and Jews, each possessing validity, were irreconcilable, and that among the solutions advanced, partition would provide the most realistic and practicable settlement. As set out, the proposed Arab state was to consist of three geographically separate areas: a southern coastal strip from Rafah through Gaza; Galilee in the north; and the country's interior, including the important towns of Nablus, Hebron and Beersheba. In contrast, the Jewish state was to be contiguous, if in places only just: much of the coastal plain, including Tel Aviv and Haifa, the Negev Desert in the south, and the Jezreel and Hule valleys in the north. There were two important refinements to the plan. While conceding that political partition was necessary, UNSCOP believed that the country's economic unity should be retained. Hence, there was to be an economic union of Palestine, responsible for distributing revenue and maintaining a common currency, customs system and communications network. Secondly, as the result of Vatican lobbying, Jerusalem was to become a corpus separatum, an international city under the United Nations (Eban, 1977; Fraser, 1984).

## The UNSCOP Report in the General Assembly

The plan was open to many objections, which its Arab and British opponents were quick to point out. If the political claims of Arabs and Jews were held to be irreconcilable, how could they be expected to cooperate in an economic union? How could two states so sinuously intertwined ever be defensible? More seriously, there was the problem of the large Arab population in the proposed Jewish state. UNSCOP admitted that it would have 498,000 Jews and 407,000 Arabs, but an ill disposed British Foreign Office soon provided figures showing that the true Arab total would be 512,000. Critics also pointed to the fact that in none of Palestine's subdistricts did Jews own a majority of the land, and that in only one of them, the heavily Jewish areas around Tel Aviv and Petah Tikva, were they a majority of the population. Had the Arabs developed these arguments with force and skill they might have won important points in the discussions that followed, but once again their leadership failed them.

Instead, Palestinian leaders attacked the principle of partition, creating an impression of mean spiritedness against a people that had recently suffered so much. Their confidence was reinforced by the knowledge that the British shared their hostility to the proposal. Concluding that partition was so unfair to the Arabs, the British government not only rejected the idea, but made it plain, publicly and in private, that they would oppose its implementation. Not so public was the policy they actually adopted of leaving the two sides to fight it out.

The partition plan inevitably fell somewhat short of Jewish hopes, especially the provisions relating to Jerusalem, for not only had the city been the focus of Jewish yearning over the centuries, but its western suburbs were one of their main centres of population. Whatever reservations were held, and whatever hopes there might have been that one day the Jewish state might be expanded, the leadership had worked hard to lead UNSCOP to this conclusion and they were now determined that partition be secured. The plan offered them statehood guaranteed in the highest international forum, the General Assembly of the United Nations. In early October, the General Assembly changed itself into the Ad Hoc Committee on the Palestinian Question to give full consideration to the UNSCOP proposals. Here would be the critical test. Interestingly support quickly came from the Soviet Union, no small matter given its three General Assembly votes and influence over the eastern European countries. Western diplomats interpreted this as nothing more than cynical support for the one plan that promised to get the British out of Palestine, but it should also be remembered that it had been the Red Army which had exposed the full extent of Jewish suffering in eastern Europe, an observation that Soviet spokesmen often made.

Significant though the Soviet response was, everyone understood that the key reaction would be that of the Americans, not least because of Washington's supposed influence over the voting intentions of other countries. Hence the consternation in Jewish circles when Secretary of State George C. Marshall announced that his government gave 'great weight' to the UNSCOP proposals, an endorsement of partition, if only just. What Marshall's guarded statement concealed was continuing bitter infighting in Washington over the prospect of Jewish statehood. At one level, there had been continuous Jewish lobbying of Truman over the summer as the President had held to a policy of non-interference with UNSCOP's work. The intensity of the campaign was not well advised, as Truman's testy response to one Zionist leader showed. There seems to be two sides to the question. He was finding it rather difficult to decide which one was right and a great many people in the country were beginning to feel just as he did. As expected, the Arab 'side' was being strongly urged by Henderson, who found a powerful new ally in Secretary of Defense James Forrestal, who was conscious of the need to keep the Arab oil-producing states on America's side. Once again, it fell to Niles to remind Truman of the political dangers of alienating Jewish voters. Any doubt about this was removed by the avalanche of lobbying which now fell upon the White House. From all over the country, leading Democrats and labour leaders wrote and telegraphed Truman urging support for partition. Power brokers like Democratic National Chairman Robert Hannegan and Paul Fitzpatrick, Chairman of the Democratic State Committee of New York, could not be ignored. On 7 October, Niles's chief contact with the Jewish Agency, Robert Nathan, sent a letter emphasising the urgency of open support for the UNSCOP proposals; failure to do this, he argued, would have an atomic impact on American Jewish voters with the Republicans the obvious winners. Three days later, on Truman's direct instructions, Herschel Johnson announced to the United Nations that the United States would support the partition plan (Fraser, 1989).

Even so, there were two important reservations. The first was to ensure proper implementation for the plan. Despite clear assurances to the contrary, the Americans continued to believe in British goodwill. The other was to reduce the Arab population in the Jewish state. A partial solution was to transfer Jaffa to the Arab state, but an attempt to do the same with the Negev was thwarted when Weizmann persuaded Truman that the desert was essential to the Jewish state's future development. On that basis, when the UNSCOP majority plan was put to the Ad Hoc Committee on the Palestinian Question on 25 November 1947, it was passed, by 25 votes to 13 but with 17 abstentions and 2 absentees. Had this been the vote of the General Assembly, the proposal would have failed, for the figures were short of the two-thirds majority needed. With the future of statehood clearly turning on the voting intentions of a few countries, the Jewish Agency mounted a desperate campaign. By themselves, they had little influence; Weizmann succeeded in changing the French vote by appealing to his old friend Léon Blum, but that seems to have been their one notable success.

Once again, the American connection was decisive. The initial instructions to the delegation in New York were to work 'independently and without restraint' to help secure the vote, but by 27 November it seems that their tactics were failing, for Jewish leaders telegraphed Truman demanding that he secure the votes of Greece, Haiti, China, Ecuador, Liberia, Honduras, Paraguay and the Philippines. Despite Truman's later denials, it is certain that clear instructions were sent out for this to be done. The crucial interventions were made in foreign capitals. The President of Haiti was told that 'for his own good' the country should vote for partition. The President of the Philippines was warned by a group of American senators of the 'adverse effect' on relations between the two countries should the vote be cast against partition. Truman's campaign had the desired effect, for when the General Assembly vote was taken on 29 November, the partition plan was endorsed by the necessary two-thirds majority: 33 votes to 13 with 10 abstentions (Louis, 1984; Fraser, 1989).

### The End of the British Mandate

This endorsement of their right to statehood was understandably greeted with great emotion by the Jews, but their exuberant celebrations in Jerusalem and Tel Aviv grated harshly on the Arabs. Their spokesman, Jamal Husseini, had already warned the United Nations that the partition line 'would be nothing but a line of fire and blood', and so it proved. The passing of the partition resolution was greeted with disturbances throughout the Arab world; more seriously, in Palestine the Arab Higher Committee proclaimed a general strike for 2–4 December 1947 which proved to be the start of an undeclared, but increasingly bitter, civil war. Arab leaders had assured the British that their protests would be peaceful but tension was too high for this to be a realistic hope and on the first day of the strike a Jewish shopping area in Jerusalem was burned. As violence grew, the real consequences of Britain's decision to do nothing to implement partition before the surrender of the Mandate on 14 May 1948 became clear. British military commanders in Palestine had no desire to see more of their men killed and injured in a quarrel that was ceasing to be of national interest. The result was a minimalist policy which allowed both Arab and Jewish irregular forces to become ever bolder and more ruthless. They were also encouraged by the total collapse of the mechanism designed to set up the two states and the economic union, the United Nations Palestine Commission. Set up on 9 January 1948 under the chairmanship of Czechoslovakia's Karl Lisicky, the Commission was intended to be the executive arm of the partition resolution, but the British made it clear that its members would not be allowed to land in the country. Frustrated by this challenge to United Nations' authority, on 16 February the Commission approached the Security Council for armed assistance, but with the collapse of relations with the Soviet Union there was no chance that the Americans would sanction such a policy against their British allies. The partition plan was dead.

The British had now cleared the way for the two sides to fight for control of Palestine and too much was at stake for either to have a monopoly on virtue, though in some parts of the country Arab and Jewish communities tried for a time to work local peace arrangements. The overall reality was civil war. From the start the Arabs were less well coordinated. In the north of the country Fawzi al-Qawuqji, a Syrian officer who had taken a prominent part in the Arab uprising of 1936–39, led the Arab Liberation Army, a mixed force of some 5000 Palestinians and Syrians. In the Jerusalem area the Husseinis had more direct control with the Mufti's cousin, Abd al-Qadr al-Husseini, who was commanding there, and Hassan Salameh, who commanded the area around Lydda, each with around 1000 men. They could count on sympathy, and some support, from neighbouring Arab countries and the departing British, but few Arabs had experience of recent fighting. Nor did they have any clear political strategy beyond the desire to thwart Jewish statehood, and even that was tempered by the ambition of Transjordan's Abdullah to secure part of Palestine for himself.

In contrast, thousands of Jews had fought in the British army or the Jewish Brigade, bringing with them a clear knowledge of what it took to fight a modern war. Over the winter of 1947–48, the Jewish Agency transformed the Haganah from an underground force into the nucleus of a field army, creating six brigades to cover key areas: the 'Golani' in eastern Galilee; the 'Carmeli' in western Galilee; the 'Givati' and 'Alexandroni' on the coastal plain; the 'Etzioni' around Jerusalem; and the 'Kiryati' around Tel Aviv. These came to number some 15,000 well organised but, because of continuing British hostility, not particularly well armed. Independent of them were several thousand members of the Irgun and Leh'i who had their own agendas. Guiding the actions of the Jewish Agency's forces was 'Plan Dallet' or 'Plan D', the successful implementation of which was to make an immeasurable contribution to the Jews' ultimate success. Briefly, 'Plan D' consisted of a series of operational orders to the six brigades to enable them to secure the area of the Jewish state and protect Jewish settlements in the Arab state. In military terms the plan was much superior to those of the Arabs. More controversially, the perceived need to protect outlying Jewish settlements had led Arabs to see in 'Plan D' a design for occupying the whole country. While this was not its purpose, its practical results were to be disastrous for the Arabs.

In the critical months before the end of the Mandate, the balance of advantage fell on the Jewish side. Particularly bitter fighting took place around the western approaches to Jerusalem, with the Jews striving to break a siege of the city and secure lines of communication to Tel Aviv. In the course of this there took place the massacre at the Arab village of Deir Yassin, one of the communities that had reached a working arrangement with its Jewish neighbours. On 9 April a mixed Irgun and Leh'i force attacked the village and, in what well may have been a premeditated act, killed 250 of its inhabitants. Despite condemnation from the Jewish Agency, a new benchmark for atrocity had been cut; retaliation soon came with an attack on a Jewish medical convoy at Mount Scopus in Jerusalem which left 77 doctors and nurses dead. Horrific though these incidents were, they tended to mask the steady advances that the Haganah forces were making on a number of fronts. In mid-April, the 'Golani' brigade took Tiberias, and then Safed and Rosh Pinna in Galilee. On 22 April, the 'Carmeli' brigade secured the key port of Haifa with its mixed Arab–Jewish population. Then, in the final days of the Mandate, the 'Kiryati', 'Givati' and 'Alexandroni' brigades took Jaffa with its 70,000 Arab inhabitants, removing the threat it posed to Tel Aviv. All these operations resulted in the flight, or removal, of tens of thousands of Arabs. The success of 'Plan D' was preparing the way for a successful declaration of Jewish statehood the moment the British left (Morris, 1987).

## The Proclamation of the State of Israel

With British authority fast disappearing and the Haganah holding the initiative in many key areas, Ben-Gurion and his colleagues prepared to proclaim statehood on the day the Mandate ended. While neither Ben-Gurion nor Weizmann, who was in the United States, had doubts about this decision, the risks were clear. The Arab states would attack, with the continuing support of the British. Much, then, would turn on the attitudes of the other major powers. Enough was known about Soviet intentions to reassure the Jewish leadership but even more critical was the likely position of the Americans. Once again, Washington was a key battlefield, with the State Department set against recognition of the new state and Truman increasingly inclined to do so. The President's aide, Clark Clifford, prepared a powerful memorandum which argued that as the Jewish state was already an 'accomplished fact', Truman should issue immediate recognition; otherwise, the Soviets and his Republican enemies at home would reap any benefit. On 12 May, Clifford presented these arguments at a meeting involving Truman, David Niles and leading State Department officials, including Secretary of State Marshall. Marshall irascibly responded that the proposal was a 'transparent dodge to win a few votes' and would have nothing to do with the idea. Truman had hoped to announce his intention to recognise the Jewish state at a press conference on the 13th but Marshall's hostile response thwarted the idea. The following day, Britain's High Commissioner, Sir Alan Cunningham, left Jerusalem and sailed from Haifa. Ben-Gurion and his colleagues assembled in the museum in Tel Aviv and announced the Declaration of Independence of the State of Israel, which was to be open to all Jews and which promised to ensure the rights of all its citizens regardless of race or religion. The honour of being first President went to Weizmann, while Ben-Gurion assumed the task of Prime Minister. The same day, the power struggle in Washington had been resolved in Truman's favour. The new state was proclaimed at 6 p.m. Washington time; Truman's de facto recognition followed 11 minutes later (Ganin, 1979).

## The First Arab–Israeli War

As American recognition was quickly followed by that of the Soviet Union, the new state could approach the dangers ahead with some confidence, for there seemed no prospect of Arab acceptance of Israel; rather their spokesman had promised 'a line of blood and fire'. The coalition of Arab League states which 'intervened' in Palestine on 15 May was neither united in its purpose nor adequately prepared for war. Four of the six Arab forces ranged against Israel – Lebanese, Syrian, Iraqi and Saudi Arabian – undertook little by way of offensive operations, though, of course, their presence tied down Israeli troops. The really hard fighting for the Israelis was against the Egyptians, who had two brigades threatening Tel Aviv, and Abdullah's British-officered Arab Legion in the Jerusalem sector. Egyptian participation in the war was problematic, despite considerable popular sympathy for the Palestinians. Indeed, it has been argued that it was the strength of public feeling that largely influenced King Farouk to intervene against the guidance of his military advisers and much of the political establishment. The Egyptian army was primarily a police force, with neither the training nor logistics to conduct a sustained offensive operation (Rogan and Shlaim, 2001). Transjordan's King Abdullah was the designated commander of the Arab League forces, but his resources were limited and his role largely meaningless. Abdullah, who had long since come to terms with the reality of the Jewish presence in Palestine, had his eye firmly fixed on securing the Arab areas of the country for his dynasty (Shlaim, 2000).

Even so, in the initial phases, the Arabs had clear advantages in terms of heavy weapons and air-power, and the Israelis had a major problem with the narrowness of the coastal plain which made in-depth strategic defence impossible. By the time the United Nations succeeded in arranging a truce on 11 June, severe fighting had taken place, especially around Jerusalem where the Jewish New City had struggled to survive Jordanian and Egyptian assaults and siege. The battles against the Arab Legion in and around Jerusalem entered Israeli military legend. The truce was to be supervised by Sweden's Count Folke Bernadotte, who had already been appointed as United Nations mediator in the conflict. It was welcomed by both sides after weeks of intense fighting which had left the balance of advantage unclear. The Arab war effort had suffered seriously from lack of a unified command, but they still held a powerful grip around Jerusalem where they had taken the ancient Jewish Quarter of the Old City, had inflicted heavy casualties in the Negev, and in the central sector were within ten miles of the Mediterranean coast. The Israelis had held their ground but desperately needed tanks, artillery and, above all, aircraft. The terms of the cease-fire did not allow them to remedy this, for neither side was to bring in men or supplies. Ben-Gurion's government honoured this in the breach. Links had already been forged with Czechoslovakia, which had access to the enormous amounts of war material left over from the war in Europe. From air-bases in Czechoslovakia, vitally needed supplies, including crated Messerschmidt fighters, arrived in Israel. Aircraft, including three American Flying Fortress bombers and several British Spitfire fighters, arrived by other routes later in the summer. During this period an episode occurred which finally brought to the surface the long-simmering tension between the Haganah and the Irgun. The latter had organised its own arms shipments in France which arrived off Tel Aviv on 20 June aboard the *Altalena*. Choosing to see this as a violation of the cease-fire and a challenge to the authority of the new government, Ben-Gurion ordered his forces to attack the vessel which was destroyed with heavy loss of Jewish life. By his action Ben-Gurion confirmed that there was now an Israeli government rather than a collection of factions, but in doing so he cut a deep wound in Israeli political life which festered for the next 30 years (Sachar, 1976).

When the war resumed on 8 July, it quickly became clear that the Israelis now held the advantage, with rapid advances being made in several key areas, notably in Galilee and the towns of Lydda and Ramle. Both these operations were accompanied by large-scale expulsions of Palestinians. In Galilee there was some distinction between Muslim villages and those with a largely Christian and Druse population; Nazareth, with its obvious significance for Christian opinion worldwide, was left untouched. Overall, some 30,000 Palestinian refugees left, many for Lebanon. Lydda and Ramle were attacked with particular ruthlessness. Under the partition plan the towns had been allotted to the Arab state. Strategically, they were important because of the airport at Lydda and their proximity to Tel Aviv. An operation which began on the night of 9 July left the towns in Israeli hands and at a meeting with army commanders on the 12th Ben-Gurion seems to have given the order for the expulsion of their inhabitants, who possibly numbered as many as 70,000. Controversy surrounds Ben-Gurion's action: there is little doubt that he wanted the Arabs expelled but that he was reluctant to be publicly identified with the action. Next to Deir Yassin, the 'Lydda Death March' which followed etched its way into the Palestinian consciousness as a symbol of their tragedy. Driven towards Ramallah in the summer heat, hundreds, especially children and the elderly, died from exhaustion and dehydration (Palumbo, 1987).

After ten days of hostilities, which left the Israelis much better positioned than before, a second truce came into operation on 18 July, giving Bernadotte the opportunity to work for a diplomatic solution. By early August, he believed he had the germ of a settlement. Talks with the Lebanese and Jordanian leaders indicated a willingness to acquiesce in Israel's existence. Discussions with Israeli leaders on the return of Palestinian refugees, whom he estimated at between 300,000 and 400,000, had been less satisfactory, but he was working towards a consolidation of Israeli territory that would reflect the way the military situation had developed. This formed the basis of the proposals he submitted on 16 September: Israel was to retain Galilee but surrender much of the Negev and return Lydda and Ramle to the Arabs; Jerusalem was to be an international city and Palestinian refugees were to have the right to return home. For some time Bernadotte had been regarded with suspicion by the Israelis. Working from an earlier draft of his plan, which had been less favourable to Israel, Leh'i members in Jerusalem decided on his death. The day after submitting his plan to the United Nations he was murdered in the city (Bernadotte, 1951).

Bernadotte's death was condemned by the Israeli government, but his proposals still threatened their plans with regard to Jerusalem, with its large Jewish population, and over the future development of the Negev. They were not reassured by General Marshall's announcement on 21 September that the United States accepted the Bernadotte plan 'in its entirety'. A determined effort had to be made to attack the plan. On 27 September, an emergency meeting was held in Oklahoma City, where Truman was campaigning, at which Clifford and others impressed upon him the disastrous consequences Marshall's statement was having on Jewish voters in the key electoral states of New York and Pennsylvania. As a result, Stephen Wise was assured that de jure recognition would be given to Israel once elections had been held there and Marshall was instructed to make no further statement without presidential clearance. Lack of American support proved fatal to the plan, even though once Truman had been re-elected on 3 November he did toy with the idea of making the Negev part of an Arab state.

Ben-Gurion's government was resolved to settle the issue of the Negev on the ground. On 15 October, having manufactured an attack on a supply convoy, Israeli forces resumed fighting in the Negev around the Faluja crossroads, the key to the road network. Although their Egyptian antagonists fought well, they had no answer to Israeli superiority in the air and it was soon clear which side had the initiative. The Egyptians were now fighting the war on their own and, by the end of the year, the Israelis were positioned to destroy the Egyptian forces and take the final stretch of territory along the coast from Rafah to Gaza, but the war was brought to an end before they could do so. In January 1949, Israeli fighters shot down five British Spitfires flying in support of the

Egyptians in the Sinai Desert across the international frontier. The prospect of war between Britain and Israel provoked the Americans into ending the conflict by warning the Israelis of British treaty obligations towards Arab countries. As a result, Ben-Gurion ordered a halt to military operations. The Negev had been secured, if not the area which soon came to be called the Gaza Strip (Fraser, 1989).

By this stage, negotiations for an Israeli–Egyptian armistice agreement were under way at Rhodes under the able direction of Ralph Bunche, Bernadotte's former deputy and successor at the United Nations. The agreement concluded on 24 February 1949 set the pattern for others with Lebanon, Syria and Jordan which defined the nature of Israel's boundaries, at least down to 1967. As these armistice agreements were seen as the forerunner of a full peace settlement, it was laid down that the 'Armistice Demarcation Line is not to be construed in any sense as a political or territorial boundary, and is delineated without prejudice to rights, claims and positions of either Party to the Armistice as regards ultimate settlement of the Palestine problem'. While this seemed to give a sense of impermanence to Israel's borders with her Arab neighbours, these came to be generally accepted as the boundaries of the state. The ending of the war and the holding of Israel's first general election were quickly followed by the coveted confirmations of statehood. In January 1949, Truman extended de jure recognition and the American Export–Import Bank provided urgently needed loans; in May, Israel took her seat at the United Nations. The contrast with the situation of the Jews a mere four years before could not have been more stark. This was equally true of the Palestinians for whom the events of 1948–49 were al-Nakba, 'the catastrophe', the full extent of which they were only just beginning to understand. The pattern of the Arab–Israeli conflict had been set.

# 2

# The Problem Consolidated

## Israel after the 1948–49 War

Israel came out of the 1948–49 war, if not yet self-confident, then at least assuming that her worst trials were over. The armistice agreements expanded her boundaries considerably beyond those set out in the 1947 partition resolution, reflecting the successes of the armed forces. The most substantial gains were Galilee and the western parts of Jerusalem with a land corridor to the coast. The Israel of 1949 was a more coherent state than could ever have come out of the partition plan. Even so, there were problems which cut into the Israelis' sense of security. Perhaps the most obvious was that these borders were still only provisional; indeed, the armistice agreements had gone out of their way to emphasise this. This reinforced the sense that Israel was still technically at war with most of her neighbours, for no peace agreement was in sight. Israel had to exist in an uneasy state of continual tension, her major settlements on the coastal plain perilously close to Jordanian territory, nine miles at the narrowest point; indeed, the main route from Tel Aviv to Jerusalem passed within yards of the border. It was a situation no general would have wanted and one that demanded a permanent state of military preparedness, which was to prove no small burden for the young country.

The other financial and human burden the state had to bear arose directly out of the reason for its creation, the desire to have an assured homeland for any Jew who wished to live there. In 1950 the Knesset passed the Law of Return which confirmed the right of every Jew to permanent settlement in the country; this was followed two years later by the Citizenship Law which gave immigrants the immediate right of citizenship. The results could not have been more dramatic, transforming both the number and the nature of the population. The new Israeli government had a problem, for the Zionist dream of providing a home for the millions of Jews of eastern Europe could not be realised: Hitler had seen to that. Although some 304,044 did arrive between 1948 and 1951, there was little further potential, not least because Stalin had become hostile to the new state, and only 4698 immigrants came from the Soviet Union. It was not until the age of Gorbachev and perestroika in the late 1980s that the prospect of mass Jewish immigration from the Soviet Union opened up. Nor did the other great diaspora, the Jews of the United States, seem much interested, for, despite vigorous support given to the Zionist cause, only 1,909 American Jews came to settle in Israel over the period 1948–51. If the population were to be built up, there was only one possible source of mass immigration: the Jewish communities of the Middle East and North Africa, which had barely featured in earlier Zionist plans. These ancient communities had long coexisted with their Muslim and Christian Arab neighbours who had generally behaved towards them with greater generosity than Europeans had afforded towards the Jews in their midst. This situation began to deteriorate after 1945. The creation of Israel was not the sole reason for this. The Ottoman, British and French Empires in the Middle East had ensured for the Jews a measure of protection, whereas the newly independent states were more concerned to assert the rights of Arabs. Even so, it is clear that the outbreak of war in May 1948 hastened the end for these communities. Between 1948 and 1951, 232,583 immigrants came from the Middle

East and a further 92,510 from North Africa, the latter continuing throughout the 1950s as France's grip on Tunisia, Morocco and Algeria began to falter. The result was a permanent change in the composition of the Israeli population which was to have the most profound political and social consequences. Oriental Jews had long been a small percentage of the world's Jewish population – only some 8 per cent before Hitler's massacres – but they came to form a bare majority of Israel's Jewish population (Sachar, 1976).

Despite the enthusiasm with which the state approached the task, the costs of forging a nation were inevitably high. Middle Eastern Jews had very different expectations from those of European origin, while many of the latter, who had survived Hitler's death camps, came physically weakened and emotionally scarred. Not all of them were capable of contributing to Israel's productive capacity. Moreover, they had to be integrated into a state which, the Dead Sea mineral deposits excepted, enjoyed none of the basic raw materials that might have generated economic development. Israel's economic priority in the early 1950s had to be the construction of housing for its new immigrant population, and while this generated good wages and stimulated demand, it did little towards building up an export sector. On the contrary, the country faced the basic need to import nearly all its essential raw materials, not least oil, with the inevitable problem of the balance of payments. While there was a conscious strategy of building up light industries which would ease transport costs and reduce the need for imported raw materials, agriculture remained the basis of the economy. Israel had inherited well-developed citrus and cotton industries, giving it primary products that could be marketed in northern Europe but even here it had obvious rivals in southern Europe who had the competitive edge after the formation of the Common Market in 1957 and its subsequent expansion. But, above all, the growth in population and the expansion of agriculture put enormous strain on that most basic of primary resources, water. Israel's need to expand its water supplies was to become a major source of tension with its Arab neighbours.

Israel could only hope to tackle these financial and economic problems with outside help. One of the earliest acts of the new state, on 25 May 1948, was to request a loan from the American Export–Import Bank. On 19 January 1949, with the ending of hostilities, the Americans granted loans of $35 million to assist agricultural development and $55 million for communications, transport, manufacturing, housing and public works. Essential though these were, they were not a solution for the country's financial situation and were to become an uncomfortable reminder of how vulnerable Israel might become to American pressure. The government looked to the continuing financial generosity of American Jews to help sustain development, but even here the omens were discouraging. Contributions through the United Jewish Appeal peaked at $148 million in 1948 but, as the danger to Israel receded, the annual totals fell away dramatically. By 1951 they were $85 million and in the first five months of 1952 only $39 million came. By this stage Israel was in such deep financial trouble that in June the government had to appeal to Washington for a refunding of its debts and allow the Americans to appoint a financial expert to sort out the confusion. This humiliation proved to be the low point, for financial relief was coming from an unexpected, and for many Israelis highly unwelcome, source. In the course of 1951 secret contacts developed between the Israelis and the new Federal Republic of Germany of Konrad Adenauer. Conscious of Germany's need for rehabilitation, on 21 September Adenauer announced acceptance of the principle of restitution to the Jews for their suffering during the war. Most Israelis were scandalised at the thought of assistance coming from the country they had come to detest, and negotiators had to be given protection from death threats. But in June 1952, the same month that the Israelis had to confess their financial collapse to Washington, the German cabinet agreed on the nature of the reparations to be paid. On 10 September representatives of the two governments met in Luxemburg to sign the Reparations Treaty. Between then and 1966, the Federal Republic supplied over 3000 million Deutschmarks to Israel, mostly in the form of goods and equipment, as well as restitution paid to individuals. It was the financial and economic breakthrough the country needed (Gillessen, n.d.).

From the start Israel was determined to establish her democratic credentials, understandably so given the disabilities Jews had suffered under authoritarian regimes. The tone of its politics was set by the first premier, David Ben-Gurion, and his left-wing Mapai party, established in 1930. Power rested with the 120-member Knesset, but the political system was far from straightforward. Elections were held under what has been described as an extreme form of proportional representation, designed to ensure that all the major groups in the country could claim an adequate say in its affairs. Elections to the first Knesset in 1949 illustrated the problem. While Mapai emerged as the largest party, it could only command 46 seats, forcing Ben-Gurion to include representatives of five other political parties in his Cabinet. The negotiations, and inevitable compromises, which this system dictated were to become a recurring feature of the political process in the years ahead. Factionalism and schism were also apparent, so that it was not until 1968 that Mapai combined with other groups to form the Labour Alignment. None of this impaired the country's political life, indeed it could be seen as a sign of health, but it did not always lend itself to clear decision-making.

## The Palestinians after the 1948–49 War

If Israel faced serious problems in the aftermath of war, the position of the Palestinians seemed hopeless – their society ravaged, their political hopes in ruins. Some 150,000 remained in Israel, largely in the north where towns like

Nazareth and Umm al-Fahm and surrounding villages remained centres of Arab life and culture. They had no choice but to reconcile themselves to life in the new state which offered toleration but could not trust them. The armistice agreements left Gaza under Egyptian control, its pre-1948 population of 70,000 increased to 270,000 through the influx of refugees. The Gaza Strip soon became a byword for deprivation as even the indigenous population had become separated from its farmlands by the armistice lines and the area was now cut off from its economic hinterland. Egypt had no resources to offer. Despite the influx of refugees and the disruption of its economic links, the West Bank seemed to offer a better prospect. In April 1950, elections were held in Transjordan and the West Bank for a new parliament in Amman. Its first act was to unite the territories as the Hashemite Kingdom of Jordan with Abdullah as its monarch. But it was at best a marriage of convenience. If most West Bank Palestinians were prepared to acquiesce in it, some were not. On 20 July 1951, Abdullah was assassinated as he came to pray at the Al-Aqsa mosque in Jerusalem. Few doubted that the Husseini interest was behind the murder.

Out of the failed political aspirations of the Palestinians came their need to accommodate themselves as Jordanians, Gazans or Israeli Arabs, while accommodation was even more difficult for those who had ended up in the other Arab states. How a sense of Palestinian identity would survive this tripartite division was serious enough, but in the immediate aftermath of the war the most pressing problem for the refugees was staying alive. Having left their farms, shops and workshops, they had no means of survival. For shelter, some found mosques, churches, schools or hospitable Arab families, but most were in temporary camps that offered the most rudimentary protection, and some were in caves. In October 1948, James McDonald, the US Ambassador to Israel, reported that the refugee situation had reached 'catastrophic proportions' and that the 'approaching winter with heavy cold will, it is estimated, kill more than 100,000 old men, women and children who are shelterless and have no food'. Out of this concern came the establishment on 19 November 1948 of the United Nations Relief for Palestine Refugees, with the United States bearing half the cost. Appeals went out for countries to provide food, clothing and shelter (Palumbo, 1987).

Initially, there was little hard information about the nature and extent of the refugee problem. As early as August 1948 Bernadotte thought that some 300,000–400,000 Palestinians had become refugees, but this was clearly impressionistic and expulsions continued long after that date. Although historians continue to debate the figures, the UN estimate of over 750,000 seems the most reliable. They were to be found in all the countries and territories surrounding Israel. The largest number, 350,000, was in Jordan and the West Bank, soon to be politically united; of these, 280,000 were located west of the River Jordan and 70,000 to the east. Gaza held some 200,000, most of them from Jaffa and the southern part of Palestine. Palestinians from Haifa and Galilee had fled in large numbers across the border: 97,000 of them into southern Lebanon and around 75,000 into Syria. A small group of 4000 was in Iraq. In addition, 25,000 Palestinians still in their homes were classed as refugees because separation from their lands had made them destitute, and there were 31,000 Arab refugees in Israel (Fraser, 1980). The Western world was slow to realise the full extent of what had happened. In part this was because of the growing preoccupation with the Cold War, the Berlin airlift of 1948–49, the 'fall' of China to Communism in 1949 and the outbreak of the Korean War in 1950. Partly, too, it was because refugees were a sadly conspicuous feature of the immediate post-Second World War world: 9,000,000 Germans had been expelled from their homes east of the Oder–Neisse Line as a result of the redrawing of the map of Poland and 3,000,000 Sudeten Germans were put out of Czechoslovakia. But whereas Germany could absorb its Prussian, Silesian and Sudeten refugees and put them to work, Palestinian national life was seemingly shattered beyond recall. The Arab economies were too poor to offer much beyond the barest assistance. Absorption, or 'resettlement' as it was known, in the surrounding Arab countries was not an option, for the refugees themselves saw this as a device to prevent them ever returning home. Their view was respected by Arab governments. Accordingly, all that remained was the hope that Israel might be prevailed upon to allow the repatriation of at least some of them, and the prospect that the international community would be sufficiently moved to provide some form of relief.

Along with the bid for immediate relief went a General Assembly resolution on 11 December 1948 stating:

> that the refugees wishing to return to their homes and live at peace with their neighbours should be permitted to do so at the earliest possible date, and that compensation should be paid for the property of those choosing not to return.

The same resolution established the Palestine Conciliation Commission which was charged with reaching agreement on the refugees, as well as borders and the status of Jerusalem. The American Government hoped that their representative on the Commission, the Louisville newspaperman Mark Ethridge, would secure concessions for the refugees, including a measure of repatriation to their homes. It was a policy that Ben-Gurion's government was determined to prevent. By the spring of 1949 it was apparent to the Americans that Arab refugee property was being cleared to make way for Jewish immigrants and that the Israeli government had no intention of increasing its Arab minority through repatriation, nor was it willing to make any form of restitution to the refugees. When an attempt to put pressure on Israel through delaying part of the Export–Import Bank loan was thwarted by a political campaign in the White House, Ethridge resigned from the Conciliation Commission. This really marked the end of the attempt to secure a measure of repatriation. Instead, the Commission set up the Economic Survey Mission which recommended that the United Nations establish an agency to provide relief and works for the refugees. Accordingly, in December 1949 the United Nations Relief and Works Agency for Palestine Refugees (UNRWA) came into being. Although intended to be a temporary measure, the establishment of UNRWA was an admission that the refugees would not be returning home. The bleak realisation that their exile was not going to be temporary was reinforced by the knowledge that the Cold War and events in Korea meant that they were no longer at the forefront of anyone's attention.

## The Egyptian Revolution

Out of the Arabs' sense of failure and humiliation came one of the Middle East's most challenging and important figures, Gamal Abdul Nasser. Born in 1918 into a lower- middle-class Egyptian family, Nasser was to become the leading Arab figure of the modern era, his portrait still proudly displayed in homes more than a generation after his death in 1970. It is easy to see why he rose to such a position, for he was instrumental in restoring Egyptian pride, which had long suffered humiliation for reasons unconnected with the Arab–Israeli conflict. Despite his immense prestige, in the long run Nasser had little positive effect on the Arab–Israeli conflict.

The completion of the Suez Canal in 1869 brought with it the unwelcome attention of the British, for whom protection of the routes to India was paramount. In 1882, the Royal Navy bombarded Alexandria, the Egyptian army was defeated, and the country passed under British control, even though still acknowledging the theoretical suzerainty of the Ottoman Empire and retaining as its Khedive the descendants of the Albanian adventurer Muhammad Ali. Under the imperious rule of such men as Lord Cromer (1882–1907) and Lord Kitchener (1911–14) Egyptians experienced the material benefits of peace and order, but hated the ways in which they were made to feel inferior in their own country. In the Second World War, Egypt was the principal battleground for control of the Middle East, and Egyptians bitterly resented the events of May 1942 when British tanks forced the young King Farouk to appoint a government of their choice. Even after the war, 80,000 British troops remained in their bases in the Suez Canal Zone, a seemingly permanent reminder of Egyptian weakness. In these circumstances the collapse of Farouk's hopes of restoring his dynasty's fortunes through a successful campaign against Israel proved to be fatal.

In Egypt, as elsewhere in the late colonial world, the army was always likely to be the revolutionary force. It had the organisational skills, the sense of grievance against a government which it felt had let it down in the recent war, and, perhaps above all, its officers included young men of comparatively humble origin, like Nasser, Anwar al-Sadat and Abd al-Hakim Amer, who had come to despise Farouk's incompetence and corruption. These men formed the kernel of the Free Officers movement, which by the summer of 1949 was plotting the regime's overthrow. Their moment came on 22 July 1952. Cairo and Alexandria were quickly seized, Farouk abdicated in favour of his son and sailed into exile. Egypt's future now lay with the young officers, led for the time being by General Muhammad Naguib, a senior general who was never intended to be more than a figurehead. Egypt's new rulers knew that their hopes for the country's future would enjoy the goodwill of the United States. The character of the regime was initially welcome to the Americans who had been looking for leaders in the Middle East with popular support who would back the Western side in the Cold War. With that in view the Central Intelligence Agency had forged links with the Free Officers well in advance of the coup. Washington and Cairo could, it seemed, form a new alliance against possible Soviet moves in the Middle East, free from the taint of imperialism that had poisoned relations with the British (Copeland, 1969; Stephens, 1971).

Naguib steadily lost ground before Nasser's superior political skills. By the spring of 1954 Egypt was a republic with Nasser its dominant figure; by the end of the year he was president and Naguib was under house arrest. For the next 16 years he was to be the key Arab player in the confrontation with Israel. It was not always obvious that this would be the case, nor perhaps was it inevitable. Nasser was an Egyptian with ambitions for his country but with little experience of the wider Arab world (Stephens, 1971). The Americans, the CIA in particular, saw Nasser as a popular leader who would not go out of his way to look for conflict with Israel and might just reach an accommodation with it. Events were to prove otherwise.

### Deteriorating Arab–Israeli Relations

In fact, the years 1952–55 were to see steadily mounting tension between Israel and her Arab neighbours, complicated by a period of frosty relations with the United States. One of the earliest sources of tension was the steady move of ministries and then the Knesset from Tel Aviv to Jerusalem. To the Israelis this was simply confirming Jerusalem's status as their eternal capital, whereas to the Americans it was a breach of the city's intended status as an international entity. Refusal to remove the American Embassy from Tel Aviv was keenly resented. This issue, and that of the Palestinian refugees, festered in the latter period of the Truman administration, but when the Republican administration of Dwight Eisenhower took office in January 1953 a noticeable chill set in. Eisenhower's election owed little to Jewish voters and his influential Secretary of State, John Foster Dulles, believed that Israel had no special call on America's affections.

In May 1953 the new Secretary of State undertook a Middle East tour, visiting all the major countries and hearing spokesmen for the refugees. Dulles was clearly anxious to enlist Arab nationalist support in the Cold War, if possible in what came to be known as a Middle East Defense Organization. A clear sign of the new direction in Washington's thinking was his indication, in both Egypt and Israel, that be believed the policy of the Truman administration had been too much influenced by Jewish groups. The new administration, he was at pains to point out, did not believe 'in building power by cultivating particular sections of populations'. This came, as was intended, as a clear signal to Ben-Gurion that he could no longer count on the kind of political leverage that had been so influential in the Truman White House. When the crisis between the two governments came, it arose over the Middle East's most precious resource, water. On 2 September 1953, the Israelis began work to divert the waters of the River Jordan at Banat Yacoub in the Syrian demilitarised zone. The United Nations' representative ordered the work to be stopped. When Israel refused to comply with this order, Dulles ordered the suspension of $26 million in aid. It was the first clear breach between the two countries since the creation of the Israeli state and, as intended, it was an uncomfortable signal that the Eisenhower administration considered itself immune to Jewish lobbying (Fraser, 1989; Oren, 2007).

This deterioration in relations between Israel and her most powerful patron came at a time of increasing tension along her borders. The 1949 armistice agreements had reflected the positions reached by the opposing armies, not the traditional landholding rights of Arab farmers. It was not surprising that the latter disregarded lines, which held little meaning for them, and crossed into Israel to inspect or farm their old lands. To the Israelis this was unwelcome 'infiltration', especially as recent Jewish immigrants had been encouraged to settle in these border areas. It was a recipe for tragedy. Israeli border patrols regularly killed Arabs who crossed the border, with the inevitable result that the Arabs themselves began to arm. As violence on the border increased, the Israelis created a new counter-terrorist force, Unit 101, commanded by the youthful Ariel Sharon. The crisis began on 13 October 1953 when an attack on the village of Tirat Yehuda killed an Israeli mother and her two children. Fearing the consequences, the Jordanians offered to help catch the killers, but instead a retaliatory raid was mounted by Unit 101 on the nearby Jordanian village of Qibya. Sixty-nine people, half of them women and children, were killed. A deeply embarrassed Ben-Gurion only added to Israel's problems with an unconvincing claim that the massacre had been the work of incensed settlers. The Americans denounced the events at Qibya, and it was only when the Israelis suspended work on the Banat Yacoub canal that Dulles released the $26 million, an uncomfortable confirmation that the benign days of the Truman administration had passed (Sachar, 1976; Fraser, 1989).

It is fair to say that the Israelis entered 1954 in a distinctly uneasy mood, made no more comfortable by the knowledge of Nasser's increasing self-assurance. In October 1954, Nasser scored his first major triumph in foreign policy by securing British withdrawal from their bases in the Suez Canal Zone, thus ending this conspicuous sign of Egypt's subordination to the old imperialism. At the same time, his relations with the Americans remained good. Fears over this situation were to lead the Israeli intelligence services into a major blunder which echoed through the country's politics for years. In an attempt to expose the instability of Nasser's regime to the British and Americans, an Israeli intelligence group began setting off bombs at American government offices in Cairo and Alexandria. Once the agents were arrested, the Egyptian police informed the Americans of their real identity. Two were executed and the rest given long prison sentences. The 'Affair', as it came to be known, badly rattled the Israeli government and dismayed the public. Once again, Israel had been shown to the Americans in a bad light: Washington refused to respond to Israeli appeals to help reduce the sentences on the agents (Black and Morris,

1991). By the end of 1954, State Department officials, together with British colleagues, were working on a secret plan, code named 'Alpha', which they hoped would stabilise the Middle East through a peace settlement between Egypt and Israel. It was rather optimistically based upon the recently concluded settlement of the Italian–Yugoslav dispute over Trieste (Kyle, 1991; Oren, 2007).

## The Gaza Raid and its Consequences

It was inevitable that the Israeli government would look for a way out of its domestic and international embarrassment and that it would do so by turning to the country's ablest leader, David Ben-Gurion, who had earlier surrendered the premiership to live in political exile in the Negev. Returning as Defence Minister in February 1955, Ben-Gurion quickly recharged the government's energy. His chosen target was Gaza which had been the source of growing Israeli irritation over the number of Palestinian guerrilla raids. The 'raid' on Gaza, which took place on 28 February 1955, was really a major military operation with the Palestinian guerrillas providing the pretext for an operation designed to show Israel's military power both to the West and to a nervous public opinion. In one sense it marked a low point in Israel's relations with the United States, for the Americans joined in condemning the operation, which had left 38 Egyptian soldiers dead. But in other respects the Gaza raid was the beginning of a chain of events which was to push the Arab–Israeli conflict in dramatic new directions.

The operation had, as intended, delivered a severe rebuff to an Egyptian army which was only beginning to recover from the defeats of 1948–49. Moreover, Nasser's was a military regime which could not sustain such humiliations. It is arguable whether the events of 28 February convinced Nasser of the need to move in new directions or simply accelerated the process. The result was the same. It had never been his purpose to act as any kind of puppet of the West. While some Americans appreciated his need to strike an independent line, others did not. Conscious of the need to build up his armed forces, and frustrated that the British and Americans were proving slow to respond, he began to look elsewhere. This did not bode well for the prospects of Plan Alpha when negotiations began in the spring of 1955. The plan attempted to address the position of the Palestinian refugees by persuading the Israelis to allow some of them to return, with financial compensation for those who could not. At its heart was the idea that Israel should surrender territory in the Negev to Egypt and Jordan with a view to facilitating contact. But Nasser's eyes were on all of the Negev, while Ben-Gurion had a passionate attachment to it. It was, after all, the Israeli leader's chosen home. Negotiations over the plan continued for the next 12 months, but these two positions were too far apart to be reconciled, and far-reaching developments were taking place on other fronts (Kyle, 1991).

Nasser's alienation from the Americans really began in March 1955 when he ignored their advice and took part in the Bandung conference of non-aligned states. As Bandung was attended by the Communist Chinese with whom Dulles was at bitter odds, his attendance had predictable results. Nasser was prepared to take his neutralism a stage further by using China's Zhou Enlai to test the possibility of securing arms supplies from the Soviet Union. The response proved positive. Despite last-minute American attempts to persuade him otherwise, on 30 September 1955 Nasser announced that he had made an arms agreement with 'Czechoslovakia', a thin cover for the Soviet Union. Although Nasser was still trying to maintain a balance between East and West that was not how his action was seen in Washington, London and Paris, and certainly not in Jerusalem. Even at this stage the American reaction was the least strident of the four (Copeland, 1969).

Clearly, the Israelis had most to fear from Egypt's acquisition of a substantial armoury. The Americans had not given up on the idea that Nasser and Ben-Gurion were strong enough leaders to strike a deal. Their efforts culminated in the early months of 1956 with the secret mission of Robert Anderson in a final attempt to explore Plan Alpha. But his report only really exposed the extent of the continuing gulf between the two countries (Kyle, 1991). Instead of moving towards a settlement, relations between them were steadily worsening. On one level there was the continuing irritation over incursions from the Gaza Strip with the inevitable Israeli retaliation, while on another there was Egypt's refusal to allow cargoes bound for Israel through the Suez Canal or the Straits of Tiran to the port of Eilat at the southern tip of the Negev. In response Israeli defence chiefs had started planning for a possible breach of the blockade by sending a secret reconnaissance mission down the Sinai Desert to mark out a route for a possible attack towards Sharm al-Shaikh, the fort dominating the Straits. But the supply of Soviet weaponry threatened to turn the military balance decisively against the Israelis. The shipments, which began in November 1955, were to include automatic light weapons, 100 self-propelled guns, 200 armoured personnel carriers and 300 tanks. Compared with these, the Israeli army had weapons which were obsolescent, but what really worried its chiefs was the supply of 200 MiG-15 jet fighters and 50 Ilyushin-28 jet bombers which put their cities in potentially mortal danger from Egyptian airbases in the Sinai. In any case, what was the purpose of this formidable arsenal? The search for a Western arms partner, particularly for the supply of modern aircraft, became imperative. Fortunately – and in a sense fortuitously – for the Israelis, such a partner existed.

## Origins of the Suez Crisis

The French view of Nasser was entirely coloured by his enthusiastic support for the nationalist rebellion that had broken out in Algeria in 1954. It was a war they were determined to win, especially as Algeria was regarded as an integral part of the French Republic with over a million French men and women living there. Still smarting from their defeats in 1940 and, more recently, in Indo-China, the French were increasingly open to suggestions from any quarter which would allow them to act against the Egyptian leader. Moreover, as veterans of the wartime resistance the French leadership was receptive to Jewish appeals for defence requirements. In April 1956, 12 Mystère IV fighters, one of the best fighter planes in the world, were flown to Israel; the following month contracts were signed for a further 72 Mystères, 120 AMX light tanks and 40 Super Sherman tanks. The Israelis could now look forward to countering the potential Egyptian threat with the active support of a major Western power. It was also a clear confirmation that the Arab–Israeli conflict had entered a more dangerous phase.

The French view of Nasser was increasingly shared by the British Prime Minister, Anthony Eden. The British had their own security network in the Middle East, the Baghdad Pact, of which Iraq was the only Arab member. The other obvious candidate was Jordan, now ruled by Abdullah's young grandson, King Hussein. Jordan was heavily subsidised by Britain, and its army, the Arab Legion, was commanded by General Sir John Glubb and other British officers. A clumsy attempt by General Sir Gerald Templer to recruit Jordan into the Pact failed when Hussein's government realised that public opinion would not stand for it. Templer's humiliating rebuff was not well received in London but worse was to come. At the end of February 1956, Glubb and the other British officers were summarily dismissed from Jordanian service. This further blow to British prestige went hard with Eden who was already being compared unfavourably with his illustrious predecessor, Winston Churchill, and was being criticised in Britain for his weakness in the face of Arab nationalism. Eden was proving to be a poor choice as Prime Minister. This was not entirely his fault, for a botched operation on his bile duct had seriously weakened his health. But he increasingly saw Nasser through the lens of the 1930s when he had been Foreign Secretary. For him the Egyptian leader had become the new Mussolini or Hitler whose ambitions needed to be curbed, just as Hitler's should have been at the time of the Rhineland crisis in 1936. However inappropriate the comparison, it came increasingly to dominate his mind and actions, with fateful consequences for Britain and the Middle East (Rhodes James, 1986).

Despite these various pressures, the Middle East crisis was not triggered by the Israelis, French or British but by the Americans who had now come round to the view that Nasser was incorrigibly anti-Western, not least because of his recent recognition of their particular *bête noire*, the People's Republic of China. The Egyptian leader's major project for improving the condition of his people was the proposed construction at Aswan on the Nile of a dam which would regulate the river's flow, providing at the same time cheap hydroelectric power and irrigation. As Egypt could only afford to bear part of the cost, the deficit was to be made up by loans from the World Bank and grants from the British and American governments. By July 1956, with Congressional opinion hardening against Nasser and claiming doubts about Egypt's ability to pay for her share of the project, Dulles had decided against financing the project. This was conveyed to an incredulous Egyptian ambassador in Washington on 19 July, the British immediately following suit. With its emphasis on Egypt's financial capacity, this was a humiliating blow for Egypt and for Nasser personally.

## Nasser's Nationalisation of the Suez Canal

The Egyptian leader responded skilfully to restore his country's pride and offer the means through which the dam might be financed. In a speech at Alexandria on 26 July, he announced the nationalisation of the Suez Canal Company. The Canal was Egypt's one major asset, but it was run by the

Paris-based company on a lease due to expire in 1968. Nasser's move was finely calculated, for shareholders were to receive compensation, care being taken to ensure that shipping in the Canal was not interrupted. Responses in London and Paris were less measured: the French now had the pretext to destroy the man believed to be behind their Algerian troubles, and Eden could indulge his 1930s analogy by pointing to the threat to Britain's imperial lifeline. The two countries began assembling a military expedition under British command. It was ill-conceived both in organisation and purpose. The latter seemed obvious enough, namely to remove Nasser from power and restore the Canal to international control. But little thought was given to who or what would replace Nasser and how any new leader would be sustained in power in the teeth of popular resentment. This confused military planning, for there was a considerable difference between an operation designed to secure the Canal and a major offensive aimed at Cairo. Nor were the British and French forces positioned for the rapid response which alone might have given the operation credibility. As the expedition slowly assembled at British bases in Cyprus and Malta, the Canal continued to work normally and the most fatal British and French miscalculation of all began to emerge: the increasingly critical attitude of Eisenhower and Dulles. As early as 31 July, the latter had flown to London with a letter from the President counselling the 'unwisdom even of contemplating the use of military force at this moment'. Despite such advice, Eden persisted in the illusion that his war-time comrade, Eisenhower, could be relied upon (Eden, 1960; Eisenhower, 1965).

## 'Collusion' and War

By late September, hectic international diplomacy seemed to be heading nowhere, the Canal was working smoothly and the excuse for launching the military forces building up in

Cyprus and Malta was draining away. Faced with this situation, the French sent out feelers to the Israelis for possible collaboration. Ben-Gurion knew that this was an irresistible chance to work closely with a major Western power, and he was ably supported by the young Shimon Peres, Director General of the Ministry of Defence. Peres, a man of wide-ranging imagination, was at the start of an extraordinary career which saw him at the heart of Israeli politics for decades. An exploratory meeting in Paris from 30 September to 1 October 1956 was followed by a French military mission to Israel; the chemistry was right and the basis for military cooperation against Egypt was laid. Even so, little could be done without the British, for the French could not act without the bases in Cyprus and Malta. Such cooperation could not be assumed. Although the worst of the bitterness left by the final phase of the Mandate had passed, Britain had widespread networks in the Arab world, not least a defence agreement with Jordan, which would be harmed by an Israeli connection. But Eden's consuming desire to destroy Nasser overrode other considerations. At a critical meeting on 14 October, the French General Maurice Challe proposed a plan which seemed to offer Eden the pretext he needed for a military operation: the Israelis would attack Egyptian positions in the Sinai Desert, allowing the British and French to seize the Canal in order to save it from damage and separate the two sides. This is what was agreed at an ultra-secret conference held at Sèvres from 22 to 24 October, attended by Ben-Gurion and representatives of the French and British governments. The 'Sèvres Protocol' committed Israel to an offensive on 29 October, to be followed by British and French appeals for a cease-fire and for the Israelis and Egyptians to withdraw their forces ten miles on either side of the Canal. If this were not done, Anglo-French hostilities against Egypt would begin on the 31st. The 'Collusion' with Israel was a highly secret affair, the true nature of which was not even confided to the British Cabinet, and soon became a matter of acute controversy in

Britain for the plot had too many transparent inconsistencies to be convincing. The Anglo-French campaign was to be launched against the victim of an attack and against a country which could hardly be expected to comply with an ultimatum that allowed the Israelis to occupy virtually the entire Sinai. The fatal omission was consideration of the American response, the Israelis seemingly assuming that as London and Washington were close, the Americans would not adopt an anti-British position.

In the early morning of 29 October, the first part of the plan unfolded with an Israeli paratroop drop on the strategic Mitla Pass in the Sinai. Although Egyptian units fought stubbornly, the Israeli operation, imaginatively conceived by Chief of Staff Moshe Dayan, soon dominated the Sinai. This was the signal for the Anglo-French ultimatums which were issued the following day, their rejection in turn permitting the start of air hostilities against Egypt in preparation for landings on the Canal scheduled for 5 November. The timing was to prove disastrous for the British and French. President Eisenhower had consistently argued against the use of force, had been kept in the dark over the Anglo-French–Israeli 'Collusion' and, facing re-election on the 6th, was now acutely embarrassed by his principal allies and furious over what they were doing. Even worse was the tragedy being played out in the streets and squares of Budapest. On 4 November, the Red Army began its occupation of the city and brutal suppression of its Freedom Fighters after Hungary's Premier, Imre Nagy, had announced the country's neutrality. While events in the Middle East probably did not influence Soviet decisions to any great extent, British and French actions were diverting attention from what was happening. The Soviets could condemn Anglo-French aggression while cynically pursuing their own. Eisenhower's inability to respond to the Hungarians' pathetic appeals stood in stark contrast to his 1952 election pledges to 'roll back' the Iron Curtain. If he could not do that, at least he could bring his allies into line.

In this unpromising climate, British and French paratroops at last dropped at Port Said on 5 November, followed the next day by the seaborne forces. Once again, delay was fatal to their hopes, for in the previous days domestic and world opinion had mounted against them, most dangerously in the White House. Even the Israelis had little real need of them any more. Aided by the Anglo-French air bombardment of Egypt, their forces controlled most of the Sinai including the cherished prize of Sharm al-Shaikh. With the fighting stopped, and Egypt and Israel accepting a ceasefire, the pretext for the Anglo-French landing had gone. Financial pressure from the Americans quickly brought the ill-starred adventure to an end. For some days Britain's sterling currency reserves had been steadily eroding, to the dismay of the Chancellor of the Exchequer, Harold Macmillan. When Macmillan learned that his American counterpart, George Humphrey, was obstructing his only hope of sustaining sterling – raising funds through the International Monetary Fund – he advised an end to hostilities. Faced with the possibility of financial collapse, Eden advised his dismayed French allies that Britain could not carry on. Thus it was, as Eden ruefully conceded in his memoirs, that the 'course of the Suez Canal crisis was decided by the American attitude to it' (Bromberger and Merry, 1957; Dayan, 1966; Nutting, 1967; Lloyd, 1978; Louis and Owen, 1989; Kyle, 1991; Eden, 1960).

### Consequences of the Suez Crisis

It is difficult to overstate the consequences of these events. Britain and France, which had acted throughout the crisis with a rare mixture of incompetence and dishonesty, rapidly ceased to be major players in the Middle East. Revolution in Iraq in 1958 removed Britain's main ally. The same year, tensions in Algeria triggered a military revolt which brought to power Charles de Gaulle in the name of 'French Algeria';

four years later he gave the country its independence. Both Britain and France now sought their futures in Europe, even though French resentment over Eden's betrayal of their joint cause was a factor in their opposition to British membership of the Common Market in the 1960s.

Their power passed to the United States and the newly re-elected Eisenhower was determined to use it. In January 1957, he announced what came to be known as the 'Eisenhower Doctrine' – a policy which decreed that the United States would use armed force to help any country in the Middle East that requested assistance against Communism. Alongside this went steady pressure to ensure that Israel did not retain its recent conquests. Ben-Gurion had hoped to use his positions in Sinai to bargain for Israeli administration of the Gaza Strip and retention of Sharm al-Shaikh, which he had long seen as vital for the future development of the southern port of Eilat and of his beloved Negev. Eisenhower and Dulles stuck to the principle of a total Israeli withdrawal, offering instead a United Nations Emergency Force (UNEF). Israel's refusal to accept this led Eisenhower in a television address on 20 February 1957 to make it clear that Israel could not 'exact conditions for withdrawal'. Privately, he threatened sanctions which included not just official aid but difficulties in the way of private Israeli fund-raising in the United States. He succeeded. After intensive negotiations, on 1 March 1957 Israel's Foreign Minister, Golda Meir, announced her country's withdrawal; any interference with Israeli shipping in the Straits of Tiran would, she made clear, be regarded as a casus belli. The ostensible guarantee Israel received was the stationing of UNEF in the Sinai, including Gaza and Sharm al-Shaikh. The secret price the Americans obtained in return for Israeli withdrawal was an assurance from Nasser that he would respect the Straits of Tiran as an international waterway (Fraser, 1989; Kyle, 1991).

Despite being prised out of her conquests by the Americans, Israel could still be pleased with the overall results of her military gamble. For the next ten years her borders were relatively stable and, despite the continuing high cost of defence, the country's economy moved steadily ahead. The military lessons of 1956, especially the importance of modern airpower, were keenly studied and were to form the basis of victory in the next war. The diplomatic lessons, if painful, were also instructive. The link with France and Britain, so eagerly grasped by Ben-Gurion, had proved to be a poisoned chalice. Such a connection was not repeated. The United States had demonstrated the extent of its leverage. The answer was to turn to Israel's lobbying machinery in Washington so that in future such pressure could be countered at source.

Nasser emerged from the crisis the hero of the Arab world, a status that he never entirely lost despite later setbacks and defeats. For a time everything he touched seemed to turn to gold. The Iraqi revolution in 1958 destroyed the pro-British monarchy there. This might have been quickly followed by revolutionary regimes in Lebanon and Jordan but for the prompt arrival of American and British troops. The same year saw the formation of the United Arab Republic when Egypt and Syria merged under Nasser's leadership. Although Nasser never believed in a politically united Arab world, he did see himself as the acknowledged voice of Arab aspirations, striking a distinctive position in world events. It was not to be. The new Iraqi regime turned out to be bitterly hostile to Nasser's ambitions. A much more severe blow came in September 1961 when the Syrians rebelled against the union. From then on, Nasser was on the decline, a hard fate for a proud man. An example of this pride came in his reaction to the American food-aid programme started by President Kennedy. Although this was feeding some 40 per cent of the Egyptian population, Nasser violently denounced this aid in a speech in December 1964, and the Americans discontinued it. Perhaps Nasser's most serious failing came in the military sphere, for the Egyptian armed forces never really learned the lessons of the Sinai campaign. Their soldiers had fought bravely and, it could be argued, had been distracted by the British bombing campaign and impending landings on the Canal. But Nasser delegated military affairs to his old colleague Abd al-Hakim Amer, who failed to take the necessary action, while nurturing political ambitions of his own. Nasser was ultimately to pay a bitter price for Amer's shortcomings.

## Fatah and the Palestinian Revival

In the immediate aftermath of the Suez Crisis these problems lay in the future; the people who felt most cheated by what had happened were the Palestinians whose name had hardly been lifted by any of the parties. This seemed to confirm two growing fears. Since 1949 there had been a gnawing suspicion that the Arab governments were not really much exercised by the fate of the Palestinians, but would manipulate them if it suited them to do so. Even worse was the fear that the world was steadily forgetting about the Palestinians or, at best, vaguely including them as one of a number of 'refugee problems'. It was in response to these depressing conclusions that a number of young Palestinians began conversations in 1957 and 1958 which were to lead to a political revival. The man who emerged as their leader was Yasser Arafat. Arafat, who came to symbolise the Palestinian cause, was born in 1929 into a Gaza family which was part of the Husseini clan. After fighting in the 1948–49 war, which left him with a poor view of his Arab allies, he trained as an engineer at university in Egypt, becoming President of the Union of Palestinian Students. Among his associates were two younger men, Khalil al-Wazir, whose family had been expelled from Ramle, and Salah Khalaf, who had been part of the flight from Jaffa. The future of the Palestinian leadership was to fall very much on these three men, broken only with the death of Khalil al-Wazir at the hands of Israeli commandos in Tunis in April 1988. In January 1991, Salah Khalaf, too, was murdered, in his case by Palestinians hostile to Arafat's leadership. Out of their discussion came the formation in 1959 of Fatah, its name derived from reversing the Arabic initials of 'The Movement for the Liberation of Palestine' (Haraka Tahrir Filastin); its journal *Filastinuna* ('Our Palestine') proclaimed the revival of Palestinian political awareness (Cobban, 1984; Hart, 1984; Gowers and Walker, 1991).

It had taken ten years after the disasters of 1948–49 for the political fortunes of the Palestinians to begin to revive, and even then progress was to be painfully slow, not least because of the hostility of the various Arab intelligence services. Developments in Israel were to stimulate the next move in Palestinian politics. By 1963, the Israelis had reached the critical stage in their plans for a National Carrier which would channel the waters of the River Jordan down to the Negev. This produced a furious Arab reaction: the scheme would transform Israel's ability to absorb immigrants and was also, it was argued, the theft of Arab water as the sources of the Jordan lay outside Israel. Nasser knew that the Arabs were in no military state to respond to the clamour for war. Instead, he convened an Arab summit in Cairo in January 1964 which took the decision to create a political organisation for the Palestinians. This was less dramatic than it seemed, for it was clear that the proposed organisation would be kept firmly under Egyptian control, not least because its chairman, Ahmad Shuqairy, was close to Nasser. In May 1964 it came into existence as the Palestine Liberation Organisation (PLO), its activities governed by the Palestine National Charter. The basic premise of the Charter was the familiar one of the illegality of the partition of Palestine and the creation of Israel. As a voice for the Palestinians, the PLO was to prove ineffective. It was never intended to have an independent life, and the haplessness of Shuqairy's leadership left Palestinians incredulous and bitter. His only obvious talent was for an extreme rhetoric that proved a gift for Israeli propagandists (Cobban, 1984).

Arafat and his associates regarded Shuqairy and the PLO with undisguised contempt, but the new organisation had one asset which caused them considerable alarm. This was the formation of the Palestine Liberation Army which started to attract recruits from the ranks of Fatah. Faced with this depressing situation, Arafat concluded that military action was needed. He believed that the only hope the Palestinians had was to escalate tension, leading to a war in which Israel would be defeated by the regular Arab armies – precisely what Nasser was trying to avoid through his control of the PLO. What saved Arafat's strategy was the continuing rivalry between Nasser and the Syrians in the aftermath of the collapse of their union. In October 1964 a military coup in Damascus brought to power the Ba'ath party which was acrimoniously opposed to Nasser's pretensions to Arab leadership. Leading Ba'athists, including the Air Force Commander Hafez al-Asad, were prepared to take up the Fatah cause. It proved to be the critical breakthrough that Fatah needed, and was to help set the Middle East on the path towards the 1967 war.

Even within Fatah there was no unanimity on the wisdom of challenging Israel. Hence, when operations began in January 1965, they were done under the *nom de guerre* of Assifa ('The Storm'). Symbolically, the first raid was against the Israeli water network and the organisation acquired its first martyr when a member of the raiding party was killed by a Jordanian patrol. These raids, which increased in frequency in the course of 1965, were never a threat to Israel's security, but nevertheless served as a source of instability and irritation. It is important to remember that by the mid-1960s most Israelis believed that their state had passed beyond the early pioneering stage. By 1965 Israel had achieved a standard of living equivalent to the countries of southern Europe, was pursuing a policy of active aid to the newly emergent states of Africa, and saw no reason why it should not be as accepted a part of the international community as, say, Belgium or the Netherlands. The state was presided over from June 1963 by Prime Minister Levi Eshkol and his Foreign Minister, Abba Eban, whose policies seemed far removed from the activism of Ben-Gurion. A former ambassador to Washington and representative at the United Nations, Eban was a sophisticated diplomat, but never seemed to carry the same weight at home as he did abroad. Their 'normalisation' of Israeli society and foreign policy was by no means to the taste of their predecessor, who, lamenting the seeming loss of pioneering urge, in November 1964 set up a new political group, Rafi, together with Shimon Peres and former Chief of Staff Moshe Dayan. Although Rafi did not attract mass support, winning only 10 seats out of 120 in the Knesset elections of November 1965, its leaders had sufficient prestige to serve as a focus for those who felt uneasy at the supposed weakness of Eshkol and Eban in the face of the Fatah raids. The presence of Ben-Gurion growling off-stage served as a significant check on the government's freedom to manoeuvre (Rodinson, 1968).

By 1966, the Arab–Israeli conflict seemed set to enter upon a more dangerous phase. Israel was now a well-established state and most Arab leaders, notably Nasser, privately acknowledged its strength and ability to defend itself, but this in turn contributed to the growing activism of the Palestinians. Terrified of being forgotten, Palestinian groups were turning to a new militancy which, if it could not threaten Israel's existence, could at least remind Israelis of the uncomfortable fact that major issues had been left unresolved. The way was clear for the third Arab–Israeli war, a volatile situation made no more stable by the Americans' almost total preoccupation with Vietnam. The one country able to influence the Arab–Israeli conflict was fixated on South East Asia.

# 3

# FROM WAR TO WAR

## Origins of the June War

The war of 1967 was to prove as decisive in its consequences as that of 1948–49. It left Israel firmly in control of all the land of mandatory Palestine, as well as extensive Egyptian and Syrian territory, and tilted the balance of Middle East power firmly in an Israeli direction. As tensions between Israel and the Syrian–Fatah alliance grew in the winter of 1966–67, the Middle East edged towards war. Two events in November 1966 stand out as marking the new levels of tension. The first was the signing of a defensive pact between Nasser and the Syrians. While this gave Syria the confidence of powerful support, it was bound to involve Nasser more closely in the increasingly tense confrontation between Damascus and Israel, even though he was careful to give private assurances to the Americans that he would not allow the agreement to drag him into war. Confirmation of the deterrent effect of the new pact seemed to come quickly when Israel mounted a large-scale raid on the Jordanian village of Samu' in retaliation for Fatah raids. In attacking Jordan rather than Syria, it seemed to the Arabs, and to his domestic critics, that Prime Minister Eshkol had taken the easy way out. By April 1967, with a major air battle over Syria and an increasing war of words between Jerusalem and Damascus, an all-out military confrontation between the two countries seemed likely; as always something was needed to provide the spark. Even so, no one was planning war. The Eshkol government had no such intention. Much of Nasser's army was fighting a sterile war in Yemen. King Hussein was not about to gamble with his kingdom, and, without Egypt and Jordan, the Syrian–Fatah alliance lacked the strength to go to war. On 4 May, Israeli intelligence reported that war was not imminent.

What actually sparked the crisis has never been in doubt. On 13 May 1967, the Soviet Union informed Nasser that the Israelis were deploying 10 to 12 brigades on their northern border with a view to attacking Syria. This seemed to confirm reports that had reached Cairo from Damascus of an Israeli concentration. What is mysterious, however, is that the report was false. Ten to twelve brigades would have accounted for half the army on full mobilisation and no such force was massing on the Syrian border. Why, then, would the Soviets send Nasser such misleading, and ultimately disastrous, information? Explanations have been offered that Moscow was trying to take some of the pressure off its increasingly embattled Syrian ally or that it was an attempt to draw the Americans into a Middle East trouble spot. The likelihood is that it was simply an inaccurate report, poorly evaluated in Moscow. Such things happen. Nasser understandably felt that he had to act swiftly to divert the Israelis from their presumed attack on Syria. When two Egyptian armoured divisions moved into the Sinai Desert on 14 May, and were immediately matched by an Israeli tank brigade, it was clear that a new crisis in the Arab–Israeli conflict might be approaching.

Dangerous though it seemed, this troop deployment did not signal that a war was imminent, only that Nasser wanted to show that he was properly positioned to discourage any possible Israeli move against Syria. Nevertheless, on 16 May Eshkol authorised the mobilisation of reserves. The same evening, Nasser prepared his position by ordering the UNEF forces in Sinai to concentrate in the Gaza Strip. Any such move by UNEF inevitably placed at risk the settlement negotiated in 1957 and raised the spectre of a renewed blockade of the Straits of Tiran, which Israel had made clear would be regarded as a casus belli. Nasser's initial demand for a UNEF withdrawal did not, however, include Sharm al-Sheikh or, indeed, Gaza. UNEF's presence, by this stage only some 1,400 men, had never been other than symbolic. The presumption had been that in the event of a crisis its position would be referred to the General Assembly of the United Nations which had authorised its presence in the first place, thus allowing diplomacy time to work. The Secretary General of the United Nations, U Thant, decided that the organisation could not keep troops in Egypt without the government's consent and that if part of UNEF were to go, then the entire force should be removed. This decision was taken without reference to the Security Council or the General Assembly. If U Thant's purpose was to put pressure on Nasser it failed, for on 17 May Egypt demanded the total withdrawal of UNEF. Although it has been strongly argued that the Secretary General had been left no alternative, U Thant's failure to use the mechanisms of the Security Council and General Assembly has been seen as opening the way to war. Nasser later claimed that he had been left no choice but to close the Straits of Tiran. While this may be so, it seems that he was also taking decisions based upon assurances from Field Marshal Amer that the Egyptian armed forces were ready for any confrontation with Israel. That prospect was now measurably closer.

Knowing this, the Israeli government ordered full mobilisation on 20 May. The following day, Nasser announced a blockade of the Straits of Tiran, in breach of the secret undertaking he had given in 1957 that it would remain an international waterway – and in the knowledge of the promised Israeli response. He had now moved several decisive steps beyond mere deterrence of an Israeli move against

Syria and no longer seemed in control of events. While Nasser's public speeches breathed defiance of Israel, heightening an increasing clamour for war in the Arab world, he sent private assurances to the Americans, through the Soviets, that there would be no attack. This was a message the Soviets were keen to reinforce for they had concluded, as had the Americans but not the Egyptian commanders, that if war came it would quickly end with an Israeli victory.

Diplomacy seemed to be leading nowhere. A mission by Israeli Foreign Minister Eban to Paris, London and Washington brought expressions of sympathy but little else. The British and French would do nothing without the Americans, who were themselves far too deeply enmeshed in Vietnam to welcome any kind of military involvement in the Middle East. While the Americans had concluded that Israel was the victim of aggression and that U Thant had seriously miscalculated, they did not believe that Egypt was about to attack. President Lyndon Johnson's advice to the Israelis was to hold back and allow time for diplomacy to work: 'You will not be alone unless you go alone', he advised them. But events in the region were developing increasing momentum. On 29 May, Nasser proclaimed to his National Assembly that what was at issue was no longer the Straits of Tiran or UNEF, but the rights of the Palestinians, not a message calculated to lower tensions in Israel. The following day, King Hussein concluded a military treaty with Egypt. As Egyptian troops arrived in Jordan, Ahmad Shuqairy pledged Israel's destruction.

Believing that they still had time to negotiate an opening of the Straits, on 3 June the Americans succeeded in arranging for Egyptian Vice President Zakariya Muhieddin to come to Washington on the 7th, but it proved to be an illusory breakthrough. Eshkol's government was faced with an increasingly fretful public opinion which did not see him as the man for the hour and had scant faith in the power of international diplomacy. On 1 June, Moshe Dayan, the hero of the 1956 Sinai campaign, became Defence Minister in a government of national unity, a clear concession to those who were demanding a decisive resolution of the crisis. The Israeli decision for war was taken on 4 June, by a divided vote in the cabinet and without informing the Americans (Laqueur, 1968; Fraser, 1989; Parker, 1992).

## The June War: Israel's Six Day Victory

Although Dayan became the public's hero during and after the war, the true architect of the victory that followed was Chief of Staff Yitzhak Rabin, under whose direction the armed forces had prepared in minute detail for the campaign that unfolded so brilliantly in the early hours of 5 June. Air power was the decisive element, and Air Force Commander General Mordechai Hod the key planner and executor. Nasser's air strength lay in modern MiG-21 fighters, and a bomber force of 30 Tupolev-16 strategic bombers and 27 Ilyushin-28 medium bombers, a force well able to devastate Israel's cities. Against them, Hod had some 250 aircraft, French-built Mirages, Super Mystères, Mystère Mark IVs and Ouragans. They could be rearmed and refuelled in eight minutes, enabling them to be back over their targets an hour after the first strike. Flying out over the Mediterranean at low level, the Israeli Air Force took its Egyptian rivals totally by surprise, striking their airfields at 07.45, just as their fighters had returned from dawn patrol. In less than three hours the Egyptian Air Force had been removed from the military equation, losing their entire bomber force and 135 fighters. Later that day, 22 Jordanian and 55 Syrian planes were also destroyed. It was probably the most decisive air strike of the post-war era, possibly of all time.

Israeli planes were now free to give full support to the army as it prepared to advance in Sinai. The Egyptian force under General Abd al-Mohsen Mortagui remained formidable, with four infantry, one mechanised and two armoured divisions. Israel's Southern Command under General Yeshayahu Gavish deployed three divisions. Key to their success was to isolate the Gaza Strip by seizing Rafah and Khan Yunis. The country's leading armoured specialist, General Israel Tal, attacked with a mixed force of tanks and paratroopers. By the evening of 5 June they had taken their objectives and advanced to El Arish in Sinai. To the south, General Ariel Sharon was charged with securing the supply route across the central Sinai at Abu Agheila, which he did by the early hours of 6 June. The third division, reservists under General Avraham Joffe, then advanced between Tal and Sharon to take another main Egyptian communications centre. The Egyptian army in Sinai was ripe for the taking. By 8 June Israeli troops were on the Suez Canal, the entire peninsula was in their hands, and seven Egyptian divisions had been defeated. The Egyptian losses were between 10,000 and 15,000 men, 800 tanks, and thousands of vehicles and artillery pieces.

On 5 June King Hussein of Jordan decided that he had to honour his commitments to the Arab cause and began to shell the Israeli enclave on Jerusalem's Mount Scopus. The Jordanians had a well-trained army of eight infantry brigades, seven of them deployed in the West Bank, and two armoured brigades held back in the Jordan valley, ready for offensive operations north and south of Jerusalem. Israeli cities were within range of Jordanian 155mm artillery. But if the dangers were obvious, so, too, was the potential opportunity of gaining Judaism's most sacred site, the Western Wall. Defence of the area fell to Central Command under General Uzi Narkiss, with a mechanised brigade and the reservists of the 16th Jerusalem Brigade. But the pace of events permitted the release from Sinai of the 55th Parachute Brigade. Hostilities began just before midnight on 5/6 June. On the morning of 7 June, the paratroopers seized the Old City, which had been left largely undefended. Their encounter with the Western Wall was an emotional high point for Israelis. They were soon followed by Rabin, Dayan, Eshkol and the chief Ashkenazi rabbi, who declared they would never leave again. By the end of the day, all of the West

Bank was in Israeli hands and a cease-fire with Jordan was in place. The short-lived Hashemite kingdom was in ruins.

So far, nothing much had stirred on the Syrian front. On 8 June, Dayan was able to order air attacks on positions on the Golan Heights. The following day, troops of Northern Command, under General David Elazar, began their ground assault on strong Syrian positions. After hard fighting, by 10 June, when a United Nations cease-fire came into effect, Israeli forces had gained the Golan, including the provincial capital of Quneitra. All that marred the Israeli victory was a sustained air and naval attack on 8 June on the American surveillance vessel *Liberty* with the loss of 34 sailors. Israel's explanation that this had been the result of mistaken identity, though possibly correct, was sceptically received in Washington and marred relations for the rest of the Johnson presidency (Kimche and Bawly, 1968; Dayan, 1976; Rabin, 1976; Ennes, 1979; Oren, 2002).

## The Aftermath of War

By any calculation Israel had gained one of the most spectacular victories of recent history. Not only had the armed forces of Egypt, Jordan and Syria been decimated, but Israel now controlled the future of east Jerusalem, the West Bank, the Sinai Desert and the Golan Heights, and enjoyed the overwhelming support of Western public opinion. A country that had felt embattled and threatened only days before was now the decisive military power in the Middle East, its people self-confident and proud of their achievements. Equally, Israel had changed in the process, for she was now an occupying power responsible for the lives and destinies of over one million Palestinians and the Arabs of the Sinai and the Golan. How Israel would resolve this was to become the central issue in the Arab–Israeli conflict over the next 40 years. Initial opinions in Israel were divided about the future of the territories. While those on the right, notably the followers of Menahem Begin, held that the West Bank was an inalienable part of the Jewish inheritance, the initial view of Eshkol and Eban was that most of the conquered land was negotiable in return for peace settlements. There was a widespread sense of relief that Israeli towns and cities were for the time being far removed from any attack, but few believed that these new positions would become the country's long-term frontier.

From the start it was clear that there were certain positions which would not be surrendered. Some were strategic. Most Israelis were agreed that Jordanian artillery should not return to the hills overlooking the coastal plain, and even before the war was over some 10,000 Arabs had been expelled from villages in the Latrun salient, which had been a constant danger to communications between Tel Aviv and Jerusalem. The future of Jerusalem transcended any strategic consideration and all political differences. Israelis felt that they had reunified their eternal capital from which they were not to be parted; hence, on 27 June the Knesset rushed through laws extending Israeli jurisdiction and administration to east Jerusalem. Two days later the partition lines that had divided the city for 19 years were removed and the integration of the two parts of the city began under its redoubtable mayor, Teddy Kollek, who was to remain in office until 1993. Evidence of Israeli intentions to stay was the immediate demolition of the medieval Mughrabi quarter in the Old City to prepare an open space in front of the Western Wall, an action condemned by UNESCO. This was completed by 12 June, but Kollek apparently rejected a suggestion from Ben-Gurion that the walls around the Old City be taken down (Kollek, 1978). The annexation of the Old City was regarded with dismay throughout the Muslim world because of its perceived threat to the Haram al-Sharif and did nothing to encourage Arabs to compromise. Nor was it recognised by the international community. On 4 July the United Nations General Assembly adopted, by 99 votes to nil with 20 abstentions, a resolution declaring Israel's actions to be invalid. Although this was followed by subsequent similar resolutions in the General Assembly and Security Council, Israeli settlements were systematically extended around east Jerusalem for the next 40 years, with Arabs becoming a minority in the eastern part of the city. Although the physical barriers had been removed, the city's Arab and Jewish citizens led separate lives (Benvenisti, 1976).

These events of May–June 1967 had been a severe jolt to the international system. To an American administration hitherto transfixed by the Vietnam War they had suddenly opened up the prospect of conflict with the Soviet Union. During the diplomatic crisis and the war the two superpowers had gone to considerable trouble to reassure each other. This reflected how seriously they regarded the possibility of escalation should events get seriously out of control. Such considerations lay behind President Johnson's broadcast on 19 June in which he set out his 'five principles' for an Arab–Israeli settlement: the removal of threats against any nation in the region; justice for the 'refugees'; freedom of navigation; an end to the arms race; and 'respect for political independence and territorial integrity of all the states in the area'. If Johnson hoped for speedy progress, he was to be disappointed. An Arab summit held in Khartoum in September seemed to underline the intractability of the problem with its resolutions on no peace, recognition or negotiation with Israel. This apparently intransigent formula concealed a willingness on the part of Egypt and Jordan to acquiesce in Israel's existence within her pre-war borders. The Arabs' problem was their hopelessly weak negotiating position. The Israelis, on the other hand, saw no reason to make easy concessions to those who had so recently threatened them. It did not make for diplomatic progress.

The way forward appeared to be the British-sponsored Security Council Resolution 242 of 22 November 1967, which embodied key aspects of President Johnson's speech, and represented a carefully negotiated compromise. The resolution recognised 'the sovereignty, territorial integrity and political independence of every State in the area and their right to live in peace within secure and recognized boundaries free from threats or acts of force': when Egypt and Jordan accepted it they acknowledged Israel's right to exist. It also affirmed that there should be 'a just settlement of the refugee problem', a concession by Israel, though Palestinians resented to being described in these terms. At the heart of Resolution 242 were the sections relating to the future shape of a peace settlement. This was to include 'Withdrawal of Israel armed forces from territories occupied in the recent conflict', a delphic clause which deliberately excluded the word 'the' from before 'territories'. Hence, while Arabs argued that it meant 'all' the territories, Israelis responded that it merely implied 'some' of the territories. The British, who had sponsored the resolution, maintained that this part of it was governed by the statement that it also emphasised 'the inadmissibility of the acquisition of territory by war', an interpretation that would have allowed Israel to retain little beyond improvements to her security in such areas as the Latrun Salient. Resolution 242 was intended to provide the basis for peace negotiations to be conducted by the Swedish diplomat Gunnar Jarring but his mission, which lasted until 1971, proved barren. The parties were still too far apart and the United Nations, its authority impaired by U Thant's actions over UNEF, could not bring them together. Even so, Resolution 242 has been the basis of all subsequent peace moves (Caradon *et al.*, 1981).

## The Palestinian Revival

Where did the Palestinians stand in regard to all of this? If some of their leaders had hoped that Israel would be broken by the armies of the Arab states, then the war had left them confounded; the conventional wisdom was that no credible Arab force would be ready to take the field again for many years. The war had also resulted in a new wave of refugees.

Although UN officials found it hard to give a precise figure, they estimated that between 350,000 and 400,000 Palestinians had fled in the course of the war, most of them from the West Bank. By the end of 1967, only some 14,000 had returned home, and although many more did in subsequent years, the overall result was another disaster for the Palestinians. Nor were they reassured by events on the ground, for the annexation of east Jerusalem seemed an ominous prelude to what might happen on the rest of the West Bank. That those on the Israeli right regarded it as an integral part of the Jewish inheritance was well known, as was the tradition, inherited from an earlier generation of Zionists, of 'building realities'. It was not long before these 'realities' began to appear with the construction of a belt of Israeli settlements along the Jordan valley and the establishment of the religious settlement of Kiryat Arba outside Hebron. Given the religious significance of Hebron for Jews and Muslims, the latter settlement proved a particular source of tension.

It was in these disheartening circumstances that the Palestinian revival began. There is little doubt that Arafat's was the decisive voice. Convinced that the spirit of resistance had to be kept alive, he personally directed a Fatah underground campaign in the West Bank in the winter of 1967–68, only just evading capture on a number of occasions. In a military sense the campaign was premature: the population was unprepared and the networks were fragile. Some 200 guerrillas were killed and 1,000 arrested, but the campaign demonstrated that sections of the Palestinians had not been cowed by defeat and Arafat's own role ensured his credibility as a leader. Stung by Fatah's revival, on 21 March 1968 some 15,000 Israeli troops mounted a major raid on the Jordanian village of Karameh just east of the River Jordan. Forewarned by the Jordanians, some 300 Fatah guerrillas put up a spirited defence that did much to restore Arab morale and increase the organisation's prestige. Fatah's new primacy was soon reflected in a major reorganisation of the PLO in the summer of 1968. The 1964 Palestine National Charter was revised to reflect Fatah's leadership and the strategy of guerrilla action which the PLO was now to follow. At the heart of the Charter was the assertion of the indivisibility of British mandatory Palestine. This reflected the Palestinians' rejection of partition, to which they had held consistently since 1937, and which held out no prospect of compromise with Israel. On the contrary, articles 9 and 10 committed the organisation to armed struggle. The way was now clear for Arafat to become chairman of the PLO, and for the various armed groups to be brought into its structure. Under Arafat's leadership the PLO was transformed into an increasingly effective voice for the Palestinians, not least because he ensured that its activities were adequately financed through a tax on the income of Palestinian employees throughout the Arab world and support from sympathetic states like Saudi Arabia and Libya (Cobban, 1984).

Under the general umbrella of the PLO, the 'armed struggle' against Israel took several forms. Although Fatah's networks in the West Bank did not survive far into 1968, it was not until 1971 that the Israelis were able to break the organisation in Gaza, where it could operate more effectively out of the crowded refugee camps. The main guerrilla base of operations, however, was Jordan, and as their power and self-confidence grew, so did the challenge they posed to the stability of what remained of Hussein's kingdom. While Fatah pursued its policy of conventional raids, the Popular Front for the Liberation of Palestine (PFLP), led by Dr George Habash, pioneered the technique of striking at the more vulnerable, but headline-catching, target of airliners. From the summer of 1968 there was a series of attacks on El Al and on other airlines flying to Israel. In one of the worst incidents, a Swissair flight to Tel Aviv was blown up in the air in February 1970. Israel inevitably retaliated, most spectacularly in December 1968 with a raid on Beirut International Airport which destroyed 13 Arab aircraft, but there seemed no obvious counter to a technique which, despite its brutality, was succeeding in bringing Palestinian grievances to the world's consciousness.

## The Israeli–American Link

If this Palestinian revival was one theme in the late 1960s, a return to active diplomacy by the Americans was the other. In the immediate aftermath of the 1967 war the Israelis had feared that Johnson might repeat Eisenhower's pressure to force a withdrawal. Despite the administration's displeasure over the *Liberty* affair, this did not happen. Instead, the two countries grew closer together. The war had proved beyond any measure of doubt that air-power was the key to military success and, as the Soviets began the urgent task of rebuilding the Egyptian and Syrian Air Forces, the Israelis looked to the Americans to replace their ageing French aircraft with the Phantom fighter. In 1968 Congress sanctioned the sale of 50 Phantoms to Israel, the first step in a relationship that was to bring a new dimension to the Arab–Israeli conflict. It was cemented by the lobbying power of the American Israel Public Affairs Committee (AIPAC), which used to powerful effect the voting potential, political commitment and readiness to donate to campaigns of the Jewish community. Local Political Action Committees ensured that such resources were deployed on behalf of politicians who were judged to have a sound record of support for Israel or against those who did not (Kenen, 1981; Findley, 1985; Tivnan, 1987).

In early 1969, the thrust of American policy changed under the direction of the new Republican President, Richard Nixon, who was set on moving away from the sterile obsession with Vietnam. As most American Jews had voted for his Democratic rival, Nixon felt that he could move forward in the Middle East with some flexibility. Even if not his immediate priority, the Arab–Israeli conflict could no longer be ignored. The Jarring Mission was clearly going nowhere, and Israel's new leader, Golda Meir, saw no reason to make compromises in face of the steady build-up of the Egyptian and Syrian armed forces. The Russian-born and American-educated Meir personified that generation of pioneering Zionists which was beginning to pass from the political scene. Assuming the premiership in March 1969 after Eshkol's sudden death, she was not a politician inclined by temperament or experience to take chances in negotiations with the Arabs (Meir, 1975; Shlaim, 2000). Such was Nasser's renewed confidence that serious fighting resumed along the Suez Canal. Despite such unpromising prospects, there were signs that a diplomatic move might be possible. Private assurances came from King Hussein that he and Nasser were willing to seek an accommodation with Israel, and the Soviets, too, were anxious to reduce tension. On that basis, Secretary of State William Rogers and his officials in the State Department began work on a framework for a peace settlement. By the end of October 1969 they were able to confirm to the Soviets that they wanted a return to the pre-1967 borders together with security guarantees.

This framework formed the basis of the peace plan which Rogers announced on 9 December 1969. It proved to be a major interpretation of how the new administration viewed a settlement based upon Resolution 242. Peace, Rogers believed, would have to be reinforced by demilitarised zones and would have to ensure freedom of navigation. Israel's frontiers 'should not reflect the weight of conquest', and any adjustments ought to be confined to 'insubstantial alterations required for mutual security'. Officials made clear that this meant an almost total withdrawal, except for some obvious security problems like the Latrun Salient. Equally worrying to Israelis were his views on Jerusalem and the Palestinians, the 'bitterness and frustration' of whom had to be addressed. It was his use of the term 'Palestinians' that marked a considerable change from Resolution 242, which had simply referred to them as 'refugees'. Jerusalem should remain a united city but with roles for both Israel and Jordan. The plan was deeply resented by the Israelis who reacted against it on a number of fronts. Moves were accelerated to consolidate control of east Jerusalem by starting the construction of 25,000 apartments for Jews on 4,000 acres of expropriated land. In Washington, AIPAC organised a lobby of 14,000 prominent Jews and pro-Israeli resolutions in Congress attracted 70 Senators and 280 Representatives (Fraser, 1989).

Even though the Rogers Plan failed to develop any momentum, it is important for two reasons. First, as it was never repudiated, it stood as a major interpretation of how the State Department saw Resolution 242. Second, its failure confirmed the pessimistic analysis of the National Security Adviser, Dr Henry Kissinger, who had discounted its chances from the start. A Bavarian Jewish refugee from Hitler's Germany, Kissinger had made a substantial reputation as an analyst of international affairs at Harvard before joining the Nixon administration. His view was that such a plan would only drive the Israelis and Arabs further apart by identifying entrenched positions. This perception was to be at the heart of his subsequent approach to the Arab–Israeli problem, though as yet that was some way off.

## 'Black September' in Jordan

With both the Jarring Mission and the Rogers Plan effectively stalled, the focus seemed to move from diplomacy to the actions of the Palestinian guerrillas who were becoming so well armed and self-confident that they seemed increasingly to dominate the affairs of Jordan. King Hussein could not indefinitely ignore their threat to his authority and, although the large Palestinian population made him move cautiously, his temper was not improved by two attempts on his life. The second of these, on 1 September 1970, was followed days later by the hijacking by the PFLP of three airliners – Swiss, American and British – to Dawson's Field near Amman. With the flaunting of his authority now dramatically exposed on the world's television screens, Hussein decided to act. On 17 September, his army began a sustained assault on the Palestinian positions. As the fighting intensified, the Syrian army, though not the Air Force, crossed Jordan's northern border to aid the guerrillas, once again threatening the region with war. Prompt counteraction by the Americans and Israelis forced a Syrian withdrawal but it had been a dangerous moment. The savage fighting was brought to an end by Nasser who brought Hussein and Arafat to a peace conference in Cairo on 27 September which succeeded in reaching a face-saving formula of sorts. But the fighting in Jordan – 'Black September' as it came to be known – had been far too bitter for the meeting to be other than stormy; the following day Nasser died of a heart attack (Cobban, 1984).

The outpouring of grief that followed Nasser's death reflected his unique position in modern Arab history, a mystique which survived even the disaster of 1967. His final years were clouded by that defeat. Field Marshal Amer died in mysterious circumstances, but not everything could be attributed to his mismanagement. As Nasser tried to rebuild his armed forces, he signalled his willingness to work for an accommodation with Israel without ever really making it clear what he meant. Nasser's successor was Anwar al-Sadat, who did not share his ambitions in the wider Arab world but concentrated instead on the needs of Egypt, particularly on how best to secure the return of the Sinai and hence the Suez Canal. In fact, Sadat's first two years in office saw yet another interlude in the diplomatic process, partly because of the need to consolidate his internal position against powerful rivals, and partly because Nixon and Kissinger were still absorbed with finding a way out of the Vietnam War. Nor did the actions of Palestinian guerrillas encourage Golda Meir's government towards compromise. Their activities reached a peak in 1972 when Japanese sympathisers killed 26 people in the terminal at Lod airport, and members of 'Black September', assumed to be a cover name for Fatah, shot 11 Israeli athletes at the Munich Olympics. That this should have happened in Germany seemed especially poignant.

Within Israel itself initiatives were unfolding which were to have the most profound effects upon political life over the next three decades. From its origins in eastern Europe, Zionism had been driven from the left, and hence it came as no surprise that, with various coalition partners, Mapai and Labour ruled the state from its inception. Excluded from power, Menahem Begin's Herut party struggled to expand its power base, forming an alliance with the Liberals to form Gahal, but still failing to make substantial progress. During the highly charged atmosphere of June 1967, Begin joined the cabinet and Gahal became part of a national unity government which lasted until August 1970 when he parted company with Golda Meir on the principle of withdrawal from the occupied territories. The catalyst for change on the right came in the unexpected form of General Ariel Sharon, hero of the 1967 Sinai offensive, in a press conference on his retirement from military service in 1973. His call for a new right-wing coalition led to intensive negotiations with Begin and others, including the remnants of Ben-Gurion's Rafi. On 14 September 1973, the new grouping, Likud (Unity) came into existence, with Begin as its leader and Sharon as election manager. Events were to demonstrate its ability to tap into the electorate, but not before Israel had survived the trauma of another war (Silver, 1984; Sharon, 2001).

## Sadat's Foreign Policy

From an early stage, Sadat's hopes for a recovery of the Sinai were focused on the United States. The Soviet Union might be rebuilding the Egyptian armed forces but had no means of exerting pressure on Israel; the Americans, by contrast, had formidable military and financial inducements should they choose to use them. The move from the Soviets, with whom Sadat had a treaty of friendship, to the Americans, with whom he did not even have diplomatic relations, was not likely to be an easy one, and it is not surprising that his first major initiative failed. In July 1972, Sadat demanded the withdrawal of all Soviet military advisers, some 15,000. Hopes that this would lead to a substantial American response were confounded by the fact that 1972 was a presidential election year in which Nixon was trying hard to win a measure of support from Jewish voters. Although unofficial channels of communication between Cairo and Washington were opened up, Sadat really needed something more substantive.

As the United States continued to supply Israel, and the Soviet leadership made plain its desire to seek détente with Washington, Sadat decided that it would take another war to force Israel to make concessions. Lack of political and diplomatic progress forced him to the realisation that Egypt would either have to accept Israel's presence on the Canal or go to war. Given the strength of the Israeli armed forces, military cooperation with Syria was of the essence. Sadat and Hafiz al-Asad, who came to power in Damascus in 1970, worked at this for two years. Once Asad and his colleagues were persuaded that this was the only way to get Israel to cede the conquered territories, serious planning could begin. On 24 October 1972, Sadat met his leading officers at his home at Giza on the outskirts of Cairo. Emphasising that he would not negotiate with the Israelis from a position of humiliation, he told them that they would have to fight and sacrifice (Arab Republic of Egypt, Ministry of Defence, 1999). The Egyptian and Syrian military had taken to heart the lessons of 1967 and the easy-going incompetence of Amer became a thing of the past. Despite their previous defeats at the hands of the Israelis, the Egyptian and Syrian soldiers had never lacked courage. What was now set in hand was the provision of efficient leadership and the means of handling the sophisticated weaponry at Arab disposal. The strategy worked out by the Egyptian and Syrian generals was simple: namely, to achieve the element of surprise and then deny the Israelis the kind of mobile warfare at which they had proved so skilled. By waging the kind of battle of attrition their Soviet patrons had used so effectively against the Germans 30 years before, Sadat and Asad hoped that an exhausted Israel would give them the concessions they wanted. Everything depended on their ability to break through on the Golan front, which was overlooked by Israeli positions on the slopes of Mount Hermon, and to cross the major obstacle of the Suez Canal. In April 1973, Asad paid a secret visit to Egypt to review Egyptian plans for an attack. He and Sadat agreed that the final plan would be drawn up by a joint supreme command. This was completed at a meeting in Alexandria on 22–23 August, with a decision for war in October. A week later, Sadat flew to Damascus where the two leaders decided on 6 October as the date (Arab Republic of Egypt, Ministry of Defence, 1999).

It was the apparent advantage of holding their positions on the Golan and the Suez Canal, combined with the sweeping nature of their victory in 1967, that gave the Israelis such confidence. Since June 1967, the fighting fronts were far away from their main centres of population. The Canal, in particular, seemed a formidable defence; it had, after all, taken the Allies weeks of preparation in 1945 to force the similar barrier of the Rhine. In fact, its advantages were somewhat illusory. Dayan had glimpsed this in 1967 when he had wanted to stop the offensive well short of the Canal, but it had proved too attractive a prize. It was stretching lines of communication across the Sinai Desert and nailing Israeli troops to static positions when their skills lay in a different form of warfare. Defying the advice of a number of experienced commanders, the Israeli Chief of Staff General Chaim Bar-Lev began the construction of defensive works along the Canal. Even then, the Israeli commanders never seemed to focus on whether the 'Bar-Lev Line' was simply a 'trip-wire', as they later claimed, or a full defensive barrier. On the Golan Heights there was no defensive line of any substance. What this situation reflected was a deterioration in the Israeli military under Dayan's stewardship, which stood in marked contrast both to the period before 1967 and to the new professionalism of the Egyptian and Syrian officer corps.

That professionalism was seen in the skill with which the Egyptian and Syrian commanders deployed their forces in preparation for the attack. It was no small achievement, given the sophisticated Israeli intelligence-gathering installations in Sinai and on Mount Hermon, and the assistance given by the Americans. Once again the Israelis' disregard for Arab fighting capacity played them false. Over the previous few years intelligence facilities had been transferred from analysis of the military and political intentions of the Arab states to countering the Palestinian guerrillas. The resulting failure to assess what the two Arab armies were preparing was to cost Israel dear. Given the overall level of tension, it was difficult to know how to separate real preparations for war from deception plans. In May the Israeli forces had been put on alert at enormous cost; it could not be repeated too often. With these advantages the Egyptians and Syrians moved their troops into position for an attack on 6 October, when conditions on the Canal would be most favourable for a crossing but also when Israelis would be observing Yom Kippur, the most sacred date in the Jewish year.

The governments in Jerusalem and Washington were also caught somewhat off balance. Golda Meir was on a visit to France and was then distracted when Palestinian gunmen attacked a train carrying Russian Jewish migrants to a transit camp at Schonau in Austria. If this was part of the deception plan, then it succeeded in drawing Meir to Vienna and Israeli eyes away from the Canal and the Golan. In addition, Foreign Minister Eban was in New York for a meeting of the United Nations. Washington was distracted for different reasons. Nixon's re-election in 1972 had been accompanied by the Watergate affair, which was reaching a crisis in early October with resolutions in Congress demanding his impeachment. As a further complication, pressure was building on Vice President Spiro Agnew to answer tax charges which culminated in his resignation on 10 October. In short, it was a badly rattled administration which had to face the developing crisis in the Middle East. Although Nixon's role cannot be discounted, it put a particular responsibility on Henry Kissinger, only just confirmed as Secretary of State (Meir, 1975; Heikal, 1976; Sadat, 1978; Kissinger, 1982).

## The Yom Kippur War

On 5 October, news reached the Israeli government that the families of Soviet personnel in Syria were being evacuated. Meir was later to concede that she should then have ordered mobilisation, but on professional advice that the Egyptian and Syrian forces were in a defensive posture she did not do so. An attempt was made to use the Americans to send warnings to Sadat and Asad but even this was mishandled. As the Israeli message was accompanied by an intelligence report saying that war was not imminent, neither the embassy in Washington nor Kissinger felt the matter was urgent. No American message was sent. On the morning of the 6th, the Israeli cabinet met to consider the news that an Egyptian and Syrian attack would come later in the day. Despite the obvious temptation, the decision was taken that there should not be a pre-emptive strike by the Air Force and that there should only be partial mobilisation. American support would be vital in the days ahead and to that end Israel had to be clearly seen as the victim of aggression.

The Egyptian and Syrian offensives began at 14.00 on 6 October 1973, with 700 tanks attacking the under-strength Israeli armoured units on the Golan, and a massive artillery barrage on the Bar-Lev Line. By nightfall the Line had fallen, engineers had put 10 bridges and 50 ferries across the Canal, and the Egyptian Second and Third Armies were deploying in force on the east bank. For some time, the Egyptians had been rehearsing on mock-ups of the Bar-Lev Line on waterways in the Nile delta (Arab Republic of Egypt, Ministry of

Defence, 1999). Defending the Canal were 600 reservists of the 16th Jerusalem Brigade, a measure of Israel's tragic overconfidence. Dramatic as this was, the more immediate threat to Israel was the situation on the Golan where the Syrians took the key positions on Mount Hermon and looked set to overwhelm the Israeli defences. It took the sacrifice of some 40 aircraft to hold the situation, a rate of attrition that could not be long sustained. Because of the closeness of the fighting to Israel's centres of population, the Golan front had to be Israel's main preoccupation in the initial stages. By 9 October, after ferocious combat, the front had been stabilised but the Syrians were still fighting hard and the cost had been high. Critically, however, they failed to seize the vital bridges across the river Jordan, enabling the Israelis to reinforce their positions (Pollack, 2002). By that date, the Egyptians had consolidated their positions along the Canal and were able to destroy the first Israeli counterattack by the 190th Armoured Brigade, the worst disaster in the country's military history. The 9th was to see the limit of Arab successes, but already the Israelis were acutely aware that this war was unlike any of its predecessors. Not only was the attack poorly coordinated, but the Egyptian forces proved unexpectedly skilled in anti-tank warfare. Of the twenty-two tanks in the Israeli spearhead, eighteen lay burning (Insight Team, 1975; Sachar, 1976; Sharon, 2001).

This was also true on the diplomatic front. From the start of hostilities Sadat sent 'back-channel' messages to the Americans that the war had been launched for limited political purposes; namely, to force an Israeli withdrawal from her 1967 conquests and then take part in a peace conference. For Kissinger this was crucial information that was to help shape his diplomacy during the crisis. On 9 October, faced with the loss of 500 tanks and 49 aircraft, the Israelis urgently requested American assistance. Nixon and Kissinger could not refuse, some have speculated because of the possible nature of Israel's response, but certainly because the Americans could not refuse their major friend in the region

(Insight Team, 1975; Hersh, 1991). The assurances that the Americans would make good their losses gave the Israelis the necessary confidence to commit their vital reserves, but the delays over the delivery of supplies gave great concern and was to lead to later accusations of bad faith. Initially, the Americans would only agree to fly material to the Azores, leaving El Al's seven jets to complete the operation, and supplies of Phantoms were limited to one and a half a day. While some Israelis have argued that this was Washington's way of ensuring that they did not win a decisive victory, Kissinger's defence was that the strategy was designed to avert the danger of an Arab oil embargo. The result was that the first American Galaxy transport aircraft did not land until the 14th.

On the same day, the decisive tank battle took place in Sinai. The Egyptian armour moved out in force from their protective screen of anti-aircraft missile batteries. It was the type of action at which the Israelis were highly skilled and in the course of one of the largest tank battles ever fought they inflicted severe losses on the Egyptians. This success allowed the Israeli commanders to exploit what they had earlier identified as the two major weaknesses in the Egyptian deployment: namely, that too many tanks had been brought across the Canal, leaving the forces on the West Bank perilously under strength; and that the most vulnerable part of the line was at the junction of the Second and Third Armies just north of the Great Bitter Lake. In the early morning of the 16th, Israeli forces under the command of General Ariel Sharon, who had been recalled to service as war was imminent, began to cross the Canal at this point, threatening to turn the entire Egyptian position (Sharon, 2001). Turning south, they advanced towards the city of Suez and across the Third Army's lines of communication. By then, superior Israeli tactical skill had pushed back the Syrian army on the Golan front, destroying some 867 tanks for the loss of 200. On 11 October, the Israelis crossed the cease-fire line to penetrate Syrian territory, and three days later were within shelling range of the capital (Pollack, 2002). The Israelis seemed poised to inflict another dramatic defeat on Egypt and Syria.

### Kissinger and the Cease-fire

Although hard fighting continued, attention now turned increasingly to diplomacy. From the American perspective, this was now urgent. Not only did they wish to avoid an Arab humiliation, but they were determined to maintain good relations with the Soviet Union, which was threatening to intervene massively on behalf of its Arab friends. Even more serious was the use of the Arab oil weapon. On 17 October, faced with America's massive airlift to Israel, the Organisation of Arab Petroleum Exporting Countries (OAPEC) announced a reduction in oil production until Israel withdrew from her 1967 conquests. This was quickly followed by a total oil embargo on the United States and on the Netherlands, which supplied a large part of Western Europe through the port of Rotterdam. As the United States had become a net importer of oil with no capacity to ease the problems of her allies, the problems likely to face the Western economies were known to be severe (Fraser, 1980).

The Soviet leaders were making their own moves. It took a visit to Cairo from Prime Minister Alexei Kosygin, armed with satellite intelligence photographs, to convince Sadat of the potentially deadly Israeli breakthrough across the Canal. Kosygin was assured that Egypt would accept a cease-fire provided it allowed for a peace conference that included the Palestinian issue, and on his return to Moscow he asked for urgent talks with the Americans. Kissinger's visit to Moscow inaugurated a distinctive period in the diplomacy of the Arab–Israeli conflict. With Nixon beset by Watergate, Kissinger went with an authority enjoyed by few Secretaries of State. His agreement with the Soviet leadership, embodied in Security Council Resolution 338, was that the two sides would observe a cease-fire in the positions that they then occupied, a formula which allowed the Egyptians and Israelis to remain for the time being in their respective bridgeheads. The aim of the resolution was to prepare for negotiations leading to a 'just and durable' peace. While this accorded with Israeli wishes for a settlement, the nation had been badly rattled by the early defeats and the government saw the proposed resolution as designed to prevent them from fully exploiting their recent gains. Knowing this, Kissinger felt it necessary to fly direct to Israel to convince Golda Meir and her ministers of the proposal's merits.

It was a cold meeting, for the Israeli commanders were aching to avenge their initial defeats, but Kissinger seemed to convince them that, as the west bank of the Canal would return to Egypt in any settlement, it was pointless to continue fighting there. His one concession was an indication that they might consolidate their positions by allowing the time of the cease-fire to overrun. The result was a major Israeli offensive from their positions on the Great Bitter Lake which succeeded in trapping Suez and the Third Army. It was a fraught situation. Capitulation of the Third Army would mean the end of Sadat and any real hopes of a diplomatic outcome, but if the Egyptians fought, then the war would be resumed with the prospect of a confrontation between the two superpowers. To emphasise the point, the Soviet leadership started to deploy 85 ships of their Mediterranean fleet and 7 airborne divisions. As a warning to the Soviets not to attempt a rescue airlift to the Third Army, Nixon ordered the state of readiness – DefCon – of all American armed forces to be increased. Although both sides acted prudently, it was a measure of how dangerous the situation on the Canal had become. Kissinger made it plain to the Israelis, threatening the supply of military aid, that there was to be no humiliation of the Third Army. On 27 October 1973, fighting finally ceased (Golan, 1976; Sheehan, 1976; Kissinger, 1982).

## Results of the War

The two sides emerged with mixed fortunes. The Israelis ended the war with some spectacular military gains, their troops powerfully positioned on the west bank of the Canal and in a salient threatening Damascus. After experiencing serious initial setbacks, their troops had proved as brave and resourceful as ever. Hence they were able to claim overall military victory. Yet their aura of invincibility had gone. The Egyptian and Syrian armies had conducted impressive offensives and had not cracked under pressure; even when the Syrians had been pushed back on the Golan front they had conducted an efficient retreat to positions protecting Damascus. In addition, the Arabs now had the 'oil weapon' with which they could pressure the West for Israeli concessions. Above all, Sadat and Asad had achieved their war aim of forcing Israel to negotiate the return of Arab territory. In doing so, they had restored Arab dignity, in itself a precondition for future diplomatic success.

Although the cease-fire had been a joint Soviet–American enterprise, from the start Kissinger was determined that the forthcoming negotiations should be under his direction. He was distrustful of any grand, overall plan, believing the two sides to be too far apart for such a thing to work, especially in the wake of such a ferociously fought war. The fate of the Rogers Plan simply confirmed his pessimistic analysis. Instead, his approach was that of 'step by step', of identifying a clearly attainable goal, the achieving of which would succeed in building up confidence between the parties. Once that degree of trust had been achieved, he could then move on to negotiate the next step. Before examining Kissinger's diplomacy at work, three things need to be kept in mind. He was working from a dispiriting domestic political base. Nixon was still fighting against Watergate until events finally overtook him in August 1974 when he resigned; his unelected successor, Gerald Ford, enjoyed goodwill but lacked authority. Secondly, between 1973 and

1975 South Vietnam collapsed, leaving people on all sides in the Middle East wondering about America's steadfastness towards her friends and allies. Finally, the Yom Kippur War left Israel politically bruised. In April 1974, the report of the Israeli inquiry into the war led to Golda Meir's resignation. Even though the experienced and capable Yitzhak Rabin replaced her, the confidence and authority of the ruling Labour Alignment never really recovered. Set against these difficulties were the encouraging indications that Sadat wanted to work for a settlement under American auspices.

## Kissinger's 'Step-by-Step' Diplomacy

The beleaguered situation of the Egyptian Third Army meant that Kissinger could not afford to delay. His first diplomatic mission to the Middle East in early November 1973 seemed to show the merits of his 'step-by-step' approach. An agreement between Egypt and Israel, signed on 11 November at Kilometre 101 on the Cairo–Suez road, provided for the movement of supplies to Suez and the Third Army, replacement of Israeli by UN checkpoints, the exchange of prisoners, and discussions for the separation of forces. In the course of these discussions Sadat confirmed to Kissinger that the fate of the Third Army was incidental to his main aims of peace with Israel and a return to the 1967 border. A visit to the main Arab oil-producing state, Saudi Arabia, confirmed that these efforts would soon bring an end to the oil embargo. Reassured that progress seemed attainable, Kissinger's next move was to convene, jointly with the Soviet Union, the peace conference at Geneva that Resolution 338 had promised. It really only provided a formal preparation for his subsequent negotiations, for it lasted a day before adjourning. Geneva's significance lay in the fact that Egypt and Jordan sat down at a conference table with Israel, and that Syria, while standing aside, had not tried to work against it. Israel's price for attending a conference whose obvious purpose was to secure its withdrawal from territory was a secret American assurance that there would be no PLO participation without Israeli consent (Kissinger, 1982).

The obvious first step was to secure the situation along the Suez Canal where the two armies remained dangerously intertwined. The glimpse of a move forward came with a visit to Washington from Moshe Dayan. Whatever his shortcomings as Minister of Defence had been, Dayan had a flexible, diplomatic mind and had never been convinced that the Canal added to Israel's security. His proposal was that Israel should withdraw its forces from the west bank, allowing Egypt to occupy the entire east bank up to a depth of 10km with a maximum of three battalions. Israel would occupy a line to the west of the Mitla and Gidi passes, the real key to control of the Sinai. The area between the two would become a 'buffer zone' under the United Nations. In return for this withdrawal, Dayan wanted an end to Egyptian belligerency, the right of Israel to send shipping through the Canal and substantial arms supplies from the Americans. These formed the basis of the proposals Kissinger brought to Egypt in January 1974. Sadat indicated his willingness to allow Israeli cargoes through the Canal, but insisted that Israel would have to withdraw east of the two passes and that he would have to station one and a half divisions east of the Canal. In what soon came to be known as 'shuttle diplomacy', Kissinger now flew to Jerusalem. The Israelis would not contemplate a withdrawal east of the passes or Egyptian 'divisions' on the east bank, for these implied the infrastructure for a military build-up. Their proposal was for Egyptian 'battalions'. A subsequent 'shuttle' between Cairo and Jerusalem produced a resolution. Sadat agreed to an Israeli line west of the passes. Israel agreed that Egypt could station 8 battalions and 30 tanks east of the Canal, while Sadat made it clear that he would not exercise his right to deploy these tanks. This formed the basis of the agreement the Egyptian and Israeli Chiefs of Staff signed on 18 January 1974. Not only did this involve the withdrawal of Israeli forces from their salient on the west bank of the Canal, it marked the first step in Israel's withdrawal from her 1967 conquests. In return, Sadat gave secret assurances that once the Canal was cleared of obstacles, Israeli cargoes would be allowed through (Kissinger, 1982).

Although the plan had started with Dayan, and Sadat had proved a willing negotiator, the agreement still bore testimony to Kissinger's skill and persistence. An agreement between Israel and Syria was likely to prove a tougher proposition. While the Suez front was remote, that on the Golan had posed a close threat to northern Israel and the new Israeli salient came to within 20 miles of Damascus. Neither side had much territory to spare. President Asad was demanding a return to the 1967 border. Knowing this to be unrealistic, his real demand was for the removal of the Israeli salient and partial evacuation of the Golan, to include the old provincial capital of Quneitra and parts of Mount Hermon. To Israelis, any concession on the Golan was problematic. Their mood was not improved by the actions of radical Palestinians hostile to the negotiations. On 11 April 1974, 18 people were killed in an attack on Kiryat Shmonah in the north of Israel, while on 15 May 16 schoolchildren died in an attack on a school bus at Maalot. Such was the context of Kissinger's attempt to reach a settlement on the Golan.

In the circumstances, Kissinger had to resort to a combination of threats and reminders that the United States was Israel's only friend. Early negotiations revealed that the issue for Israel was not Quneitra but the strategic positions in the hills around the town. Kissinger's plan then hinged around a line to the west of Quneitra with a demilitarised zone between the two sides. The actual negotiations proved less straightforward than this apparently simple formula might suggest, for the Syrians still felt the Israeli threat to Damascus while the Israelis demanded a mechanism to prevent future Palestinian raids. These matters were resolved by an agreement that the Syrians could position nine brigades in front of Damascus and an assurance by Asad that the frontier would not be violated, something that he scrupulously upheld. When the final agreement was signed on 31 May 1974, Israeli forces withdrew from their salient and the ghostly ruins of Quneitra were returned to Syria (Kissinger, 1982).

## 'Reassessment' and the Return to Diplomacy

Despite his enviable prestige as an international superstar, Kissinger's position began to deteriorate after the summer of 1974. Nixon's resignation followed by the death agonies of South Vietnam seemed to signal the retreat, if not quite collapse, of American power and authority. It was not until March 1975 that Kissinger felt able to return to the Middle East, this time with a view to securing further advances in Sinai. Inevitably, the Israeli Government saw his mission as an attempt by a feeble administration to secure a foreign policy success at their expense and, once again, their attitudes were hardened by a Fatah raid on a hotel on the Tel Aviv waterfront on 5 March which killed 18 people. What was at stake was the extent of a further Israeli withdrawal. Israel wanted to keep its forces west of the Mitla and Gidi passes, with their electronic early warning systems, and wanted Sadat to make a public statement ending belligerency. Egypt demanded the return of the passes and the Abu Rudeis oilfield in return for private assurances; Sadat would not make public declarations of goodwill while Israel occupied any Egyptian territory. Agreement proved elusive. On 22 March, Kissinger declared his mission at an end, blaming Israel and threatening a 'reassessment' of American Middle East policy on his return to Washington.

As the Israeli government well knew, such a 'reassessment' could only work to their disadvantage. Signals of the new climate in Washington were not long in coming: Jordan was allowed to buy a Hawk missile system, while an Israeli attempt to buy F-16 jets was held at arm's length. The real pressure that Ford and Kissinger sought to exert, however, was the $2.5 billion aid package to Israel about to be put before Congress. Such a threat could only be challenged at source. The result was an impressive display of political muscle by AIPAC. The Israeli lobby's tactic was to pull the teeth from any possible threat to the aid package. This was done in the form of a letter to President Ford which emphasised Israel's value as an ally and urged that any aid package be 'responsive' to her needs. This was signed by 76 senators – 51 Democrats and 25 Republicans – including such eminent figures as Walter Mondale, Edward Kennedy, John Glenn, George McGovern, John Tower, Barry Goldwater and Robert Dole. The letter is generally regarded as a triumph for the power of the lobbyists, for it seemed to end any prospect of a 'reassessment' hostile to Israeli interests (Fraser, 1989).

Yet this is to misunderstand the realities of the relationship between the two countries, not to mention the dynamics of American decision-making. Ford's response was that while such tactics might scare someone else they did not work for him. When Ford met Sadat near Salzburg on 1 June, he assured the Egyptian leader that the letter's impact was negligible (Kissinger, 1999). Ford and Kissinger kept up the pressure, only less publicly, until the Israeli Treasury began to buckle. Kissinger later recorded that no president since Eisenhower had talked to the Israelis so abruptly (Kissinger, 1999). When Kissinger returned to the Middle East on 21 August 1975, on what proved to be his final mission, Israeli concessions were forthcoming, however hard the issue of where the line east of the passes might be.

Israel agreed to withdraw her forces east of the passes and to return Abu Rudeis; in return, Sadat only conceded a public declaration that Israeli cargoes would be allowed through the Canal. What really persuaded the Israelis was Kissinger's clever mixture of threats and secret assurances which, he believed, would secure their position against possible future dangers. The loss of Abu Rudeis, which had been supplying over half of Israel's oil requirements, was made good by a guarantee to secure their position for five years and funds to build greater oil-storage facilities. Kissinger also promised that the United States would be fully responsive to Israel's defence and economic needs. Finally, he agreed that the next step would be negotiations for a peace settlement and assured the Israelis that the Americans would neither recognize nor negotiate with the PLO as long as the organisation did not accept Security Council Resolutions 242 and 338. These were far-reaching guarantees which secured the Israeli–American relationship, perhaps too securely for many Israelis who still felt potentially vulnerable to their powerful patron (Quandt, 1977; Fraser, 1989). At all events, the second Sinai agreement, initialled on 1 September 1975, brought to an end one of the most distinctive phases of the Arab–Israeli conflict. Kissinger had brought a degree of stability out of the 1973 war. The agreements he had brokered meant that the United States was henceforward linked with Egypt in the search for a peace agreement. But the Syrians and Jordanians were unconvinced (Kissinger, 1999). While the worst danger between Israel and her two main Arab antagonists appeared to have passed, the Palestinians were once again the missing element.

# 4

# The Search for a Settlement

## The PLO after the 1973 War

While Kissinger's diplomacy had been vigorous and imaginative, critics complained that he had neglected or ignored the central issue of the Arab–Israeli conflict: the future of the Palestinians – in short, that he had succeeded in stabilising Israel's fronts with Egypt and Syria without addressing the future of Jerusalem, the West Bank and Gaza. Curiously, the period when Kissinger was at his most active coincided with a rise and fall in the PLO's fortunes. The end of the 1973 war produced a general expectation that there would be some progress for the Palestinians. The war had succeeded in restoring Arab pride and the oil weapon, which seemingly gave the Gulf States such leverage over Western economies, had ostensibly been mounted on the Palestinians' behalf. The reality was rather different, for the PLO leadership knew the uncomfortable truth that Sadat had fought the war for limited diplomatic aims, that he was engaged in a diplomatic process aimed at producing a settlement with Israel, and that such an agreement would leave the Israelis invulnerable to military attack. Moreover, it was clear in the summer of 1974 that Kissinger saw a settlement with Jordan as the logical next step after his agreements involving Egypt and Syria. His view was that the barrier of distrust between Israel and the PLO was so wide that negotiations were impossible and that progress could only be made with King Hussein. In the circumstances it was vital for Arafat and his colleagues to define their diplomatic position. Not to do so risked being left aside if an overall settlement involving Israel, Egypt, Syria and Jordan were to emerge. To do so risked exposing the fundamental dilemmas in the PLO's position, with incalculable consequences.

Most Palestinians could unite behind the rhetoric of the National Charter which had talked of the indivisible nature of Palestine, but there had been a growing realisation in the Arab world, seen as early as the autumn of 1967 by the signals coming from Cairo and Amman, that Israel's presence in the Middle East could not simply be wished away. The 1973 war and the subsequent diplomacy had simply confirmed this. If the reality of Israel were accepted, then the best the Palestinians could hope for was a 'mini-state' on the West Bank and Gaza, in effect a belated acceptance of partition. But such an outcome could do little or nothing for the hundreds of thousands of Palestinians in Jordan or the refugee camps in Lebanon from whom Fatah had drawn its most ardent volunteers. People who looked back to their homes in Acre, Haifa, Jaffa, or villages long since destroyed, could only look with despair on a possible solution which condemned them to permanent exile. Such was the harsh dilemma facing the PLO leadership and it is not surprising that they were reluctant to confront it.

After much heart-searching and internal debate, the Twelfth Palestine National Council in July 1974 adopted a formula allowing it to establish sovereignty 'on every part of Palestinian land to be liberated', should circumstances so permit. This was an acknowledged code for a 'mini-state' solution, and it could be represented to Palestinians outside the West Bank and Gaza as the creation of a base from which the future liberation of the entire country could be organised. Even so, the inhabitants of the refugee camps in

Lebanon were not convinced and many found a spokesman for their rejection of the formula in George Habash and his PFLP. Clearly, it was a very fine line for Arafat and his colleagues to tread (Cobban, 1984). But they had to do so, for Kissinger appeared to be pressing ahead with his ideas for introducing some form of Hashemite rule on the West Bank. He conceived the idea of restoring Jordanian administration to the city of Jericho, thus reintroducing at least some Arab rule in part of the West Bank. His plan foundered on the reluctance of the Israeli government to contemplate the idea, but it pointed to the need for the PLO to counter the Hashemites. As a result, on 28 October 1974 the Arab summit at Rabat in Morocco affirmed the position of the PLO as the sole legitimate representative of the Palestinians, acknowledging it as, in effect, a government in exile (Cobban, 1984).

Arafat's opportunity to underline that fact came just two weeks later before the General Assembly of the United Nations in New York. In September, a number of states had proposed that 'The Question of Palestine' be debated by the Assembly and a subsequent vote invited the PLO to take part. The extent of that vote, 82 in favour, 4 against and 20 abstentions, showed how far the organisation had come in terms of international acceptance. The idea that Arafat should come to New York aroused furious opposition in the city's Jewish community for whom he represented nothing more than terrorism, but the American government, aware of its obligations to the United Nations, allowed him to come. Those who hoped that he would use the occasion to signal the PLO's acquiescence in a 'mini-state' solution were disappointed, but the reality of Arafat's position as head of a broad coalition made that impossible. Instead, he chose to set before the world body a full statement of the Palestinians' grievances and his dream of a future state in which Palestinians and Jews would live together. Dramatic as his appearance was, its impact was somewhat diminished by media speculation as to whether he had carried his gun to the rostrum (he had not) and, as was almost always to be the case in the future, the lack of any clear proposals for a way forward. Even so, advances were made (Hart, 1984). The PLO was accorded observer status in the United Nations, thus allowing its representatives an opportunity to take part in the secret discussions that go on in the corridors of the world body, and the Committee on the Exercise of the Inalienable Rights of the Palestinian People was set up. Support for the Palestinians amongst the countries of Africa and Asia was high. In the summer of 1975 a concerted campaign to deprive Israel of her UN membership only just failed, but in November a resolution was passed in the General Assembly in which Zionism was identified as 'a form of racialism'. As the United Nations had ceased to be an actor of any consequence in the Arab–Israeli conflict, such things had little practical result, but they helped bring to the surface Israeli fears that the world's hand would always turn against the Jews and hence did nothing to encourage a spirit of compromise.

## The PLO and the Lebanese Civil War

The years 1974–75, then, saw a considerable transformation in the PLO's fortunes but this was soon to be confounded by events in Lebanon. In the 1950s and into the 1960s Lebanon had created the image of itself as the 'Switzerland of the Middle East', Beirut being the Zurich of the region, with its Christians, Muslims and Druses sharing power and cooperating in the manner of German-, French- and Italian-speaking Swiss. It was, in fact, a cruel illusion. There was, indeed, a power-sharing arrangement based upon the unwritten National Pact of 1943, itself based upon the census of 1932 through which the French mandatory authorities had contrived to show that the Christians were a slight majority in the country. The Pact really reflected the hegemony of the most powerful groups within each community, the Maronites on the Christian side and the Sunnis on the Muslim side. By the 1970s this arrangement had become dangerously unrealistic. Not only were the Muslims generally acknowledged to be a majority, but within the Muslim community there was a growing assertiveness amongst the Shi'as. As elsewhere in the Middle East, the Shi'as were the 'have nots' of the Muslim community, cultivating the poor hill land of southern Lebanon. By the 1960s, their high birth-rate was causing them to migrate in large numbers to Beirut where they concentrated in large numbers in the south-western quarters, forming an alliance of deprivation with the Palestinians of the refugee camps. This population shift coincided with an increase in assertiveness by the Palestinians. After 'Black September' in Jordan, the Palestinian guerrillas made Lebanon the main focus of their activities, not least because they had a steady stream of recruits from amongst the 400,000 inhabitants of the country's refugee camps.

The growing strength of the Shi'as and Palestinians brought to the surface the gnawing fear amongst the Maronites that their privileged position in the country's political and economic life was fated to disappear. The cutting edge of the Maronites was the right-wing Phalangist party and its armed militia, led by the powerful Gemayel family. On 13 April 1975, an attack on Pierre Gemayel, the veteran founder of the Phalange, led to a massacre of Palestinian passengers travelling by bus through a Christian part of Beirut. The Lebanese civil war, which was to involve all religious groups and devastate the country in the years ahead, had begun. The Palestinians were amongst its principal victims, most dramatically in the siege of their Tel al-Zaatar refugee camp in Christian east Beirut in the summer of 1976. The slaughter which accompanied the fall of Tel al-Zaatar seemed to symbolise once again the Palestinian tragedy. On the international front, the inevitable preoccupation of the PLO with the Lebanese civil war meant that it was unable to build upon the diplomatic advances made in 1974–75. It meant that the organisation could be pushed aside in the dramatic new phase of diplomatic activity which was about to begin, and which was to result in a realignment of forces in the Middle East (Cobban, 1984). Civil war continued to plague Lebanon until the Taif Accord of November 1989 set new terms for the constitution. By then the once-elegant streets of Beirut had long been reduced to ruins. There were, inevitably, wider ramifications. In 1976, Syria intervened in massive strength on the Maronite Christian side under the banner of the Arab League, while contacts were opened up between the Israelis and the Maronite leaders, united in their hatred of the PLO. The significance of these developments would become apparent in 1982 (Shlaim, 2000).

## Carter and the Return to Diplomacy

This diplomatic revolution had several sources. It had been apparent for some time that the only logical outcome of Sadat's policy would be some kind of accommodation with Israel which would see the Sinai returned to Egypt, even if the means by which this would be brought about were much less clear. There were still many doubters in the Egyptian military and diplomatic establishment whom Sadat would have to confront. There were also problems and divisions on the Israeli side. Israel's Prime Minister was the distinguished former general and ambassador to Washington, Yitzhak Rabin. Although he could appear stiff in public and in negotiations, this concealed a flexibility of mind linked to a cool grasp of reality which might have enabled him to make imaginative moves but for a series of problems afflicting his government. The Labour Party, which had never quite recovered public confidence after the disasters at the start of the 1973 war, was riven by bitter feuding between Rabin and its other leading figure, Shimon Peres, and then in the spring of 1977 Rabin's wife was fined for having a bank account in the United States in breach of Treasury regulations.

Despite these obstacles, there was a new spirit in US government circles that an attempt should be made to address the central issues of the Arab–Israeli problem. The presidential election of 1976 was won by the Democratic candidate Jimmy Carter who was determined to pull America out of the depressing legacy of the Watergate scandal and the Vietnam War. Central to his view of foreign affairs was a determination that the United States had to stand for human rights. A man of deep Christian faith, he also had an instinctive interest in the Holy Land and was likely to respond to an appeal to help address its problems. The Democratic Party, too, had been rethinking its positions, some of its foreign policy experts believing that Kissinger had failed to address the core issues. The key to Democrat strategy towards a settlement came from a report of the Brookings Institution, an influential Washington 'think tank', in 1975. Its findings represented several radical new dimensions in American thinking and among its authors were two men likely to exert considerable influence on the administration's policy, Zbigniew Brzezinski, who became Carter's National Security Adviser, and William B. Quandt, who assumed particular responsibility for Arab–Israeli affairs. Their report advocated an Israeli return to the 1967 borders, with demilitarised zones under UN supervision to guarantee security. More far-reaching was the recognition of the need for some kind of Palestinian state, possibly in federation with Jordan. In the course of the election campaign Carter privately accepted the findings of the Brookings report, the tone of which seemed to sit well with his avowed concern for human rights (Carter, 1982, 1985; Brzezinski, 1983; Quandt, 1986).

### Menahem Begin's Electoral Triumph

It was in this spirit that early in his presidency Carter began to make significant moves. At meetings with Rabin in early March 1977, he informed a dismayed Israeli leader that he believed the PLO should be involved in negotiations and then kept up this pressure by publicly referring to the need for a Palestinian homeland and shaking the hand of the PLO representative at a UN reception. A meeting with Sadat in early April began a warm relationship which lasted throughout the Carter presidency. What the Americans were not prepared for was the change of government brought about in Israel as the result of the general election in May, which altered the whole ideological thrust of the country's foreign policy. For three decades the world had been accustomed to Mapai and Labour's dominance of Israeli politics, but in 1977, beset by internal rivalry and financial scandal, the party had lost its sureness of touch. In contrast, the right-wing Likud, led by Menahem Begin and Ariel Sharon, fought an intelligent campaign. Its principal appeal was to the oriental Jews who now formed half the population and felt undervalued by the predominantly European Labour party. Support from the oriental Jews throughout Israel proved enough to bring Begin the premiership, though it pointed to an uneasy split in the country's Jewish population. It was an odd commentary on Israeli politics that the country's 'have nots' turned to the right (Pappe, 2004).

Under Begin, Likud was the heir to the traditions and ideology of the Irgun, and beyond that to Jabotinsky and the pre-war Revisionists for whom the territorial integrity of 'Greater Israel' was beyond question. While the Labour Party had taken a pragmatic approach to the Occupied Territories, for Begin the West Bank constituted the 'Liberated Territories' of Judea and Samaria which in his view had never ceased to be part of the Jewish inheritance; in contrast, he had little interest in Gaza. The stated policy of Likud was that Israeli sovereignty should extend from the Mediterranean to the River Jordan. Begin's profound emotional commitment to 'Judea and Samaria' was a new factor in the Arab–Israeli problem and one that the Carter administration took some time to understand. Nor was Begin an easy man to deal with on the personal level. Haunted by the Holocaust, which had claimed the lives of almost all his family, he was determined to make no mistake, or make any concession, that might once again place the Jews at risk. As a result, his negotiating style was formal and legalistic. Once he had made an agreement, however, he stuck to it, or at least to his interpretation. There had been those in the Labour Party, Ben-Gurion and Dayan for example, who had taken an active interest in the Arab world and its civilisation. Begin had no such curiosity, the Arabs, and the Palestinians in particular, being closed to him. In the circumstances his choice as Foreign Minister, Moshe Dayan, was bold and unexpected, for not only had Dayan fought the election on the Labour ticket but he was known to favour peace moves with the Arabs. Dayan accepted the offer on condition that it was not government policy to extend sovereignty to the Occupied Territories, at least while peace talks were in progress. Assailed by his former Labour colleagues as a turncoat, his appointment proved to be a conspicuous success, for in negotiation he had the imagination to range beyond the confines of Begin's seemingly invincible stubbornness (Silver, 1984).

The Americans were slow to discover the depth of Begin's commitment to the West Bank, but the Israeli leader was open enough in signalling his intentions. In July 1977 he flew to Washington to consult Carter. While there was agreement on the need for a peace settlement based upon Resolution 242, Begin persuaded Carter to agree to stop using the term 'Palestinian homeland', something to which he was totally opposed. Hopes in Washington that a positive relationship had begun were quickly dispelled when Begin legalised three Jewish settlements on the West Bank on his return home. These settlements were seen by Likud as the keystone of their policy. Labour had proceeded cautiously with regard to settlements, largely confining them to the eastern suburbs of Jerusalem and the Jordan valley, the total number of settlers amounting to no more than a few thousand. This had not satisfied those on the religious right for whom Judea and Samaria were inalienably Jewish, and even less those for whom this land was bound up with the redemption of the Jewish people by the Messiah. In 1974, supporters of this view formed Gush Emunim ('The Block of the Faithful'), dedicated to extending and defending the Jewish presence in the territories. Their settlements, highly provocative to the Arabs, were half-empty, even at times allegedly constructed for the benefit of visiting journalists. Few Israelis felt the urge to live in such obviously hostile surroundings, but the activities of Gush Emunim were the spearhead of Likud policies. 'Building realities' was a tradition which reached back to the early history of Zionist settlement and Likud was happy to annex the idea and to cast a benign eye over Gush Emunim activities. It soon became clear that the government had plans of a more far-reaching nature than Gush Emunim's haphazard enterprises could ever have achieved (Palumbo, 1990).

## Sadat's Visit to Jerusalem

The issue of the settlements clouded relations between Jerusalem and Washington over the summer of 1977, with American initiatives achieving nothing. The real contacts were taking place elsewhere in conditions of the utmost secrecy. In late August, Dayan met King Hussein in London where the two men explored the possibilities of settlement between the two countries. The following month even more significant meetings were arranged in Morocco by King Hassan who brought together Dayan and the Egyptian Deputy Prime Minister, Dr Hassan Tuhami. Sadat had long been frustrated at the seemingly interminable pace of Middle East negotiations and was convinced that at its heart lay the 'psychological barrier' of distrust which had built up between Arabs and Israelis. The secret meetings in Morocco convinced Dayan that Sadat genuinely wanted peace, while Tuhami took back the message that the Begin government was strong enough to reach an agreement. Sadat remained wary of Begin's reputation for extremism, but his growing belief that a bold move should be made was reinforced by a letter from Carter and discussions with the Romanian leader, Nicolae Ceausescu, who reinforced his growing feeling that Begin was a leader capable of reaching an agreement.

In a speech to his People's Assembly on 9 November 1977, Sadat astonished the world, including many of his closest advisers and the American Government, by his announcement that he was ready to address the Knesset. It was the dramatic move that he believed would break down the psychological barriers and enable both sides to make the concessions necessary to achieve peace. While many applauded his boldness, others feared that his move had been insufficiently thought through and failed to take account of the depth of Israeli suspicion. The doubters were reinforced by the resignation of his Foreign Minister, Ismail Fahmy. The American Government was highly dubious that Sadat and Begin could reach agreement without outside mediation. But the move had been made, and between 19 and 21 November the world was treated to the sight of the Egyptian leader in Israel. The climax of his historic visit was his speech to the Knesset on the 20th. Central to his message was the need to break down what he believed had been the psychological barrier between the two sides. For his part, he was ready to assure the Israelis that were welcome to live in the Middle East. Peace, he was careful to assure his audience, could not be based upon a bilateral agreement between the two countries but had to incorporate a solution for the Palestinians, which would include their right to statehood. Begin was determined that he should not be swayed by the emotion of the moment into making concessions he would later regret. Conceding only that everything would be open to negotiation, his speech was seen outside Israel as failing to match the undoubted drama of the occasion. Whatever the outcome, however, the presence in Israel of the leader of the most powerful Arab country ensured that the pattern of Arab–Israeli relations would never be quite the same (Fraser, 1980; Dayan, 1981).

Subsequent negotiations between the two parties confirmed the Americans' worst fears, for they generated neither progress nor personal warmth. The chief reason for lack of progress was that the two sides wanted very different things. Sadat's purpose was to work towards an overall peace settlement which would see Israel return to her pre-1967 border and include provision for the Palestinians; not to achieve this would leave him dangerously isolated at home and abroad. This aim was broadly supported by the Americans, so much so that Carter paid a brief visit to Egypt in January 1978 in which he pointedly referred to the need to take into account 'the legitimate rights of the Palestinian people'. Such an outcome, with its obvious consequences for the West Bank, was what the Begin government wished to avoid. Begin's strategy was to negotiate for a bilateral peace treaty with Egypt which would ensure Israel's security by removing her most powerful enemy. To that end he was prepared to negotiate a full withdrawal from the Sinai, for many Israelis the surrender of a major asset in return for a signature on a piece of paper. The most he would concede on the West Bank and Gaza was a proposal for the personal 'autonomy' of the inhabitants under which Israeli military rule would continue while the Palestinians ran their everyday lives. The problem for Sadat and Carter was whether this represented a genuine concession or was simply a device to perpetuate Israeli control of the territories. Their situation was not eased by the accelerated expansion of a cluster of Israeli settlements in the Sinai on territory undeniably Egyptian. By the end of January 1978, not only had the 'psychological barrier' between the two sides not been removed, but the goodwill seemingly generated by Sadat's journey to Jerusalem was threatening to turn to mutual antipathy.

Despite the fact that the Americans had feared this from the start, they had no option but to follow the path Sadat had set. Before this could be done, however, the murderous nature of the Arab–Israeli conflict once again erupted. On

11 March 1978, a group of Palestinians landed on the Israeli coast and killed 35 people in two buses. Three days later, the Israeli army began a major offensive into southern Lebanon inflicting a death toll of hundreds and occupying the country south of the Litani River. Fearing an Israeli plan to annex the area, Carter denounced their invasion as an overreaction and threatened to cut off military aid. Whether Congress would have sanctioned such a move may be doubted but Carter's obvious displeasure was enough to ensure a withdrawal. The Americans knew that anything less would kill off the floundering Egyptian–Israeli peace process. The invasion was followed by a bitter three days in Washington when Carter charged Begin with his obstinacy over the West Bank and the future of the Palestinians, something the Israeli leader did not trouble to deny (Quandt, 1986).

## The Camp David Summit

Despairing of progress, Carter decided in July that the only possible way forward was to bring Sadat, Begin and their advisers to Camp David, the presidential retreat in Maryland. The Camp David Summit, which took place from 5 to 17 September 1978, was a concentrated attempt by the Americans to salvage something from the 'peace process' which Sadat had started the previous November. Of the three leaders, Begin came with certain clear advantages. His purpose was to secure a bilateral peace treaty with Egypt while giving away nothing of substance on the West Bank and Gaza. Stirrings amongst Jewish supporters of the Democratic Party earlier in the year signalled certain limits to Carter's ability to put pressure on the Israelis. Failure to reach an acceptable agreement would have minimal consequences for Israel. In contrast, Sadat desperately needed to come away from Camp David with something that would justify his efforts. While still determined to achieve progress for the Palestinians, he was ultimately ready to concede a bilateral peace treaty at the price of a total Israeli evacuation of the Sinai desert. Carter, too, needed a diplomatic success to justify the full exercise of his prestige behind the Camp David Summit.

For ten days the negotiations merely seemed to confirm the extent of the gulf between Begin and Sadat. It was only when the Americans learned on 15 September that the latter had ordered a helicopter to start his journey that the summit was jolted into life. Over the next three days two 'frameworks' were agreed, each seeming to give the Egyptians and Israelis the essence of what they needed to claim success. The 'Framework for the Conclusion of a Peace between Egypt and Israel' set out the terms for 'normal relations' between the two countries, in return for which Israel conceded full evacuation of the Sinai. A peace treaty was to be signed within three months. Potentially more ambitious, but inevitably more problematic, was the 'Framework for Peace in the Middle East', which sought to accommodate Sadat's desire to come away with something positive for the Palestinians. This laid down that:

> there should be transitional arrangements for the West Bank and Gaza for a period not exceeding five years. In order to provide full autonomy to the inhabitants, under these arrangements the Israeli military government and its administration will be withdrawn as soon as a self-governing authority has been freely elected by the inhabitants of these areas to replace the existing military government. (Department of State, 1978)

Carter and his team genuinely believed they had gained a major concession on the West Bank and Gaza but events were to confound their hopes. On his return to Israel, Begin insisted that all he had agreed to was the kind of 'personal autonomy' he had alluded to earlier in the year. Moreover, the Americans and Israelis had very different interpretations of an agreement for a moratorium on further settlements in the territories. Begin and Dayan claimed this was only for three months, while Carter had come away with the belief that it was to be for the five years of the transitional arrangements. Thus the 'Spirit of Camp David', applauded as a breakthrough for peace in the region, was soured almost from the start (Carter, 1982; Kamel, 1986; Quandt, 1986).

The Palestinians of the West Bank and Gaza saw Camp David as the ultimate betrayal by their most powerful ally, condemning them to permanent Israeli military occupation. Their view was widely shared in the Middle East. Even Jordan and Saudi Arabia joined the Syrians in condemning the agreements. Nor was the atmosphere helped by Begin's clear intention to press ahead with more settlements. As the weeks turned to months with little progress on the signing of the peace treaty, it became vital for Carter to salvage something from what had seemed to be the major foreign-policy triumph of his presidency. This became even more urgent after January 1979 when the Shah of Iran, America's principal ally in the Middle East, was forced into exile. The Islamic government inspired by Ayatollah Khomenei was to prove deeply hostile to American interests. In these depressing circumstances Carter flew to the Middle East in March 1979, only to find Begin as immovable as ever. Carter was now forced to the conclusion that the Israeli leader was so opposed to progress over the West Bank that he was prepared to sacrifice the treaty with Egypt. It took vigorous and flexible diplomacy by Dayan to save Carter's mission and with it the peace treaty.

On 26 March 1979, Begin and Sadat signed the 'Treaty of Peace between the Arab Republic of Egypt and the State of Israel' in Washington. On one level it was a major development. Israel was now at peace with her strongest potential enemy. Israelis felt that they were no longer an island in the Middle East. Posters in Tel Aviv travel agencies could now proclaim the attractions of visiting the pyramids. The reality was that the goodwill generated by Sadat's visit to Jerusalem had long since been dissipated. What had been achieved was a 'Cold Peace' which survived the trials of the next three decades, even the death of its author. On 6 October 1981, as he reviewed a parade to commemorate the crossing of the Suez Canal, Sadat was assassinated by disaffected soldiers. He was succeeded by Husni Mubarak, an air-force officer, who, if he exhibited little of the fire of Nasser or Sadat, had a marked feel for Egypt's internal and external needs. Nor was progress made on the promised autonomy for the West Bank and Gaza, for the Carter administration had other problems which took priority. On 4 November 1979, the American embassy in Tehran was seized and 69 Americans held hostage. It was a disaster for Carter, compounded by the ignominious failure of a rescue mission, which dominated the final year of his presidency and contributed to his defeat by Ronald Reagan. If Carter had ultimately failed to find an overall settlement of the Arab–Israeli conflict, it had not been for want of effort, and the Egyptian–Israeli peace treaty stood as his principal foreign policy achievement (Carter, 1982).

## Reagan's Middle East Policy

Ronald Reagan's foreign policy agenda was to have profound consequences for the Arab–Israeli conflict. He later recorded that one of his strongest convictions was his belief that America had to ensure Israel's survival (Reagan, 1990). The recent events in Tehran reinforced what was already an intense dislike of 'terrorism' in American government and society and this was not to the Palestinians' advantage, however much the PLO leadership might argue that violence belonged to an earlier phase of its development. The Soviet invasion of Afghanistan in 1979 appeared to usher in a new phase of East–West confrontation and revived the old Cold War strategy of 'containment' of Moscow's ambitions, not least because airbases in western Afghanistan could potentially threaten Western oil supplies in the Gulf. An early priority for the new American administration was the building of a 'strategic consensus' around Israel, Egypt,

Saudi Arabia, Oman, Somalia and Kenya – a fanciful idea at best but again one in which the Palestinians were likely to be ignored. A visit to the region in April 1981 by Reagan's Secretary of State, Alexander Haig, revealed that only the Israelis were attracted by the idea. The Israelis were quick to grasp that Washington's new priorities offered the possibility of a much more positive relationship than they had enjoyed with Carter, with his tiresome concern over the West Bank and Gaza. Their bargaining cards were the stability of their democratic regime and the proven effectiveness of their armed forces, the latter particularly attractive to the Americans because of the mutual dislike of their other two allies in the eastern Mediterranean, Greece and Turkey. In November 1981, an agreement for strategic cooperation was signed in Washington by Israel's Defence Minister, Ariel Sharon, and a rather hesitant American Defense Secretary, Casper Weinberger, who was unhappy about the effect this might have elsewhere in the Middle East (Fraser, 1989).

In other respects, 1981 seemed to show Israel becoming increasingly assertive. On 7 June, Israeli jets destroyed the nuclear reactor at Osirak that Iraq had been building with Soviet and French help. This attack was a breach of the agreement under which the United States had supplied the aircraft and the Americans were forced publicly to rebuke the Israelis; privately, they were quite pleased. A more serious issue between Jerusalem and Washington was the Pentagon's desire to supply five Airborne Warning and Control System (AWACS) aircraft to Saudi Arabia. Seen in Washington as a necessary reinforcement for Western security in the Gulf, it was viewed in Israel as a potential threat to her vital air superiority. The result was a bruising eight-month battle in Congress with Reagan's authority pitted against the lobbying strength of AIPAC. Reagan's eventual Senate majority of 52 votes to 48 seemed to emphasise Israel's power in Washington. The Israeli government's response was to claim that the administration was anti-Semitic (Tivnan, 1987; Reagan, 1990). Finally, on 14 December 1981 the Knesset voted for the de facto annexation of the Golan Heights, in defiance both of the views of its remaining inhabitants and the known American position that it should be returned to Syria in an eventual peace settlement. Fearing that this was the prelude to a similar move over the West Bank, the Americans suspended the agreement for strategic cooperation. By the end of 1981, it was hard to escape the view that Begin's government was holding the initiative, with the Reagan administration being forced to react.

## Israel's Lebanon War

These events in 1981 proved to be the prelude to the tragedy that unfolded the following year: Israel's invasion of Lebanon. The immediate background was instability on Israel's border with Lebanon from which Palestinians had been launching rockets against Israeli towns, especially Kiryat Shmonah. In July 1981, the Americans arranged a cease-fire and, although this had been observed, many Israelis felt nervous about the PLO's accumulation of weapons in southern Lebanon. While no one pretended they were a threat to the state, they were enough to build up pressure for action. There were other anxieties. On 25 April 1982, a major phase of the Camp David agreements was completed with Israel's final withdrawal from Sinai; promptings from the Americans for progress on autonomy for the West Bank and Gaza were bound to follow. In these circumstances, pressure began to grow in the Begin government for a major move in Lebanon which would have as its immediate aim the removal of the PLO threat to the northern border and the expulsion of the organisation from Lebanon. But even more ambitious prospects were in mind. Breaking the PLO in Lebanon would, it was felt, make the Palestinians of the West Bank more pliable, thus making some form of de facto annexation easier. A successful campaign might also bring about another dream: the establishment of a regime in

Beirut which would sign a peace treaty. While Lebanon was never a military threat, such a treaty would stabilise the border with a second Arab state. This took surprisingly little account of the country's instability, or of Syria's special relationship with it. The chosen instrument was the Phalangist leader Bashir Gemayal, who had long been in contact with key Israeli figures. Not every member of the Begin Cabinet thought the same way, or was even aware of such plans, but these were all considerations influencing key figures in the government and army. Reagan's view was that Israeli Defence Minister Ariel Sharon, the veteran of the 1967 and 1973 wars who had been appointed in August 1981, was 'chomping at the bit to start a war' (Feldman and Rechnitz-Kijner, 1984; Reagan, 1990; Shlaim, 2000). Chief of Staff Raful Eitan later recorded his view that war in Lebanon was inevitable in order to curb the growing strength of the PLO (Eitan, 1992).

By May 1982, there was an expectation in informed circles that an Israeli move into Lebanon was imminent. Faced with this, the Reagan administration gave out signals that the Israeli government allowed itself to misinterpret. Warnings against action in Lebanon were so diplomatically couched as to encourage Begin and his key advisers in the belief that they were being given a 'green light' by Washington. A speech by Haig on 26 May failed to hit its mark, though it is fair to say that he could not have anticipated the event which within days was to trigger the invasion. On 3 June, Israel's ambassador to London, Shlomo Argov, was shot and seriously wounded by Palestinians. One of his country's most promising diplomats, Argov spent the next two decades on a life-support machine, dying in February 2003. Despite intelligence from London that the attempted assassination was the work of men hostile to Arafat and the PLO, on 6 June Israel began a full-scale invasion of Lebanon. Entitled 'Operation Peace for Galilee', its declared purpose was the creation of a 40-km security zone in southern Lebanon, but it soon became clear that the terms of the operation extended far beyond 40km. Although outnumbered by the well-equipped Israeli forces, the PLO men fought back hard. Tyre, Sidon and Nabatiyeh were badly damaged and villages and refugee camps were abandoned, with thousands dead and wounded. By 9 June, Israeli and Syrian ground forces were also engaged, and this escalated into a major air battle (Shlaim, 2000). The following day the Israelis were approaching Beirut, and three days later they were in control of its western and southern approaches. The prospect now opened up of an assault on west Beirut with its largely Muslim population of 500,000 amongst whom were some 6,000 embattled PLO defenders. Such a development was unwelcome in Washington, where Haig resigned as Secretary of State, and was to be regarded with increasing unease by sections of the Israeli public. Whereas every other war in Israel's history had enjoyed total public support, from July public confidence began perceptibly to erode. Even in the army, which had taken substantial casualties, questions were beginning to be asked, especially amongst reservists (Schiff and Ya'ari, 1985).

## America Intervenes: The Multinational Force

By early July, with Israeli artillery bombarding west Beirut, the Americans were trying to negotiate a disengagement agreement. Both Begin and the PLO were talking in terms of a multinational force to supervise such an agreement and the delicate question of the inclusion of American troops was beginning to arise. Arafat in particular saw American soldiers as the guarantee for the security of the Palestinian refugee camps in Beirut, should he agree to his fighters evacuating the city. While thoughts increasingly turned to the concept of a PLO evacuation under cover of a multinational force, the new American Secretary of State, George Shultz, began to prepare plans for a more wide-ranging peace initiative. On 1 August, however, Israel began a major assault on west Beirut, flying 127 sorties over the city on that day alone. Two weeks of intensive bombardment followed, devastating whole areas of the city, which were believed to be the prelude to a full-scale assault. Repeated attempts by the Americans to bring about a cease-fire were ignored until, on 12 August, Reagan's patience finally snapped. Believing that Israeli actions were designed to thwart a peaceful outcome, he telephoned Begin demanding an end to the 'needless destruction and bloodshed', deliberately using the word 'Holocaust' because of its resonance with the Israeli Premier; a cease-fire came into operation that day (Jansen, 1982; Reagan, 1990).

The way was now open for an evacuation of PLO guerrillas, supervised by a Multinational Force in which France and Italy had confirmed they would join with the Americans. On 13 August, the PLO submitted a list of 7,100 guerrillas with a timetable for their evacuation by sea and land to various sympathetic Arab countries. On the 21st, paratroopers of the French Foreign Legion were to arrive in Beirut to supervise a seaborne evacuation to Tunisia and Yemen. Five days later they were to be joined by Americans and Italians who would help ensure the departure of PLO fighters to Syria. At the time it was seen as a triumph of crisis management. An Israeli attack on west Beirut, with incalculable civilian casualties, had been avoided; instead, by 9 September 8,144 PLO fighters had left Beirut by sea and 6,254 had gone overland to Damascus. Although Israeli spokesmen tried to claim the demise of the PLO, they failed to convince, for the nature of the opposition the outnumbered Palestinians had put up and the jubilant nature of their departure ensured that the organisation's standing remained intact. If Begin and his colleagues had believed that the expulsion of the PLO from Lebanon would destroy its credibility, at the very least events had conspired to confound them. Believing they had averted a slaughter, on 9 September the troops of the Multinational Force left Beirut.

## The Reagan Peace Plan

A successful evacuation of the PLO had been one prong of American policy; the other was the peace plan which President Reagan announced on 1 September. Its essence was 'that only self-government by the Palestinians of the West Bank and Gaza in association with Jordan offers the best chance for a durable, just and lasting peace'. While stressing his personal commitment to Israel, Reagan warned that the United States opposed any further settlements in the territories. It was a strategy close to the heart of the Labour leader, Shimon Peres, but was in clear contrast to Likud hopes over the West Bank, and Begin's rejection of the plan was both immediate and sulphurous. In rejecting the plan, Begin emphasised that what for some was the West Bank was for him Judea and Samaria (Fraser, 1989; Reagan, 1990). The Americans had been well aware that the plan would need time to mature but could not have been prepared for the bloody events in Beirut which stifled it. On 14 September, Bashir Gemayel was assassinated, destroying yet another element in Israel's Lebanese strategy. The following morning the Israeli army began to occupy west Beirut, in violation of assurances given to the Americans. With the Israeli army now in unfettered control of west Beirut, Arafat's nightmare of the defenceless nature of the refugee camps had come true.

## The Sabra and Shatila Massacres

Even so, the signs did not necessarily point to tragedy, for the Israeli army was assumed to be a disciplined force. The critical decision was taken not only to allow Phalangist militia into west Beirut alongside the Israelis but to assign them the task of seeking out 'terrorists' in the Sabra and Shatila refugee camps. The likely consequences should have been predictable by anyone aware of the murderous passions that had been stoked up in the course of the Lebanese civil war, now at a new intensity as a result of Gemayel's death. On the evening of 16 September, Phalangists entered Sabra and Shatila, which were illuminated by flares fired by the Israeli army. For two days the militiamen killed defenceless men, women and children in the camps. Despite the graphic accounts of newspaper and television reporters, no one yet knows how many were killed. Palestinian sources put the figure at 2,000; Israeli intelligence conceded 800 (Fisk, 1990). Israel could not escape the blame for introducing the militiamen into the camps nor for seeming to be indifferent to massacres being carried on over so long a period in an area under their control. Pictures of the slaughter shocked opinion throughout the world, but Begin seemed immune to the enormity of what had happened until a demonstration of 400,000 people in Tel Aviv forced him to concede an independent inquiry. In fact, Sabra and Shatila marked the beginning of the end of Israel's Lebanese adventure. Within days Israeli troops had left west Beirut and from then on Israel was on the political and military defensive.

The Israeli army was replaced in west Beirut by a hastily contrived revival of the Multinational Force. American, French and Italian troops, later joined by a small British contingent, deployed to protect the refugee camps, separate the combatants and attempt to fulfil a hopelessly optimistic brief that they assist with the reconstruction of the Lebanese state. In the meantime, American diplomats tried to press ahead with the Reagan Plan. But the whole Lebanese affair, culminating in the Sabra and Shatila massacres, had shattered what little stability the region possessed. The Israeli committee of inquiry chaired by Chief Justice Yitzhak Kahan reported in February 1983 and shook the country's political establishment. While Begin was criticised for his lack of involvement and a number of officers were censured, including the Chief of Staff, it was Defence Minister Ariel Sharon who drew the principal condemnation for allowing the Phalangists into the camps. As Sharon declined to resign, Begin was forced to dismiss him. From then on, Begin went into visible decline. Long prone to depression, he was devastated by the death of his wife. In September 1983, he resigned and became a recluse, dying in March 1992. His successor, Yitzhak Shamir, a former leader of Leh'i, was to prove no less inflexible in his interpretation and defence of Israel's interests.

## America's Lebanese Débâcle

Events on the Arab side were just as discouraging. American officials had looked to King Hussein to open the way forward but on 10 April 1983 the Jordanians announced that agreement on the future of the Palestinians would have to be made by the PLO. Ten days later, key American intelligence personnel – including the CIA station chief in Lebanon and Robert C. Ames, its leading Middle East analyst – were killed in a massive car bomb at the embassy in Beirut. As a result of this double blow, George Shultz flew to the Middle East. On 17 May, he concluded an agreement for an Israeli withdrawal from Lebanon in return for a security zone in the south of the country, but as he could not get Syrian agreement, this, too, failed. Just as Shultz was becoming discouraged by these setbacks, the Multinational Force in Beirut fell victim to the lethal passions of Middle East politics. The American marine contingent around Beirut International Airport was threatened by two powerful groups which saw the Multinational Force as favouring the Christian side, the Druse militia in the Chouf mountains and the Shi'as of south Beirut. On 23 October 1983, Shi'ite suicide car bombers hit the French and American bases: 78 French troops and 241 American marines were killed. Their action had the desired effect: on 8 February 1984, President Reagan, faced with the prospect of re-election, announced the 'redeployment' of the marines to ships offshore. The French, Italians and British had no choice but to follow (Fraser, 1989).

With the departure of the Multinational Force, and the effective demise of the Reagan Plan, yet another phase of Middle East diplomacy had ended in frustration. But not quite, for the Israeli armed forces were still in Lebanon in positions that were under pressure from two directions. The Israeli public, which had initially supported the invasion in 1982, now largely saw the affair as pointless. More seriously, the Shi'ite population of southern Lebanon and south Beirut were fiercely anti-Israeli. In fact, one major consequence of the invasion was the formation of the strongly Islamic movement, Hizbollah, 'The Party of God', whose activities came to torment the Israelis in the years ahead. Israel's policy of the 'iron fist' against them seemed only to inspire more resistance, including suicide car bombs against which conventional resistance was hopeless. In 1985, the Israeli army withdrew from most of the country, maintaining a presence only in the 'security zone' along the southern border. Thus ended a war that had cost thousands of Arab, Israeli, American and French lives, completed the devastation of Lebanon, divided Israeli society as never before, and achieved nothing, beyond the security zone, which lasted until 2000.

## The Intifada

Diplomacy never entirely died out between 1984 and 1987, but it is fair to say that it languished. State Department officials tried to ensure that Israelis and Palestinians had opportunities for exploring each other's positions against the day when the conflict would return to the top of the agenda, as they knew it must before too long. This feeling of neglect in the era when Reagan and Gorbachev were presiding over the end of the Cold War contributed in no small measure to the growing sense of frustration amongst the Palestinians. This was particularly felt in the Occupied Territories which were about to enter their third decade under Israeli rule. The twentieth anniversary of the Six Day War seemed to emphasise both the permanent nature of the occupation and the failure of international diplomacy to bring about change. Behind this façade, however, profound forces were at work which were to change the nature of the Arab–Israeli conflict. A new generation had grown up in the West Bank and Gaza that had known nothing but occupation with its daily frustrations and humiliations; some 50 per cent of the population had been born under Israeli rule. It was a generation which had a new potential leadership fostered in the schools and universities of the West Bank and Gaza. These young men and women no longer looked to Jordan, and if they overwhelmingly gave their allegiance to the PLO, it was in the knowledge that its leadership was of an older generation remote from the everyday realities of life in the territories. Significant pointers to the new political spirit were the numbers of community groups, cultural associations, women's organisations and other grass-root activities which sought to build the Palestinian community from the bottom up; there was, of course, a political subtext to much of what they did. Above all, by the late 1980s this generation had ceased to fear the Israelis – a telling factor behind any uprising.

What they did fear was Israel's intention with regard to the West Bank and Gaza. For much of the 1980s the pace of settlement policy seemed unrelenting. The ideological thrust behind government policy in the West Bank, and to a much lesser degree Gaza, was to build up the Jewish presence to such an extent that it would be indissolubly bound to the rest of the country. The key to this was land, access to which was largely secured through the old Ottoman concept of 'state land', continued during the British and Jordanian periods. By designating certain areas as 'state land', it is estimated that by 1987 Israel had secured just over 50 per cent of the West Bank and 30 per cent of the Gaza Strip, though only part of this was settled. To the Palestinians who had farmed these lands for generations this amounted to expropriation under thin legal cover. By the same date, some

70,000 Israelis had settled on the West Bank and 2,000 in the Gaza Strip. Their motivation varied. Some were undoubtedly attracted by keen religious and political fervour, seeing their presence as a fulfillment of Jewish destiny. Others were more prosaic. Many of the settlements were within easy commuting distance of Jerusalem and Tel Aviv and their inhabitants could travel to the cities along a road network designed to bypass Arab towns and villages. Whether there by conviction or convenience, the Palestinians saw them as the most obvious obstacle to their own political hopes. Above all, they saw them as a threat to the land.

The Intifada which broke out on 8 December 1987 was not planned but it was the culmination of all these factors. It was sparked by an Israeli army vehicle in the Gaza Strip, crashing into a truck with Palestinian workers, causing four deaths. Rumours spread that this was deliberate retaliation for the fatal stabbing of an Israeli in Gaza two days before. The funerals became large-scale demonstrations, Israeli soldiers opened fire in the Jabalya refugee camp and a youth was killed. Over the following days, unrest spread across the Gaza Strip and then into the West Bank. It soon became clear that the scale of what was happening far surpassed any previous form of protest in the Occupied Territories and that the Israeli authorities were not well prepared to deal with it. The sight of security forces using live ammunition against demonstrators armed with stones was damaging to the country's reputation, which was only just beginning to recover from Sabra and Shatila. In January 1988, Defence Minister Yitzhak Rabin announced a policy of 'might, power and beatings' as an alternative to the use of live ammunition but this gave rise to serious allegations of brutality, backed up by television images (Siniora, 1988; Schiff and Ya'ari, 1989; Parker, 1992).

The Israelis were not alone in being surprised by the nature and extent of the Intifada. The PLO, too, had to define its political response, not least because of the growth of a potential rival, the Islamic Resistance Movement, Harakat al-Muqawama al-Islamia, or Hamas. Founded by the religious teacher Sheikh Ahmed Yassin, Hamas first emerged at the start of the Intifada in December 1987, and owed much of its inspiration to the Muslim Brotherhood. In its Charter of the following year it clearly defined its strongly religious foundations, and looked forward to the establishment of an Islamic state in the whole of Palestine. The movement developed in two ways. Its religious, social and educational work steadily attracted support, especially in the Gaza Strip, while its military wing, the Izz al-Din al-Qassam Brigade, named after the Arab leader killed in 1935, was to become a formidable opponent of the Israelis and a powerful rival to Fatah. As such, it posed a nascent, but growing, challenge, not just to Israel, but to the secular PLO. Even Yassin's imprisonment by Israel from 1989 to 1997 failed to stifle the movement's growth (Shlaim, 2000). If the PLO were to retain its predominant position, then contact had to made with those who were emerging as the leaders of the uprising. This led the Israelis in April 1988 to organise the assassination in Tunis of the PLO leader believed to be coordinating what was happening in the occupied territories, Arafat's long-time confidant, Khalil Wazir. His death did not serve its intended purpose, not least because the underground leadership of the Intifada, the Unified National Leadership of the Uprising, was firmly rooted inside the territories. In fact, the death of such a popular figure acted as an incentive to greater acts of defiance. As the number of deaths mounted, so did the pressure on the various parties to work towards a resolution of the conflict. In July, King Hussein gave a clear impetus to this by severing his links with the West Bank, thus leaving it clear that the PLO was central to any negotiation. The PLO leadership was aware that it would have to make political gains from the Intifada. Equally, the Americans were coming under pressure from their friends in Europe and the Middle East to make some moves towards easing the situation.

## Moves towards a Settlement

Delicate contacts between the PLO leadership and the Americans led to the declaration by the PLO national council on 15 February of an independent Palestine on the West Bank and Gaza. While this implied recognition of Israel, it did not go as far as Shultz wanted – namely acceptance of Resolution 242 and a renunciation of terrorism. Weeks of hectic negotiation followed, including Swedes and a group of American Jews, before Arafat seemed ready to make a major pronouncement along these lines to the United Nations in Geneva. In fact, his speech on 15 December 1988 fell short of what the Americans felt he had agreed and it took further mediation to bring him to a press conference the next day to announce his rejection of terrorism and acknowledgement of the right of all parties in the Middle East to live in peace and security. A major obstacle to negotiations with the United States had been removed.

## The Gulf War

The 'substantive dialogue' that Shultz had promised the PLO did not go well. From the start the two sides were far apart on the issue of what was 'terrorism' and what were attacks on 'legitimate targets' in Israel. On 20 June 1990, President Bush suspended the dialogue in the wake of a Palestinian raid on Tel Aviv, itself almost certainly designed to put an end to the talks. Then, on 2 August, came Iraq's invasion of Kuwait, beginning months of tension as the United States painstakingly assembled a coalition to expel Saddam Hussein's forces from the country. America's allies did not just include her traditional friends in Europe – Britain, France and Italy – but also Egypt, Syria and, of course, Saudi Arabia on whose territory the forces for 'Operation Desert Storm' assembled. When their offensive ended, on 28 February 1991, Iraq's armed forces had been expelled from Kuwait, even though, contrary to American hopes, Saddam's regime survived. Prospects for the PLO seemed dim. In the course of the war, Iraq had fired missiles at Israel in the hope that by retaliating she would shatter the unity of the allied coalition. That Israel did not do so gave it a claim on American goodwill in the post-war period. Even more serious was Arafat's clear endorsement of Saddam Hussein's actions. In many respects it was not surprising, for sentiment in the West Bank and Gaza was strongly behind the Iraqi President as the one Arab leader apparently standing up to Israel and the Americans; moreover, Palestinians contrasted the West's prompt action over Kuwait, where economic interests were strongly engaged, with 25 years' inaction over the Occupied Territories. But the war left Arafat on the losing side, his judgement in question, his hard-won links with the United States in tatters, and estranged from his former patrons in Saudi Arabia and the Gulf who had provided very substantial financial backing for his movement for a quarter of a century.

## The Bush–Baker Initiative

President Bush and his Secretary of State James Baker sought to build quickly on their success in the Gulf War by working for a Middle East peace conference. It was none too soon, for the Intifada had claimed over 1,000 lives and neither side looked likely to compromise. The easing of restrictions in the Soviet Union after 1989 had led to a sudden surge of some 370,000 immigrants and the Shamir government responded with an expanded building and settlement programme in the West Bank, which the Americans saw as a further obstacle to prospects for peace. By 1992 it was estimated that the Jewish population in the West Bank had grown to 97,000 and in Gaza to 3,600, in addition to 14,000 on the Golan Heights and 129,000 Jews in and around east Jerusalem. So alarmed was Bush by the pace of events that in September 1991 he publicly threatened to veto $10 billion in loan guarantees requested by Israel to help settle the new Soviet Jewish immigrants, initiating a new confrontation with the government in Jerusalem and AIPAC in Washington. Relentless diplomacy by Baker was pushing and cajoling the parties towards a peace conference, which convened at Madrid on 30 October 1991 under the joint presidency of Bush and Gorbachev. It was a remarkable occasion for Israel was now sitting down in face-to-face negotiations with Syria and Lebanon, as well as the Egyptians. Important as this was, everyone knew that the key issue was the role of the Palestinians. Delicate negotiation had produced a formula by which Israel accepted a joint Palestinian–Jordanian delegation with certain conditions attached, namely that the Palestinian members must come from the West Bank and Gaza and that they should have no links with the PLO. The 14 members of the delegation, led by the veteran Dr Haydar Abd al-Shafi, did reflect this territorial provision, but the Americans also permitted a steering committee representing Palestinians from east Jerusalem and outside the Occupied Territories. Two members of that committee, Faisal Husseini and Dr Hannan Ashrawi, were to emerge as the key figures on the Palestinian side.

But even when the talks moved to Washington, progress proved virtually impossible. The temper of the Shamir government was not improved by the unrelenting pressure from Bush over the loan guarantees; when Congress passed its foreign-aid bill on 1 April 1992 the $10 billion in guarantees requested by Israel was not included. A breakthrough seemed to beckon when on 23 June Labour, once again under Yitzhak Rabin, won the Israeli general election and proceeded to form a coalition government. Israeli voters were alarmed at Shamir's breach with Washington and disappointed by Likud's economic performance, but were also attracted by Rabin's pledge to work for a peace settlement that would include Palestinian autonomy. Rabin was soon rewarded by the warmer attitude coming from Washington.

On 11 August, Bush announced that he would place a revised Israeli loan-guarantee proposal before Congress; surplus American military equipment was to be transferred to Israel. On 5 October, Congress approved the loan guarantees, just in time to see power pass to Bill Clinton who had claimed in the course of the presidential election campaign that the Bush administration had gravely harmed the Israeli–American relationship.

## The Breakthrough

For much of 1993 the diplomatic process appeared to be stagnant. Palestinian negotiators seemed to lack the authority to make significant moves and a frustrated Rabin's attempt to expel 400 Hamas activists led him nowhere. Despite Clinton's success, the Israeli Government knew that the collapse of Communism meant that they could not call for much longer on the strategic relationship with the United States. Fresh thinking was called for. The PLO leadership also realised this. The Arabs, too, had been profoundly affected by the disappearance of the Soviet Union. At a stroke Syria, the main military power confronting Israel, had lost its patron and arms supplier. Iraq, the only other significant Arab power likely to confront the Israelis, had been ravaged by the Gulf War. The Gulf War had also deprived the PLO of its vital sources of Saudi finance. Both Rabin and Arafat had strong reasons for looking favourably on highly secret moves which had been maturing for months in Norway, initially sponsored by individuals and then taken up by the Norwegian government. These talks between PLO and Israeli officials had become so promising that they had been enthusiastically adopted by the Israeli Foreign Minister, Shimon Peres.

The secrecy of Norway allowed for the exploration of highly sensitive issues in a manner that would have been difficult, if not impossible, in the full glare of Washington publicity. It enabled the Israelis to explore the vexed, but central, issue of the PLO, which successive governments had condemned as a 'terrorist' organisation but which the Washington talks were confirming as essential to any settlement. The realisation was there that without Arafat's active cooperation no settlement could have a realistic hope of success, but this was something for which Israeli public opinion would have to be prepared with some finesse. The key to Arafat's participation in any proposed settlement would be land; the PLO would have to be given territory on which it could begin to exert its authority and from which it could hope to build. In short, Israel would have to contemplate some form of withdrawal from the West Bank and Gaza, and the PLO would have to acknowledge that this could only come about in stages.

At first sight Gaza seemed the likely option. With the exception of the few thousand settlers who lived there, Israelis held no affection for Gaza. It was a dangerous and unpopular military posting with soldiers in a state of constant alert and regular confrontation with its 800,000 inhabitants. With its miserable refugee camps and constant tension, it continually reproached Israel's international position. To turn Gaza over to the PLO was an obvious step, but not one that Arafat would respond to without some concession on the West Bank. The PLO leadership was understandably wary of any suggestion which would allow Israel to divest itself of Gaza while allowing unfettered control of the West Bank. The solution was to include Jericho on the West Bank in the proposed agreement. This would allow the PLO to establish its presence on an historic West Bank city close to Jordan; it was a return to an idea floated by Kissinger nearly 20 years before. Withdrawal from Gaza and Jericho was intended to be the first stage in a wider transfer of authority to the Palestinians of the West Bank. While Israeli negotiators made it clear that Israel would maintain responsibility for the security of the settlements on the West Bank and their inhabitants, it was also apparent that the settlers, many of whom saw themselves as the advance guard of Zionism, would have to come to terms with life in an Arab entity. After years of sterile and bloody confrontation, the Israeli government and the PLO were charting a path that offered the possibility of a way forward.

Under the auspices of the Norwegian Foreign Minister, Johann Jorgen Holst, on 9 September 1993 Arafat and Rabin exchanged letters which marked the historic beginning of an attempt to arrive at a settlement. Arafat's letter assured Rabin that the PLO recognised 'the right of the State of Israel to exist in peace and security', renounced terrorism and pledged to remove the sections of the Palestine National Charter which denied Israel's right to exist; in a separate letter to Holst he called on the inhabitants of the West Bank and Gaza to reject violence – in effect to call off the Intifada. Rabin's reply recognised 'the PLO as the representative of the Palestinian people'. The essence of the agreement to which the two men committed themselves looked forward to the imminent withdrawal of Israeli troops and administration from Jericho on the West Bank and from Gaza, followed by elections for a Palestinian Council to run the West Bank and Gaza for a five-year period, during which the two sides would negotiate a final settlement. When the two leaders signed their agreement at the White House on 13 September and then, with Clinton's encouragement, shook hands it was clear that the Arab–Israeli conflict had taken a new turn. No one, not least Arafat and Rabin, was prepared to underestimate the difficulties that might lie ahead.

It was soon apparent that, despite the goodwill generated in Norway and the international acclaim that had greeted the signing ceremony in Washington, serious problems remained. Neither side found it easy to agree to the precise dimensions of the Jericho enclave which was to pass under PLO control, the Israelis arguing that it should be confined to the city, while the Palestinians argued for a larger administrative district. The nature of border controls meant hard bargaining for both sides. The PLO saw control of the border crossings into Gaza and Jericho as a test of its sovereignty; the Israelis, concerned for security, insisted upon some kind of monitoring of their own. Ultimately, these issues were resolvable. The real tests for the agreement were the future of the Israeli settlements and the extent to which Rabin and Arafat could hold their positions internally in the face of the challenges which would arise. It was inevitable that Arafat's concessions would be challenged by those who wanted no compromise with Israel. Chief among them were the supporters of Hamas. Together with Islamic Jihad, Hamas was to provide the spearhead of Palestinian opposition to the Oslo process. Its tactics were to resort to violence in order to provoke an Israeli response, and hence discredit the PLO's concessions. Attacks on Israelis increased as a result, putting the agreement under strain. In order to combat Hamas's challenge, Arafat had to secure the loyalty of his own Fatah members, not all of whom agreed with what he had done. Central to the concerns and reservations held by many Palestinians were the disparity in power between the two signatories, reinforced by Israel's close relationship with Washington, and the fact that the key issues of Jerusalem, the refugees and the future of the settlements would only be addressed at some future point. A noted critic was the Palestinian scholar Edward Said, whose articles made uncomfortable reading for those who saw the agreement as the way forward but whose views were listened to with respect by many in the West and the Middle East (Said, 2000; Fisk, 2005). In the end it would be the PLO's own policemen who would have to confront Palestinian dissidents of whatever persuasion.

From the Israeli perspective, this was precisely the issue that cut at the heart of their concerns. In recognising the PLO and Arafat in the way that they did, the Israeli team seemingly believed that he could control violence coming from the Palestinian territories, a matter of substance on which they believed that they had been reassured in the course of the negotiations. This belief was to be sorely tested, and was to prove fundamental in the erosion of support for the Accord (Makovsky, 1996). Rabin's government, with its small Knesset majority, had to face the opposition of Likud, which had done so much to build up the Jewish presence on the West Bank. Right-wing leaders pointed to the attacks on Jews as proof that no concessions should be made to the Arabs. The Knesset vote approving the agreement of 61 to 50 but with 9 abstentions exposed the fault line amongst the country's politicians. But it was amongst the settlers on the West Bank that emotions ran highest. While a majority of the settlers had come there as the result of economic inducements and could probably be persuaded to resettle elsewhere, this was not true of a determined group for whom the territory held a very different significance. For these settlers the area was an inalienable part of the Jewish inheritance which they were determined to retain.

At the heart of this sentiment were the settlers of Kiryat Arba on the outskirts of Hebron. Kiryat Arba, the first settlement allowed for non-security reasons after the 1967 war, set out to recreate the Jewish presence in Hebron, one of the four Holy Cities of Judaism, whose Jewish community had been wiped out by the Arabs in the 1929 disturbances with the loss of 60 lives. The city itself was deeply holy both to Jews and Muslims, because of the presence of the Tombs of the Patriarchs, Abraham, Isaac and Jacob, with their wives Sarah, Rebecca and Leah. By Jewish tradition, too, Adam and Eve rested there: hence the ancient name Kiryat Arba ('The Town-of the Four', in honour of the four couples), which the modern settlement's name revived. The atmosphere in the city was invariably uneasy, the prime focus of tension being that what to Jews was the Tomb of the Patriarchs was to Muslims the Mosque of Ibrahim. Undeterred by the hostile population around them, the Jewish settlers were heavily armed for their own protection. Hence, the attack on the Hebron mosque on 25 February 1994 by a Jewish doctor in which 29 Palestinian worshippers were killed before the gunman was himself beaten to death was a tragedy waiting to happen. The scale of the killing seemed only to spur the Israeli government and the PLO towards a more urgent conclusion of the deadlines set out in the 13 September agreement. But even as the Israeli army and administration began its evacuation of Gaza, on 6 April 1994 the expected retaliation for the Hebron massacre took place when a suicide car bomber drove into a school bus line in Afula, killing 7 and injuring over 50 people.

The Israeli government and the PLO leadership had invested too much of their credibility to allow themselves to be deflected by such acts, however appalling. In May 1994, Rabin, Peres and Arafat came to Cairo to resolve the simmering dispute over what had actually been agreed the previous September. Despite a final public wrangle over the dimensions of the Jericho enclave, the two sides reached agreement over the nature of the Israeli withdrawal and the powers of the Palestinian Authority. In the case of Gaza there was to be a military redeployment to guard the remaining Jewish settlers; otherwise, the new Authority was to acquire the symbols, and some of the reality, of Palestinian sovereignty. The way was now clear for Arafat's emotional return to Gaza and Jericho in July, an event that observers of the Arab–Israeli conflict had in the not-too-distant past believed unthinkable.

Behind that emotion lay stern realities. While the PLO had a wealth of educated and dedicated talent at its command, Arafat's background had been that of a revolutionary leader rather than an administrator. His penchant for keeping the threads of administration in his own hands, and heeding his own counsel, led a number of respected figures, like Haydar Abd al-Shafi and Hannan Ashrawi, to keep their distance. The inevitable compromises with Israel, the more powerful partner in the relationship, steadily increased the appeal Hamas and other Islamic groups held for young Palestinians. Continuing attacks inside Israel, most spectacularly a suicide car bomb aboard a Tel Aviv bus which killed 22 people, were designed both to embarrass Arafat and harden Israeli opposition to the agreement. Although the PLO and Hamas were anxious to avoid a civil war, no one seemed to know how to attract the Islamic groups into a Palestinian political consensus, short of concessions beyond Arafat's, and Rabin's, reach. With Israeli public opinion hovering around 50 per cent for their peace strategy, and dependent on Arab and Communist votes for their Knesset majority, the Rabin–Peres combination had precariously little room for manoeuvre in the face of a sustained Likud opposition, which also drew strength from public unease over the government's domestic policies. It was hardly surprising that Rabin would not be drawn on such critical issues as the future of the settlements and their inhabitants. The continuing settlements in Gaza were especially galling to the Palestinians.

But the Israeli leaders were sophisticated political veterans who were working on another diplomatic track to which their right-wing critics would find it hard to object. The Labour leadership, Peres in particular, had for some time held views close to those of King Hussein of Jordan and his brother Crown Prince Hassan, and there had long been contacts between them. The King could not afford to be left behind by Arafat and the PLO. Intricate negotiations led to the signing of a peace treaty between the two countries on 26 October 1994. From this, Israel gained security on its eastern flank, for not only did Jordan renounce force but it was committed to ensuring that acts of violence would 'not originate from' its territory, though this simply confirmed what had been the case for years. Only Israel's northern border with Syria and Lebanon remained to be secured. Jordan could show some tangible benefits in return, not least $980 million of American debts written off by President Clinton as an inducement to sign. Boundary disputes were apparently resolved in Jordan's favour; 135 square miles were returned to Jordanian sovereignty with certain areas leased back to Israel, a precedent viewed somewhat uneasily in other Arab countries. Jordan was accorded a special position with regard to the holy sites of Jerusalem, to the fury of the PLO leadership. The ultimate benefit to both parties was thought to be economic, for all discriminatory trade barriers were to be removed and that most precious of resources, water, was to be carefully regulated between them. While this agreement had its bitter opponents, not least inside Jordan, it seemed to mark yet another key stage in the Arab–Israeli conflict.

# 5

# An Uncertain Path

## The Peace Process under Arafat, Rabin and Peres

It was clear that the fate of the peace process would be determined by the ability of Arafat and Rabin to convince a majority of Palestinians and Israelis that their plan held out the prospect of substantial progress on the political, security and economic fronts. Security continued to present the most acute and immediate danger. 1995 had barely begun when suicide bombers detonated two car bombs at Nardiya, killing 20 people, mostly young soldiers. Realising the effect of this on a grieving Israeli public, Rabin went on television to vow that such attacks would not deflect him from his negotiations with the Palestinians, but it was an open question how long his credibility could be sustained in the face of such tragedies. In April, a further suicide attack in the Gaza Strip killed seven Israeli soldiers and an American female student. This, in turn, increased the difficulties faced by the Palestinian Authority, as it carried out arrests of members of Islamic groups at the same time as Israeli security measures prevented workers from Gaza crossing to jobs in Israel, and Gazan farmers were unable to market their crops. Palestinians inevitably questioned what tangible benefits the new arrangements were bringing them, despite the efforts of the Authority to create an administration where none had existed before. The sense of disappointment was compounded when the date of 1 July 1995 set for expanding self-government in the West Bank came and went.

These unpromising events set the context for fresh American and Egyptian attempts to nudge the two sides forward on the issue of the West Bank. Their efforts bore fruit on 28 September 1995 with the signing in Washington, in the presence of Presidents Clinton and Mubarak and King Hussein, of a new agreement which was at least as significant as the one confirmed at a similar ceremony almost exactly two years before. Its purpose was to give substance to much of what had been implicit in the earlier document. Under its terms the Israelis agreed to withdraw their troops from most towns and villages in the West Bank by 30 March 1996, civil control passing to an elected Palestinian council. Balancing this were the continuation of an Israeli security role and a Palestinian agreement to amend their National Charter by removing the sections which called for Israel's destruction. Clinton believed that the ceremony in Washington ushered in the beginning of a personal relationship between Arafat and Rabin, hitherto notably lacking. How any such relationship might have developed was fated to be one of the great 'ifs' of the Arab–Israeli conflict (Clinton, 2004).

While most Israelis seemed content with what had been agreed, angry demonstrations by settlers in Hebron against the concessions over the West Bank were a portent of opposition to come. Such was the strength of feeling generated by the settlers and their supporters that Rabin and Peres decided to address a peace rally in Tel Aviv on 4 November 1995. Attended by an estimated 100,000 people, it probably amply met their expectations, but as he left the rally Rabin was shot dead by a student opposed to his concessions on the West Bank. Possibly the ablest soldier in the country's history, Rabin's death was seen as a political tragedy of major dimensions, confirmed by the world leaders, including Clinton, Mubarak and King Hussein, who assembled in

Jerusalem for his funeral. Arafat's presence at the funeral was regarded as too much of a security risk but he later paid his respects to Rabin's widow. The Israeli leader's death invited unavoidable comparisons with that of President Sadat 14 years before. It is difficult, if not impossible, to estimate the impact Rabin's assassination had on the subsequent course of events. In one sense, the feelings of shock it created, not just in Israel, might have created the conditions for diplomatic movement. But the reality was that the peace process had been deprived of a pivotal figure.

Rabin was immediately succeeded by his long-standing colleague and former rival, Shimon Peres. Perhaps if Peres had gone to the electorate immediately after the assassination he might have gained a mandate for the course he and Rabin had charted, but he chose not to do that. Instead, Peres pressed ahead with implementing the agreements he had done so much to bring into being. By the end of the year such key West Bank cities as Jenin, Tulkarm, Qalqilya, Bethlehem, Ramallah, and perhaps above all, Nablus had returned to Palestinian authority after almost three decades of Israeli occupation. Peres was also signalling his desire to include Syria in an overall peace settlement, a sentiment which Clinton shared. This, of course, called into question the future of the Golan, which many Israelis felt to be an essential element in their security and which, like the West Bank and Gaza, was home to settlers.

On one level, the expectations of progress appeared to be reinforced by the elections for the Palestinian Council held in the West Bank and Gaza on 20 January 1996. With a broad endorsement from the electorate, Arafat's position as the acknowledged leader of Palestine was confirmed. But another agenda was at work. On 5 January, the man alleged by Israel to have directed the bombing campaign against it was killed in the Gaza Strip; on 25 February, bombs in buses in Ashkelon and Jerusalem killed 25 people. Messages to the press claimed the attacks were in retaliation. The following week, a further suicide bomb in Jerusalem resulted in 19 deaths. Then, on 4 March, a fourth suicide bomb at a shopping centre in Tel Aviv killed 14 people and injured over 100. Over the same period there were a number of fatal attacks on Israeli patrols in southern Lebanon. The cumulative effect was to undermine public confidence in Peres's government and its peace strategy. In the circumstances, it was inevitable that Likud, under Binyamin Netanyahu, would press home security concerns.

In an attempt to show solidarity with Israel and its government, President Clinton paid a flying visit to the country on his return from a Middle East peace summit in Egypt at which the recent suicide bombings were condemned. As Israel prepared to go to the polls in May, the Palestine Liberation Organisation fulfilled its obligations by revoking the clauses in the National Charter which referred to Israel's destruction and there were sustained Israeli air and artillery attacks on guerrilla positions in southern Lebanon. The election followed the now familar pattern of a close result made more complex by the strength of support for minority parties, but the veteran Peres was defeated by the youthful Netanyahu. Although a native-born Israeli, Netanyahu was familiar with the United States, where he had attended Massachusetts Institute of Technology and Harvard, and had later served in the Washington embassy. As a professional soldier from 1967 to 1972, he specialised in counter-terrorism.

## The Peace Process in Crisis

Netanyahu assumed office as Prime Minister of a Likud-led coalition, pledged to continue the peace process and defend Israel's battered security. He inherited a peace process which was already in crisis. Palestinian alarm and dismay at the defeat of Peres, who had done so much to bring the agreements into being, was only to be expected. In August 1996, Arafat and Netanyahu met for the first time, shook hands and pledged to continue to work for the peace process, but the following month saw Israeli–Palestinian relations come close to collapse. The occasion was the opening by the Israelis of an entrance to an ancient Hasmonean tunnel running close to the Haram al-Sharif/Temple Mount in Jerusalem, the site sacred both to Jews and Muslims. The action provoked serious disturbances on the West Bank and Gaza Strip, which took on a new and more dangerous dimension as the Israeli army and Palestinian police exchanged fire (Ross, 2004). With 39 Palestinians and 11 Israelis killed, Clinton brought the two leaders to Washington for a crisis meeting in an attempt to defuse the situation, but he had to admit that little progress had been made.

Relations did not improve subsequently, with tension coming to focus on the timing and extent of an Israeli withdrawal from Hebron, where the situation had become even more volatile since the February 1994 massacre. It was not until 14 January 1997 that American mediation produced an agreement by which Israel agreed to evacuate 80 per cent of the city. With Labour support, Netanyahu had no difficulty in securing endorsement in the Knesset, but at the cost of a high-profile resignation from his cabinet. Arafat's tumultuous welcome to the city four days later marked the establishment of Palestinian authority in the last major population centre in the West Bank, even if the areas they controlled still resembled something of a patchwork and its deep-seated economic problems, especially those of Gaza, showed no signs of easing. In fact, 1997 saw no improvement in Israeli–Palestinian relations, while tragedies continued to mount. In one of the most traumatic of these, 73 Israeli soldiers were killed in a helicopter collision in February, a disaster without equal in the country's history. What exercised the Palestinians most was the announcement that the Israeli government planned a new housing development of 6,500 apartments in east Jerusalem. Not only did this threaten the Arab village of Umm Tuba, but it was seen as cementing Israeli control of the city. Both President Clinton and King Hussein opposed the move. In these unpromising circumstances a further tragedy occurred when a Jordanian soldier killed seven Israeli schoolgirls, an act which impelled King Hussein to visit the grieving families.

These events set the tone for the rest of the year. Suicide bombs continued, including one in Jerusalem's Ben Yehuda Street, the centre of the city's social and commercial life, while in September an Israeli attempt to assassinate an Islamic leader in Jordan plunged relations between the two countries into crisis. A meeting between Clinton and Netanyahu in April failed to produce any progress, and in a subsequent visit to the United States by the Israeli leader in November the two men did not meet. The White House claimed this was the result of scheduling problems, but it was widely perceived as a snub to the Israeli Premier. Clinton's Secretary of State, Madeleine Albright, saw the need for direct involvement in view of the increasingly unsatisfactory nature of Israeli–Palestinian relations. In a major speech in August 1997, she spelled out the need for increased American involvement, and for accelerating the dialogue between the two sides, but a visit to the region the following month, in which she stressed the need for Israeli–Palestinian security cooperation and counselled the Israelis against unilateral actions, seemed to generate little momentum.

In fact, it was not to be until October 1998 that the next substantial advance could be made when Arafat and Netanyahu came together at the Wye Conference Center in Maryland. It took nine days of intensive effort personally brokered by Clinton and a terminally ill King Hussein to produce an agreement. It set out the stages for a further Israeli evacuation from the West Bank, which would put some 40 per cent of the territory under Palestinian control, and pledged Arafat to a programme of measures to combat attacks on Israel, including a role for the Central Intelligence Agency. The Wye Agreement was rightly seen as a significant advance after a long period of stagnation, though essentially it was only giving precision to what had been agreed in 1993 and 1995. This time, however, it was Likud which was cementing an agreement with the Palestinians. Arafat's role in agreeing to the new security programme was assailed by Hamas, but it was Netanyahu who faced the greater domestic crisis, since the agreement struck at the heart of Likud's long-standing hopes for the West Bank. Once again, he won a substantial Knesset majority with the help of Labour, but at the price of serious dissent in his own ranks. Two of his ministers voted against the agreement, while five others left the Knesset rather than vote. On 13 December, Clinton arrived on a three-day visit to set his seal on the agreement. The climax was a visit to Gaza, where he addressed the Palestinian National Council, watched the Council confirm the elimination from the National Charter of the sections calling for Israel's destruction, and with Arafat at his side opened a new terminal at Gaza Airport. His visit seemed to signal that full Palestinian statehood could not be far off. The Israeli leader's political troubles increased with the resignation of his Finance Minister. Faced with the erosion of his political base and the possibility of losing a vote of confidence in the Knesset, Netanyahu was left with no alternative but to agree to hold elections on 17 May 1999.

## New Agendas

With Israeli politics in disarray, further moves were not to be expected before the May elections, but as the parties manoeuvred for position it became increasingly clear that King Hussein of Jordan was losing his battle with cancer. In a surprise move, the King returned home from his treatment in the United States to replace his brother Prince Hassan as Crown Prince with his son Prince Abdullah. The King, for so long a key intermediary in the Arab–Israeli conflict, died in February 1999. His funeral, attended by world leaders, including Presidents Clinton, Yeltsin, Asad and Mubarak as well as Yasser Arafat and Israel's President Weizman, was a unique event, which indicated how pivotal the Jordanian ruler had been. There was a sense that an era in Middle East politics had ended. This was compounded in July with the death of another veteran of Arab–Israeli diplomacy, King Hassan of Morocco.

Netanyahu's challenger in the May elections was Ehud Barak, who had replaced Peres as Labour leader in June 1997. Born in a kibbutz, a highly decorated soldier and a former Chief of Staff, Barak was cast in the Rabin mould, both likely to appeal to the traditional Labour constituency, and unlikely to compromise the basic integrity of the Israeli state. As such, he was well placed to mount a powerful challenge to the embattled Likud, even though observers were aware that the voting intentions of the newly arrived Russian Jewish immigrants, now numbering some 800,000, had introduced a powerful new variable in electoral calculations. In the event, the Israeli electorate endorsed Barak by a decisive margin of 56 per cent, giving him a more secure mandate than any recent Israeli leader had been able to enjoy. His first task was to build a broad-based coalition, which would secure a Knesset majority for any new peace initiative. On 7 July Barak was sworn in as leader of an administration which brought together Labour with six other political parties intended to emphasise national unity. Within days he had met with Arafat in Gaza, pledging to work for the removal of obstacles to a peace settlement. Central to Labour's analysis was the desire to separate, partition in effect, Israelis and Palestinians in a manner which would allow Israel to develop its potential as a Jewish state in the new century. In September, renewed negotiations, presided over by US Secretary of State Albright, resulted in an agreement to reach final borders and a settlement for Jerusalem within a year. The following month the opening of a 40 km land route connecting the West Bank with the Gaza Strip was a further gesture which allowed safe passage between the two parts of the Palestinian Authority, reuniting Palestinians after years of separation. It was another indicator of the shape a future settlement would take, suggesting that a new agenda might be taking hold.

## Attempts to Restore the Peace Process

At first, progress seemed possible. On 5 January 2000, peace talks between Israel and Syria began in the United States, but they soon stalled, frustrating Barak's hopes for an overall settlement. At the same time, Israel was coming under increasing pressure in southern Lebanon as Hizbollah militiamen mounted attacks on its soldiers. Barak's government seemed to be vulnerable on a variety of fronts, of which the vulnerability of Israeli troops in southern Lebanon was only the most acute. In March, his cabinet voted for a withdrawal from the southern Lebanon security zone. This actually took place on 22 May, ending the last legacy of Begin's bloody and ill-fated invasion of the country 18 years before. For many Israelis this was not a reassuring move, since Hizbollah forces could now deploy along Israel's northern border. For Palestinians, it seemed to confirm that Israel was vulnerable to sustained attacks, even to the extent of abandoning her long-standing Lebanese allies.

The decision to evacuate southern Lebanon was quickly followed by one to hand a further 6.1 per cent of the West Bank to the Palestinian Authority, clearly seen by the Israeli government as an intent of goodwill. Then, on 22 March, a powerful voice in favour of a Palestinian homeland was raised by Pope John Paul II, who was making his first pilgrimage to the scenes of the Bible. Despite Jewish resentments over Pope Pius XII's attitude to the Holocaust, John Paul II was widely respected for his acknowledgement of the need for Christian–Jewish reconciliation. His support was important to the predominantly Muslim Palestinians, not least because their case for statehood was being acknowledged by the head of the world's largest, and most influential, Christian denomination. But tension was never far away. On 15 May, the anniversary of Israel's foundation was marked by widespread violence, which included shooting between Israeli and Palestinian security forces, a clear sign of the continuing intensity of feeling on the ground. In the circumstances, cracks in Barak's coalition government were perhaps inevitable. Faced with these pressures, Barak requested a high-level meeting of the key parties. Clinton's response was an invitation to a summit at Camp David (Blumenthal, 2003).

Clinton and his advisers had worked patiently and constructively to help ensure the success of the peace negotiations concluded in Northern Ireland in 1998. It is reasonable to assume that when he announced on 5 July 2000 that Arafat and Barak had accepted his invitation to come to Camp David, Clinton hoped to rescue the struggling peace process. But the Northern Ireland agreement, while it showed the possibilities of accommodation after decades of strife, was a cruel mirage, since the issues dividing Israel and Palestine were of a different order (Fraser and Murray, 2002). Even so, there were grounds for optimism. Clinton had been closely engaged at various stages of the process, notably at the Wye Conference, and his chief peace negotiator, Dennis Ross, had in the course of more than a decade acquired a unique knowledge of the issues and personalities. The Camp David summit, held from 11 to 25 July 2000, illustrated just how tantalisingly close the Israelis and Americans believed they were to an agreement, and the vast gulf of incomprehension which actually divided the two opposing sides. At the start, Clinton outlined for the Israeli leader how the Americans saw a settlement unfolding. The western borders of the Palestinian state would reflect the pre-1967 position, but with modifications which would see the bulk of the settlements transferred to Israel. The possibility of territorial compensation for the Palestinians was to be held open. The border with Jordan would try to reconcile Israeli security concerns with Palestinian sovereignty. They also anticipated an international fund to address the future of the refugees whether in Palestine, in other countries, or, in limited numbers, in Israel. Jerusalem, as ever, the most contentious issue, was to be approached from the standpoint that it had administrative needs, that it was sacred to Jews,

Muslims and Christians, and that there were political considerations. As an analysis of a realistic settlement, it was hard to fault, and set a benchmark for any future negotiations (Ross, 2004). From the Israeli perspective, Barak's proposals were bold and far-reaching; arguably no Israeli leader had ever gone further. In effect, he offered the Palestinians a contiguous area comprising over 90 per cent of the West Bank, a Palestinian capital in part of Jerusalem, some kind of shared sovereignty on the Haram al-Sharif/Temple Mount, and the return of refugees to a Palestinian state, but not to Israel. Barak's offer over Jerusalem marked a major shift for the Israelis. Realising how far Barak had come, Clinton offered to campaign on his behalf, and tried to entice Arafat by pledging to raise tens of billions of dollars for Palestine (Blumenthal, 2003). But Arafat had argued from the start that the summit was premature. He was being pressured into accepting what for the Palestinian leader were fundamental issues, which would inevitably lead to new stresses and strains within the Palestinian movement, something he wished to avoid. The Israeli offer held out no hope for the refugees who saw their homes as lying within Israel's pre-1967 border. It was also asking him to settle for less than the 22 per cent rump of Palestine which had been left after the war of 1948–49, something he argued that his acceptance of Security Council Resolution 242 in 1988 precluded. Finally, compromise formulas over Jerusalem proved intractable. Clinton's final bid to rescue the summit was an attempt to secure agreement that there would be full Palestinian sovereignty over the outer areas of east Jerusalem, limited sovereignty elsewhere, and what he termed 'custodial' sovereignty on the Haram al-Sharif. But the Palestinian leader proved immune to the argument that this was the best offer he was likely to get. At that point, Clinton saw no sense in continuing (Clinton, 2004). Since tragedy was soon to follow, the Camp David summit came to be seen as one of the great missed opportunities of the Arab–Israeli conflict. Whether its failure lay with Arafat, or with Barak and Clinton, became a matter of acrid debate. The commitment of Clinton and his team could hardly be faulted, however.

## The Al Aqsa Intifada

This was more than reflected on the ground, where the summit's failure led to an appreciable rise in tension. The Israeli government later claimed that the Palestinian Authority planned an uprising with the aim of regaining the initiative, a view dismissed by the committee led by former American Senator George Mitchell. The catalyst for what happened was provided by the Likud leader Ariel Sharon, who made known his intention of visiting the Haram al-Sharif/Temple Mount. Knowing the unique sensitivities of a site sacred to Jew and Muslim, and how bitterly Sharon was perceived by the Palestinians as a result of his association with what had happened in Lebanon in 1982, American officials pleaded with Barak to ban the visit. Clinton's highly experienced envoy Dennis Ross reportedly commented that he could think of a lot of bad ideas, but that he could not think of a worse one (Mitchell, 2001) An embattled Barak took the view that Sharon's move was a domestic political matter directed against him, and would not intervene. On 28 September 2000, Sharon entered the site, accompanied by 1,000 police. Sharon's visit did not cause the outburst which followed, but it did bring to the surface the tensions within the Palestinian community. The following day, unarmed Palestinians held a massive demonstration in protest; the Israeli police killed 4 and injured 200. Thus began what for Palestinians was the 'al Aqsa Intifada'. Unlike the Intifada of the late 1980s, the Palestinian security forces now had arms. More critically, the suicide bomb was to become the weapon of resistance for those who felt they had no other option. The suicide bomber, who had no need to prepare a line of escape after an attack, proved to be a deadly foe. The only obvious method of defence was pre-emption, to kill people believed by the Israeli security forces to be a 'ticking bomb'. Even so, the preponderance of power still lay with the Israelis, who responded in time with tanks and helicopter gunships (Mitchell, 2001). Within days, over 50 people had been killed in a climate of violence which seemed to mock any notion of a peace process. World opinion was shocked by the sight of a Palestinian boy dying in his father's arms in Gaza, and of the lynching of two Israeli soldiers in Ramallah.

Faced with this descent into violence, Clinton tried desperately to retrieve the situation. On 17 October 2000, a summit at Sharm al-Sheikh involving the Israeli and Palestinian Authority governments, as well as the Americans, Egyptians and Jordanians, and the United Nations and the European Union, tried to chart a way forward. Instead, Clinton announced that there would be an international fact-finding committee, which would report on 'the events of the past weeks and how to prevent their recurrence'. Senator George Mitchell, who had worked tirelessly for a peace settlement in Northern Ireland, chaired a high-level committee which comprised the European Union's Javier Solana, Turkish President Suleyman Demirel, Norwegian Foreign Affairs Minister Thorbjoern Jagland, and former Senator Warren B. Rudman. When it reported on 30 April 2001, the political landscapes of Israel and the United States looked totally different. In the previous December, faced with the prospect of a no-confidence vote in the Knesset, Barak had announced elections for 6 February 2001. Meanwhile, the American presidential elections of November 2000 had resulted in the narrowest of victories for the Republican George W. Bush, who had failed to command the popular vote. As Governor of Texas, Bush had paid a visit to Israel where he had been impressed by the narrowness of the country's border, less than Dallas–Fort Worth Airport was how he later described it. All the instincts of the new administration were to back away from the kind of intense involvement Clinton's team had devoted to the Northern Ireland and Arab–Israeli peace processes and move towards a new unilateralism (Frum,

2003). How Palestinian concerns and perspectives would be heard in the new administration was unclear.

In his final days in office, Clinton made a final brave, but fruitless, attempt to bring the two sides together. From leaked documents it would appear that the essence of the plan was that Israel would withdraw from some 95 per cent of the West Bank, but would annex the remainder, accounting for around 80 per cent of the settlers. The Palestinian state would then be compensated by a transfer of 1–3 per cent of Israeli territory. The West Bank and Gaza would have a guaranteed land link. The Palestinians would have a presence in east Jerusalem, and authority over the Muslim holy places in the city. Once again, Arafat could not agree. At issue were the familiar tests; namely, the right of return of the refugees and the extent of Palestinian authority in the Old City. To Clinton's evident amazement, Arafat demanded several blocks of the Armenian quarter in addition to the Christian and Muslim quarters. Clinton would have been less than human had he not felt frustration at the way his hopes for a final agreement had been confounded. (Wasserstein, 2001; Fraser and Murray, 2002; Blumenthal, 2003; Clinton, 2004). Representatives of Israel and the Palestinian Authority met to explore these ideas at Taba in Egypt in January 2001. But the talks broke up on 27 January without agreement, days before the Israeli election. The overwhelming victor was Ariel Sharon, *bête noire* of the Palestinians, but hero of the settlers and the Israeli right, a man who, they felt, would ensure the country's security. Sharon was, however, aware of the need to sustain a national consensus, and included Shimon Peres, architect of the Oslo agreements, as his Foreign Minister.

## The Mitchell and Tenet Plans

Central to Mitchell's analysis was the 'profound disillusionment' of each side with the Oslo peace process. At the heart of Palestinian alienation was the continuing growth in Israeli settlements, the Palestinian Authority claiming that since the signing of the Oslo accords 30 new settlements had been constructed, and existing settlements had been expanded, doubling the settler population to 200,000. The Palestinians also complained of their deteriorating economic circumstances, and the fact that nothing was being done for the refugees. For its part, the Israeli government focused on the issue of security, something which was not negotiable, accusing the Palestinian Authority of failing to control illegal weapons and of actually conducting violent operations. Trust was felt to be central to progress. In order to achieve this, Mitchell believed that the Palestinian Authority had to make it clear 'that terrorism is reprehensible and unacceptable, and… prevent terrorist operations and to punish perpetrators'. On the Israeli side, Mitchell called for a settlement freeze, emphasising that 'settlement activities must not be allowed to undermine the restoration of calm and the resumption of negotiations'. Mitchell ended with a dire, and prophetic, warning: 'The parties are at a crossroads. If they do not return to the negotiating table, they face the prospect of fighting it out for years on end, with many of their citizens leaving for distant shores to live their lives and raise their children. We pray they make the right choice. That means stopping the violence now' (Mitchell, 2001). Mitchell's report was a finely crafted attempt to defuse the issues of most burning concern to the two sides, while skirting around some highly sensitive issues.

Since nothing could be done without an end to violence, the Central Intelligence Agency's chief George Tenet was sent to broker a cease-fire. Tenet drafted a plan for the Israelis and Palestinians to institute a realistic security policy based upon cooperation, but, despite a tentative agreement in June, violence soon spiralled to new levels. Palestinian hopes for an international monitoring force to oversee a cease-fire were accepted by the Americans, and by the G8 summit in Genoa on 19 July, but firmly rejected by the Israelis. By July, the Israeli strategy had become one of targeting prominent Palestinians they believed were instrumental in orchestrating the violence. On 31 July, a helicopter gunship attacked Hamas offices in Nablus, killing 8 people, including 2 children and a leading member of the movement. Hamas promised revenge. On 9 August, a suicide bomber attacked a restaurant in Jerusalem, killing 15 people, including 6 children. Five days later, Israeli forces entered Jenin, followed by Nablus on 22 August, and Beit Jallah on 28 August, actions condemned by the Bush administration.

## 11 September

On 11 September 2001, Israeli operations in the West Bank seemed to move into a dramatic new phase when a major armoured force deployed around the city of Jenin and its adjoining refugee camp. Seven Palestinians were killed in serious fighting, but these events were completely overshadowed by barely imaginable events elsewhere. On the same day, America and the world were rocked when suicide attacks damaged the Pentagon in Washington and demolished the twin towers of the World Trade Center in New York, with horrific loss of life. Bush and his advisers identified the perpetrators as an Islamic terrorist group, al-Qa'ida, largely Arab in composition but based in Afghanistan. Declaring a 'war on terror', the United States prepared for an assault on al-Qa'ida's Afghan bases. It was a war with which Israelis instinctively identified, but as America and her allies engaged in Afghanistan, al-Qa'ida's roots in the tensions and frustrations of the Middle East, of which the Palestinian issue was only one, at first seemed pushed to one side. The following day, Israeli tanks entered Jericho, followed by Ramallah, and then launched missile attacks on Gaza and Rafah. For Bush, anxious to engage Middle Eastern and Islamic countries behind his Afghan campaign, an end to the seemingly unending cycle of violence was imperative.

Knowing the significance of the Arab–Israeli conflict for their Afghan expedition, Bush and his principal ally, British Prime Minister Tony Blair, both affirmed their support for Palestinian statehood, but events were running strongly against them. The Israeli government seemed instinctively to grasp the language of anti-terrorism, and violence never lurked far away. On 17 October, Israel's right-wing Minister for Tourism, Rehavam Zeevi, was shot dead in Jerusalem, apparently by the Popular Front for the Liberation of Palestine. Once again, the Israeli army moved in force into cities in the West Bank, provoking a major crisis with Washington. A visit to the region by Blair proved fruitless, as did an American attempt to secure a cease-fire brokered by General Anthony Zinni. Zinni's mission seemed fated from the start. On 23 November, a senior Hamas official was killed in an Israeli attack. This was followed, on 1 and 2 December, by suicide bomb attacks, claimed by Hamas, which killed 11 people in Jerusalem city centre and 15 in Haifa. Israel responded with air strikes against Palestinian Authority buildings in the West Bank and Gaza, and severed its remaining links with Arafat. Faced with American pressure to act, Arafat ordered the arrest of Hamas and other Islamic militants, to the fury of their supporters. Israelis were unconvinced. As violence reached a new peak, Zinni returned to Washington. The failure of his mission seemed to highlight the limits to the Bush administration's influence.

### Violence and Peace Moves

The early weeks of 2002 saw no improvement in a seemingly intractable conflict. In fact, it was taking on new dimensions with the interception of a ship, the *Karine A*, which the Israelis claimed was carrying a major consignment of arms, including rockets, from Iran, and, on 27 January, the first attack by a female suicide bomber. While Arafat denied to Bush that he was involved with the arms shipment, the affair affected American attitudes towards him (Frum, 2003). On 1 February, Sharon revealed his feelings for his adversary when he confessed his regret at not having eliminated Arafat 20 years before. At the end of February, a new peace plan began to surface, inspired by Saudi Arabia's Crown Prince Abdullah. It was basically the 'land for peace' formula which had been around since 1967, but it held out the prospect of Arab recognition of Israel beyond Egypt and Jordan, and at least it seemed to inject some hope into what was a fast-deteriorating situation, in which there seemed no end to the cycle of violence.

On 28 February, the Israeli army began a major operation against the Jenin and Balata refugee camps on the West Bank. On 2 March, a suicide bomber attacked an orthodox Jewish district of Jerusalem, killing 9 people, including 6 children, while the following day 10 Israelis, including 7 soldiers, were killed by a Palestinian gunman. Israel's response was swift. On 4 March, 11 people were killed in the Jenin and Ramallah camps, 17, including 5 children, in Ramallah, and a further 6, including 2 children, in an attack on a Hamas leader. The following day, a Palestinian gunman opened fire in a Tel Aviv nightclub, and there were further attacks on Israelis in Jerusalem and the West Bank. Then, in a series of incidents beginning on 8 March, when 5 Israeli officer cadets were killed in the Gaza Strip and an estimated 40 Palestinians in Israeli attacks, the situation seemed to touch rock bottom. Two days later, another suicide bomber killed 11 people in a Jerusalem cafe, followed by a large-scale Israeli operation against Gaza and Ramallah in which over 30 Palestinians were reported killed. By then, Arafat was effectively confined to his Ramallah headquarters, the *Muqata*, and passions on both sides were seriously inflamed.

In an attempt to retrieve what was clearly a fast-deteriorating situation, on 12 March the Security Council of the United Nations adopted Resolution 1397, which demanded an end to all acts of violence, and called upon the two sides to implement the Mitchell and Tenet plans. More importantly, for the first time it affirmed a future in which two states of Israel and Palestine could live together. Hopes for progress rested on the United States, where Zinni renewed his mission, and on the Arab summit due to convene in Beirut on 27 March, but the omens could not have been worse. When Sharon made it his condition that Arafat could only attend on condition he could not return if there were terrorist attacks while he was in Beirut, the Palestinian leader refused. President Mubarak of Egypt and Jordan's King Abdullah also stayed away. The summit broadly endorsed the Saudi peace initiative, but by the time it did so this had become largely irrelevant. As the conference was convening, a suicide bomber struck at a Passover gathering at the coastal city of Netanya, killing 28 and injuring 140, enraging an Israeli public opinion already stretched to the limit of its endurance.

## 'Operation Defensive Shield'

Two days later, castigating Arafat as an enemy who was part of a coalition of terror against his country, Sharon announced that the Israel Defence Forces would conduct an extensive campaign against the centres of terrorism. Termed 'Operation Defensive Shield', the operation's initial target was Ramallah, where Arafat's headquarters were surrounded, effectively confining the President to a room. His fate had been the subject of a vigorous debate in the Israeli cabinet, with some, including it seems the Prime Minister, advocating his exile. Others argued that he would be less of a danger if he were kept under surveillance in his Ramallah headquarters. The latter course won the day, and for the time that remained to him Arafat was effectively confined in the *Muqata*, only leaving with his final illness (Halevy, 2006). Prompt action by the international community seemed to be of the essence. On 30 March, the Security Council adopted Resolution 1402, which, while recognizing its grave concern over the suicide attacks and the attack on Arafat's headquarters, called for an immediate cease-fire and an Israeli withdrawal from Palestinian cities. This was a message reinforced by Bush in a statement on 4 April, announcing that Secretary of State Colin Powell would go to the Middle East the following week. Bush attempted to balance the issues, castigating Arafat as having not 'consistently opposed or confronted terrorists', as well as having 'missed his opportunities'. Suicide bombers were, he emphasised, not martyrs but murderers. But, for its part, Israel had to stop its settlement activity and acknowledge the need for an economically and politically viable Palestinian state. While acknowledging Israel's right to defend herself against terrorist attacks, he nevertheless emphasised that 'to lay the foundations of future peace, I ask Israel to halt incursions into Palestinian-controlled areas and begin the withdrawal from those cities it has recently occupied' (White House, 2002a). While Bush's comments seemed pointed enough, many congressmen were expressing their sympathy for Sharon's action, and Jewish organisations were busy rallying support for Israel. On 15 April, a mass rally was held in Washington addressed by prominent Democrat and Republican politicians, as well as former New York Mayor Rudy Giuliani and former Israeli Premier Netanyahu. Deputy Secretary of Defense Paul Wolfowitz represented President Bush. The dominant theme of the speeches was the common purpose of the United States and Israel in defeating terrorism in the aftermath of the 11 September and Palestinian suicide attacks. One of the more curious features of PLO strategy at this time was its evident reluctance to appreciate just how much its failure to condemn suicide bombing would increase support for Israel in the post-9/11 United States.

Impervious to the demands of Bush and the United Nations, the Israeli government pressed ahead with sustained military operations, largely out of sight of the world's press and international observers. Major attacks were mounted on Ramallah and Bethlehem, where some 200 Palestinian gunmen and Christian clergy and nuns came under siege in the Church of the Nativity, the reputed birthplace of Christ. But the most intense fighting took place in Nablus and in the Jenin refugee camp, believed by the Israelis to be at the heart of the suicide-bombing campaign. To the consternation of an Arab world increasingly incensed by reports coming out of the West Bank, Powell did not reach Israel until 11 April. His progress through Morocco and Spain did not convince Arabs that the administration saw the situation as urgent. Powell's arrival in Jerusalem was marked by a female suicide bomber from Jenin who killed six people in the city. Immediate talks with Sharon failed to secure any cessation of the Israeli military campaign. In the light of the Jerusalem bomb, Powell refused to talk to Arafat until the Palestinian President denounced terrorism. Arafat's statement condemning attacks targeting civilians, and specifically the Jerusalem bomb, did enough to allow Powell to travel to Ramallah on the 13th. But the negotiations in Arafat's shattered headquarters were no more productive than those with the Israeli leader, who had said that the meeting would be a tragic mistake.

As Powell pursued his quest for a diplomatic breakthrough in Damascus and Beirut, the course of events on the ground was starting to become clearer. Israeli special forces in Ramallah arrested one of Arafat's most senior aides, whom Israeli government sources claimed had been behind many of the suicide attacks. On 13 April, the International Committee of the Red Cross, which had been attempting to gain access to the Jenin refugee camp for almost a week, appealed to the United States for assistance with humanitarian aid. The Israeli Defence Forces admitted that the fighting in the camp had claimed 23 of their men, including 13 in a single ambush, and estimated the Palestinian dead at about 70, a number later revised to 52 (UN, 2002). The Palestinians accused Israel of committing a massacre in the camp. In the atmosphere of claim and counterclaim, Powell's mission was visibly crumbling. No one disputed the ferocity of what had occurred. Further meetings with Shimon Peres and Arafat produced no movement, the latter protesting against his confinement in Ramallah. Egyptian President Mubarak apparently snubbed the Secretary of State by claiming he was unable to meet him. The best Powell could secure as he returned home on 18 April was an assurance from Sharon that Israel was preparing to withdraw. The Secretary of State conceded that the withdrawal was not going 'as quickly as we would have liked', though Sharon had apparently given him a timetable. Powell appealed to Arafat to instruct his security forces to 'arrest and prosecute terrorists, disrupt terrorist financing, dismantle terrorist infrastructure and stop incitement'. His message to Israel was 'to look beyond the destructive impact of settlements and occupation, both of which must end' (Department of State, 2002).

But the immediate focus of international attention was on what had happened in Jenin. Visiting the devastated camp on 18 April, the senior United Nations official in the West Bank, Terje Roed Larsen, said that he was horrified by what he had seen. The following day, the Security Council adopted Resolution 1405, noting its concern at 'the dire humanitarian situation of the Palestinian civilian population, in particular reports from the Jenin refugee camp of an unknown number of deaths and destruction', calling for an end to Israeli restrictions on the operations of humanitarian organizations, and accepting a recommendation from Secretary General Kofi Annan that a fact-finding mission be sent to the Jenin camp. As Israeli politicians attacked Larsen for his comments, American Assistant Secretary of State for the Near East, William Burns, visited the camp, as did Russian diplomat Andrei Vdovin. Echoing Larsen, Burns said that what had happened was a tragedy. The nature and scale of what had happened remained in dispute. Israeli objections to the membership of the United Nations fact-finding mission led to its collapse. Later United Nations reports suggested that 497 Palestinians had been killed in the course of the Israeli operation, and that 17,000 people were left homeless (UN, 2002). What was clear was that the political structures and economic life of the Palestinian Authority had been shattered by the Israeli offensive. While their security officials listed key Palestinian activists killed or captured in the course of 'Operation Defensive Shield', the Israeli press conceded that what had happened would only fuel the desire for revenge.

As complex negotiations took place to resolve the immediate crises in Ramallah and Bethlehem, that response took the form of a suicide bomb near Tel Aviv which claimed 15 lives. In a complex choreography, the siege of Arafat's headquarters was ended when six Palestinians wanted by Israel were put under Anglo–American guard, while on 10 May, 13 Palestinians from the Church of the Nativity were flown to Cyprus for exile in the European Union. But the cycle of terror and reaction seemed unrelenting. On 5 June, a suicide attack at Megiddo in northern Israel killed 17 people. Once again Jenin and Ramallah bore the brunt of Israeli anger, Arafat's headquarters being wrecked in a sustained attack by Israeli tanks. As the American administration signalled that a fresh initiative was being prepared, Israel was dealt a further blow when a suicide bomber killed 20 people on a Jerusalem bus.

## The Iraq Crisis and the 'Roadmap for Peace'

On 24 June, Bush made his much-awaited statement on how his administration saw the way ahead. It embodied ideas that he had been formulating for some time, and has to be seen in the context of his 'war against terror'. Emphasizing the need to secure a settlement based upon Resolutions 242 and 338, the President outlined his vision of 'two states, living side by side in peace and security'. In order to bring this about, he demanded that Israel withdraw to the positions held before 28 September 2000, bring an end to settlement policy in the Occupied Territories, and 'take concrete steps to support the emergence of a viable, credible Palestinian state'. The Palestinians were challenged more directly. 'I've said in the past that nations are either with us or against us in the war on terror', he said, claiming that 'today, Palestinian authorities are encouraging, not opposing terrorism. This is unacceptable'. 'Peace', he believed, 'requires a new and different Palestinian leadership, so that a Palestinian state can be born. I call on the Palestinian people to elect new leaders, leaders not compromised by terror'. His emphasis on new leadership both reflected the administration's sense of frustration with Arafat, as well as that of the Israelis who had been lobbying for a new leadership in the Palestinian Authority (White House, 2002b; Halevy, 2006). The reality of change, when it came, was to be notably different to what the Americans and Israelis had hoped for. Notably absent from Bush's speech was any mention of international monitors, which some had been hoping for, or, more importantly, any timetable for the creation of a Palestinian state, although 2005 emerged as a likely date. Inevitably, each side picked on what it liked. The Israeli government signalled its willingness to negotiate with a new Palestinian leadership, while Palestinians angrily rejected the notion that Washington could dictate whom they should elect.

Despite expectations, Bush's speech did not yet signal a major American attempt to resolve the crisis. Washington's eyes were now firmly fixed on a different part of the Middle East. In his State of the Union message of 29 January 2002, Bush had made it clear that his attention would be focused on an 'axis of evil', including Iran and North Korea, but featuring particularly Iraq, which, he claimed, 'has something to hide from the civilized world' (Fraser and Murray, 2002). As Bush's military chiefs mustered their forces in the Gulf, and his diplomats tried to rally support in the United Nations, any hope that his speech would be the prelude to rapid progress on the Israeli–Palestinian front was confounded. Over the following months, Iraq would dominate the American agenda. Even so, work went ahead with Russia, the European Union and the United Nations, the 'quartet', to produce a 'roadmap' for a peace settlement.

Realising that any Western action over Iraq would be compared with lack of progress over the future of the Palestinians, European leaders, notably Britain's Tony Blair, pressed for action (Halevy, 2006). As the crisis in the Gulf developed, it was clear that the Arab–Israeli issue still held centre stage. The dreary litany of killings in Israel and the Palestinian Authority continued unabated. Then, on 28 November, the conflict assumed a new dimension when three Israelis and ten Kenyans were killed in a suicide bombing on an Israeli-owned hotel in Kenya, and an attempt to shoot down an Israeli airliner taking off from Nairobi airport narrowly failed. The same day, six Israelis were killed in an attack on Likud party offices in Beit Shean. Nowhere, it seemed, was safe.

All of this coincided with new moves in Israeli politics. On 30 October 2002, the Labour party resigned from Sharon's governing coalition, forcing him to call an election. The probable outcome of the collapse of the coalition was a more hardline government. Facing Sharon was a new Labour leader, Amram Mitzna, another former general and now Mayor of Haifa. Veteran of the 1967 and 1973 wars, Mitzna had protested over the Sabra and Shatila massacres before going on to confront the Intifada of the late 1980s. His policy was to set a deadline for agreement with the Palestinians, failing which Israel would retire behind a security fence, evacuating many of the settlements. His strongest card was Israel's serious economic and financial situation in the wake of the renewed Intifada. In response, Sharon set out his vision of a demilitarised Palestinian state which would take in 42 per cent of the West Bank and 70 per cent of the Gaza strip, and which would have no place for Yasser Arafat. This could not have been further removed from the Palestinian position. Arafat's New Year speech called for an independent state with Jerusalem as its capital, the deployment of international observers, and an end to attacks on Israeli and Palestinian civilians.

At the beginning of 2003, as the unfolding crisis over Iraq dominated the international agenda, Israel went to the polls on 28 January. Mitzna's message failed to strike home with an Israeli public fearful of its security, and unwilling to take risks. Reduced to 18 seats in the Knesset, its worst-ever result, Labour could only lick its wounds. With 40 seats, Sharon could, given the complex nature of the voting system, legitimately claim a landslide. After four weeks of negotiations, on 27 February he was able to announce his new government, which was an intriguing combination. His coalition partners included the National Religious Party with 6 seats, and the strongly nationalist National Union Party with 7 seats, each opposed to the creation of a Palestinian state. But the key partner was Shinui, with 15 seats. Shinui described itself as a middle-class secular party. It supported the peace process, though not with Arafat as a partner, called for settlement blocks to be integrated inside Israel, but conceded that isolated settlements would have to be abandoned. In a dramatic development, Sharon dropped his party rival, Netanyahu, as Foreign Minister, giving him responsibility for finance. The new government's guidelines included working for peace on the basis of Security Council Resolutions 242 and 338, promised that there would be no new settlements, and conceded that any negotiations likely to include a Palestinian state would first be discussed by the government. This meant that his colleagues in the National Religious Party and National Union Party would have to be satisfied with any proposal.

As Sharon was concluding his negotiations for his governing coalition, Bush made a speech on 26 February, linking his policies on Iraq to the prospects for progress on the Israeli–Palestinian issue. 'Success in Iraq', he declared, 'could also begin a new stage for Middle Eastern peace, and set in motion progress towards a truly democratic Palestinian state'. The scenario he presented was that the removal of

Saddam Hussein's regime would deprive terrorist networks of a patron, and hence encourage Palestinians to choose new leaders, 'leaders who strive for peace'. As the threat of terror was removed, Israel would 'be expected to support the creation of a viable Palestinian state', and to bring an end to settlement activity (White House, 2003a). Although his speech was seen as code for the emergence of a contiguous Palestinian state on the West Bank, the overall thrust of what he said confirmed that the future of Iraq remained his overriding concern. Nor was it clear what influence would be brought to bear on Israel to accept Palestinian statehood. Progress would have to await the outcome of events in Iraq.

However dramatic the military and diplomatic events connected with the unfolding crisis over Iraq, the Arab–Israeli conflict retained its own grim integrity. A suicide bomb on a Haifa bus on 5 March killed 15 and injured another 40 people, many of them university students. While Hamas did not claim responsibility for the attack, in an apparent retaliation Israeli helicopters struck hard at the organisation on 8 March, killing one of its founders, Ibrahim al-Makadme, in Gaza. In response, the organisation pledged to target Israeli leaders. As it did so, the Central Council of the PLO confirmed the appointment of Mahmoud Abbas as Prime Minister. A veteran both of Fatah and of diplomacy associated with the peace process, his appointment was seen as marking a fresh start on the part of the Palestinian Authority, not least since it implied that Arafat would no longer be its sole voice.

On 14 March 2003, with the last attempts at a diplomatic solution to the Iraq crisis being played out in the United Nations, Bush made his much-awaited statement on his 'roadmap' to resolve the Arab–Israeli conflict. Confirming his support for a Palestinian state 'that abandons forever the use of terror', he called upon the Israelis to end settlement activities and 'take concrete steps to support the emergence of a viable and credible Palestinian state'. Once the Palestinian prime minister had been confirmed in office, the roadmap would be presented to the two governments. 'America', he emphasised, 'will be the active partner of every party that seeks true peace' (White House, 2003b). What role the other members of the 'quartet' might assume was less clear, but the part of first violin was in no doubt. The following week, on 19 March, American forces, with British support, began their offensive against Saddam Hussein's government in Iraq, ushering in a dramatic new phase in Middle Eastern affairs. On 9 April, Baghdad was judged to have fallen to the American forces, and although the reconstruction of Iraq promised to be a long and costly affair, the toppling of Saddam's regime meant that the unveiling of the roadmap could not be long delayed.

The final element fell into place on 29 April when the Palestinian parliament voted to confirm Mahmoud Abbas as Prime Minister. The following day the Americans released the text of the 'Performance-Based Roadmap to a Permanent Two-State Solution to the Israeli–Palestinian Conflict', which had as its aim 'a final and comprehensive settlement of the Israel–Palestinian conflict by 2005'. Under Phase I of the plan, the two sides were to issue immediate commitments, the Palestinians were to issue an 'unequivocal statement reiterating Israel's right to exist in peace and security and calling for an immediate and unconditional ceasefire to end armed activity and all acts of violence against Israelis anywhere', and Israel was to issue 'an unequivocal statement affirming its commitment to the two-state vision of an independent, viable, sovereign Palestinian state living in peace and security alongside Israel, as expressed by President Bush, and calling for an immediate end to violence against Palestinians everywhere'. On the security front, the Palestinian security forces were to begin 'sustained, targeted, and effective operations aimed at confronting all those engaged in terror and dismantlement of terrorist capabilities and infrastructure'. The Israeli government was to take no action which would undermine trust, 'including deportations, attacks on civilians; confiscation and/or demolition of

Palestinian homes and property, as a punitive measure or to facilitate Israeli construction'. Palestinian institution-building was to be facilitated by the production of a draft constitution, the appointment of an interim prime minister or Cabinet with executive authority, and an early move to hold 'free, open and fair elections'. For its part, the Israeli Government was to dismantle settlement outposts erected since March 2001, and freeze 'all settlement activity (including natural growth of settlements)'. This initial phase, to be in place by June 2003, was intended to address the fundamental fears of the Israelis over security and the Palestinians over settlement expansion.

Phase II of the roadmap, to be completed by December 2003, was to be triggered by Palestinian elections. These were to be followed by an international conference, brokered by the quartet, the aim of which would be to aid Palestinian economic recovery and 'launch a process, leading to the establishment of an independent Palestinian state with provisional borders'. More ambitiously, it was also to have as its goal a 'comprehensive Middle East peace (including between Israel and Syria, and Israel and Lebanon)'. A key element of this phase was to enhance territorial contiguity, 'including further action on settlements in conjunction with establishment of a Palestinian state with provisional borders'. Phase III was to open with a second international conference, early in 2004, intended to lead 'to a final, permanent status resolution in 2005, including on borders, Jerusalem, refugees, settlements; and, to support progress toward a comprehensive Middle East settlement between Israel and Lebanon and Israel and Syria, to be achieved as soon as possible'. The overall aim was to end the Israeli–Palestinian conflict in 2005 (Department of State, 30 April 2003). It was a highly optimistic timetable given the fate of previous peace plans The lack of detail over key issues such as borders, refugees and Jerusalem, or whether a state meant an independent country, gave endless possibilities for prolonged negotiation, but there were more immediate threats to the roadmap's prospects, especially since these were so dependent upon security and a mutual confidence which was almost wholly lacking. Hamas and Islamic Jihad rejected the plan. The following day, a suicide bomb killed 3 people in Tel Aviv, and 12 Palestinians were killed in Gaza. There were also rumblings on the Israeli right, unhappy at the implications for settlement activity.

Any hope that Phase I might be in place by the end of May was devastated when a suicide attack in Jerusalem led Sharon to call off a planned visit to Washington. Despite the deep unhappiness felt by many in his coalition, Sharon persuaded his Cabinet to endorse the roadmap, albeit on a divided vote and with a number of qualifications. With victory over Saddam Hussein apparently behind him, Bush put his personal authority behind the plan at a summit in Aqaba with Abbas and Sharon on 4 June. While the Palestinian premier confirmed his commitment to end the armed Intifada, Sharon conceded the importance of territorial contiguity for the Palestinian state and pledged to dismantle what he termed unauthorised outposts. Significantly, too, he acknowledged that it was not in Israel's interests to govern the Palestinians. But any optimism which might have surrounded the summit was once again dashed on 11 June when a suicide bombing caused carnage in central Jerusalem. Israelis responded with a rocket attack on Gaza, killing a Hamas leader.

Although the June deadline for Phase I of the roadmap, like most other deadlines set over the years, came and went, the summer of 2003 seemed to throw out some prospect that movement might be possible. On 1 May, President Bush proclaimed success in the Iraq war, holding out the hope that the weight of his administration would now be thrown behind the peace plan. But the situation in Iraq remained unsettled, with recurring attacks inflicting significant casualties on American and British troops, as well as amongst the population. Just how unstable the situation remained was tragically confirmed on 19 August when a car bomb killed

United Nations Special Representative Sergio Viera de Mello together with many of his staff, and again ten days later when another bomb killed Ayatollah Mohammed Baqir al-Hakim and scores of others at the Imam Ali Mosque in the Shi'ite holy city of Najaf. Iraq would continue to be the Americans' clear priority. Certainly, separate meetings in July between Bush and the two prime ministers yielded little of substance.

On 29 June, the main Palestinian armed groups, including Hamas, agreed to a three-month cease-fire, but this was linked to an Israeli concession on the release of Palestinian prisoners. Experience elsewhere, notably in Northern Ireland, had taught that prisoner releases, however upsetting to victims and their families, were an essential element in a peace settlement, but hard to bring about in practice. Israeli and Palestinian expectations of the numbers to be released were, predictably, far apart, with the former talking of hundreds and the latter thousands. Although there was some progress on the issue, with Israel beginning prisoner releases in early August, it was already being overshadowed by another matter which was casting a lengthening shadow across a future Palestinian state.

Israeli military and political circles had debated for some time the desirability of a barrier with the West Bank, beyond the existing network of checkpoints. This was clearly accelerated by the heightening level of violence, not least the security nightmare of how to prevent penetration by determined suicide bombers. Approval for the construction of a security fence was given in August 2002, initially in the north-west of the West Bank. As work proceeded, the formidable nature of the barrier became apparent, with the fence's deterrent effect enhanced by a patrol road and tracking roads to detect intrusions. On completion, it would extend over 600 kilometres. By the following year, the barrier was also under construction around east Jerusalem. Here it assumed even more formidable dimensions, since it comprised a concrete wall between four and eight metres in height. Rejecting Israeli claims that what was being constructed was a security fence, Palestinians termed it a wall of annexation, since it quickly became clear that its line extended significantly beyond the 1967 border to take in Israeli settlement blocks, in all some 7–8 per cent of the territory. The Palestinians saw this as Israel deciding unilaterally where the future new border would lie. They particularly resented the barrier's construction around Jerusalem, not least since it appeared to threaten their hopes of east Jerusalem becoming their capital. It also cut into the economic and social life of adjacent communities like Abu Dis and Ar Ram, whose inhabitants depended upon access to the facilities of east Jerusalem. To the south of Jerusalem, there was a dramatic impact on Bethlehem, whose livelihood depended to a large extent upon the tourist and pilgrim trade. The combination of the barrier and the Intifada led to the virtual collapse of the city's economy. To the east of Jerusalem, the barrier's proposed extension to include the Israeli settlement town of Ma'ale Adumim, was a particular cause for concern to the Palestinians: inclusion of this area would further isolate the Palestinians of east Jerusalem, but would also threaten to turn the West Bank into two cantons, stultifying a future Palestinian state (Brooks *et al.*, 2005; Migdalovitz, 2006).

As these issues were festering, a renewed spiral of violence threatened to stifle the roadmap altogether. What appears to have sparked this was the death of two Hamas members at the hands of the Israeli army in Nablus, as a result of which the organisation threatened revenge. On 12 August, two Israelis were killed in two suicide bombings, one inside the country, the other in the West Bank. Two days later, a leading figure in Islamic Jihad was shot dead by the Israeli army in Hebron; here, too, revenge was the watchword. On 19 August, a bus carrying religious Jews was blown up in Jerusalem by a suicide bomber from Hebron, killing 22 people. Israel responded with a series of strikes, in the course of which a leading Hamas figure in Gaza, Ismail Abu Shanab, was killed in a missile attack. The cease-fire was effectively at an end.

In the face of these pressures, the political situation also threatened to disintegrate. On 6 September, Mahmoud Abbas, on whom the American administration had pinned such hopes but who had lacked any independent power base, resigned the Palestinian premiership, accusing the Americans of lack of support. Once again the spotlight fell on Arafat, still confined to his Ramallah headquarters, and blamed by the Americans for undercutting Abbas (Department of State, 7 September 2003). Abbas's successor was Ahmed Qureia, a veteran supporter of Arafat who had helped start the Oslo peace process. The change in leadership demonstrated once again Arafat's continuing hold over Palestinian politics. Equally, no one could ignore what was happening on the ground. A failed Israeli attack on Sheikh Ahmed Yassin, Hamas's spiritual leader, was answered with suicide bombings near Tel Aviv and in Jerusalem which killed 15 people. For its part, Israel's security Cabinet voted in principle for Arafat's expulsion from the Palestinian Authority. As the Americans warned against any such action, and thousands of Palestinians rallied to his support in Ramallah and elsewhere, Arafat replied that he would rather die than be expelled. A new and potentially volatile situation had been created in which a power vacuum would open up if the Palestinian president were removed, but the Israeli government would lose credibility if it did not do so in the event of further attacks. The latter was not long in coming. On 4 October, a young woman lawyer exploded a suicide bomb in Haifa, killing 20 people. The next day, the Israeli Air Force struck at what their government claimed was a training camp near Damascus. The attack on Syria was both a stark warning, and carried the threat that the conflict could once again assume wider dimensions.

## New Political Realities

With the Intifada continuing unabated, and the uncertain nature of both Palestinian and Israeli politics, scant hope seemed to beckon on the political front. Arafat's relations with the new premier proved to be uneasy, while his own health gave increasing cause for concern. Unhappy with the lack of progress, on 1 December 2003 a group of well known Israelis and Palestinians signed what became known as the Geneva Accord, a high-profile, albeit unofficial, attempt to put flesh on the bones of a two-state solution (Migdalowitz, 2006). Their initiative was soon upstaged when, on 18 December, Sharon began to signal his intention to move ahead unilaterally in Gaza in what was, for the Israelis at least, a political vacuum, but uncertainty over what this might mean rang alarm bells amongst some members of his own party. These would soon intensify, as Sharon's intentions began to emerge more clearly. On 12 January 2004, the government indicated that it would begin the process of withdrawal from areas of the Occupied Territories, and then, on 2 February, Sharon announced that Israel would evacuate her 21 settlements in Gaza, whose inhabitants were now estimated to be 7,500, but whose cause had a powerful constituency in the country. Sharon's policies also involved a strengthening of the security fence, or wall, between Israel and the West Bank, notwithstanding international condemnation of its construction which had culminated in a United Nations resolution calling for it to be dismantled. While many on the Israeli right, Sharon's natural constituency, castigated this as the abandonment of established positions for no return, Palestinians feared that withdrawal from Gaza might simply herald tougher policies on the West Bank. Crucial American backing for these initiatives was secured in April, and attention now rested on Sharon's scheme rather than on the roadmap, which had been, in truth, moribund for months. The roadmap was now archived along with the previous American initiatives of the Rogers Plan, Carter's Framework and the Reagan Plan (Quandt, 2005). While Bush's support was welcome, that of Sharon's own party was less assured, since on 2 May Likud members voted against their leader's proposal by 60 per cent to 40 (Mark, 2005).

Violence remained an incessant counterpoint to these political developments. On 14 March 2004, two suicide bombers targeted the town of Asdod, leading the Israeli government to threaten the Islamic leadership in Gaza. This was soon put to deadly effect on 22 March when a missile killed the 67-year-old quadriplegic Sheikh Ahmed Yassin, whose work had inspired Hamas members but who was detested by Israelis. His place in the Hamas leadership was assumed by the paediatrician Dr Abd al-Aziz al-Rantissi, whose career lasted less than a month until he, too, was killed by an Israeli missile on 17 April. While the Israeli government evidently hoped that it was decapitating Hamas's leadership in Gaza, and hence undermining its ability to strike, it was also running a grave risk of creating martyrs whose deaths others would seek to avenge. Faced with the Israeli challenge, Hamas embarked upon a disaggregated leadership structure, which would be less vulnerable to such attacks. Over the next two years support for the movement was to grow appreciably, not just in its Gaza stronghold, but also in the West Bank, until it proved capable of upsetting the calculations of those who had hitherto dismissed it as the militant fringe of Palestinian politics.

Gaza never receded far from the headlines, whether politically or militarily. In mid-May, serious fighting there resulted in the death of 15 Israeli soldiers. In response, the IDF mounted a major operation against the Gaza and Rafah refugee camps, killing scores of people, including many children, and destroying hundreds of homes. While these events pointed once again to the human and political costs of the continuing Israeli occupation, Sharon's party's unease over the implications of his withdrawal proposals was intensifying apace. As formulated on 16 April 2004, and then revised on 28 May, the plan reaffirmed Israel's continuing commitment to President Bush's vision, but went on to say that because of the lack of a credible Palestinian partner it was necessary to set in hand a plan of unilateral disengagement. Accordingly, by the end of 2005 she would evacuate all towns and villages in the Gaza Strip and redeploy her forces apart from those along the border with Egypt, though this aspect was later rescinded. The absence of Israeli troops or civilians would mean the end of any Israeli responsibility towards its inhabitants, though the plan was careful to retain the right of preventive and reactive defence. On the West Bank, Israel would continue constructing her security fence, but would evacuate four settlement villages in the north, Ganim, Kadim, Sa-Nur and Homesh, together with associated military installations (State of Israel, 2004). This was the plan approved in the Knesset on 3 November 2004 by 64 votes to 44, with 9 abstentions (Mark, 2005). The International Court of Justice in The Hague had by then demanded the dismantling of the security fence, a decision which cut no ice with the Sharon government nor with the Israeli public, which had mourned the death of 16 people at the hands of suicide bombers in Beersheba earlier in the summer. Unhappiness within Likud forced Sharon into coalition with Labour at the end of the year with his old adversary Peres as his deputy.

The Knesset vote on 3 November coincided with a sharp deterioration in Arafat's health, which observers had been watching with concern for some time. Fearing that Sharon's government would not permit his return, Arafat had resisted calls that he seek more sophisticated medical treatment overseas than could be provided in Ramallah. On 29 October, reassured on this issue, he was flown to Amman by Jordanian helicopter and then to a military hospital in France. But in the early hours of 11 November 2004, the man who had for a generation embodied the Palestinian cause died. After a formal funeral in Cairo, his body was greeted by thousands of mourning Palestinians for burial, not in Jerusalem as he had wished, but in the grounds of the *Muqata* in Ramallah (Bregman, 2005; Fisk, 2005).

In fact, for many in Israel and elsewhere who had despaired of reaching a settlement while he remained in office, his death appeared to open up new avenues. Former premier Mahmoud Abbas was confirmed as PLO Chairman, becoming the leading contender to succeed Arafat as President of the Palestinian Authority. When the elections for president were held on 9 January 2005, the strong support of his Fatah members ensured that he was endorsed by some 60 per cent of those who voted. His victory was widely seen as a triumph for Fatah pragmatism, a view seemingly confirmed by a congratulatory telephone call from Sharon. But for those who cared to look at the figures, his win was not quite so emphatic. Hamas, Fatah's chief rival for popular affection, had boycotted the election, large numbers were not registered and the turnout was low, notably so in the Gaza Strip. The shadow of Arafat, and Fatah's continuing place at the centre of affairs, had helped the veteran and well-respected Abbas to power, but clearly many Palestinians were having reservations over the performance of the Palestinian Authority.

Nevertheless, the Palestinians had a new leader, raising expectations that political dialogue could now resume. One of the new President's first actions was to call for implementation of the roadmap. On 8 February 2005, Abbas and Sharon met at Sharm al-Sheikh, together with President Mubarak and Jordan's King Abdullah II, to proclaim an end to the Intifada and military operations (Migdalovitz, 2006). Hamas, for its part, refused to be bound by their agreement. On 25 February a suicide bomb at a popular waterfront bar and club in Tel Aviv killed five people and caused widespread other casualties. Despite the deeply held reservations of party colleagues, including Netanyahu who resigned over the policy, and large-scale public protests, Sharon pressed ahead with the disengagement plan. On 15 August 2005, the border to the Gaza Strip was closed, and the settlers given 48 hours to leave their homes. In the event, a strong military presence proved unnecessary. While some settlers made a vigorous protest, most left peacefully enough, and by the 19th the operation was complete. On 12 September, Israel's military presence in Gaza also came to an end. With the exception of the Sinai settlements abandoned under the peace treaty with Egypt, this was the first major Israeli withdrawal since 1967. As such, it was bitterly assailed on the right, arousing fears over what might be conceded on the West Bank. For Palestinians, the pullout was largely cosmetic, given the surrounding Israeli military presence, and could only be the first step to further moves elsewhere.

The Israeli public's sense of security, brittle at the best of times, was further tested from a new direction. The Iranian presidential elections of June 2005 saw the success of Tehran mayor, Mahmoud Ahmadinejad, who soon began expressing controversial anti-Israeli sentiments. On 26 October, he made remarks which Israelis found deeply alarming and followed this by apparently challenging the truth of the Holocaust. While such anti-Israeli rhetoric was nothing new in the Middle East, there were dimensions to his stance which the Israelis, and the American administration, could not but find troubling. The practical effect of the removal of Saddam Hussein's regime in Baghdad, and the subsequent turn of events in Iraq, was to remove the only real counterweight to Iran's regional power. Iran, the world's major Shi'ite power, was the obvious point of attraction for the Shi'ite Hizbollah militia in southern Lebanon, strongly entrenched as it was just across Israel's northern border. Finally, there was the issue of Iran's nuclear programme, the disputed purpose of which had set Tehran and Washington at odds and triggered fears in Israel. The signing of a defence pact between Iran and Syria did nothing to reassure a febrile Israeli public (Katzmann, 2006).

As these events were unfolding, seismic changes took place in the Israeli body politic. In November 2005, the veteran Shimon Peres was, by the narrowest of margins, defeated for the Labour leadership by Amir Peretz, a trade unionist of Moroccan origin whose first move was to end the coalition. Peretz's move was soon eclipsed when, on 21 November, Sharon shook Israeli politics to their foundation. Resigning as leader of Likud, the party he had been instrumental in founding, Sharon announced the formation of Kadima ('Forward'), which proclaimed itself a centrist and secular party. His move was, perhaps, simply the logical result of the schisms which had beset Likud since he had embarked upon his disengagement strategy. He was joined by Ehud Olmert, a lawyer who had served for nearly ten years as mayor of Jerusalem, and then by Peres, who severed his long-standing links with Labour. Kadima, dedicated to Israel as the eternal national home for the Jewish people, nevertheless defined the peace process with the Palestinians as a primary goal, for which it was willing to make concessions. Its basic principle was that there should be two nation states. On future borders between these states, Kadima was determined that Israel would retain areas necessary for her security, the Jewish holy places, a unified Jerusalem and the large settlement areas in the West Bank. In addition, the party was committed to the completion of the security fence. By splitting Likud and establishing this new centrist party committed to pursuing a peace strategy, Sharon had made one of the most dramatic moves in Israeli politics since the establishment of the state. Where he would have taken it was to remain a matter for conjecture, however. On 18 December 2005, Sharon suffered a minor stroke, but on 4 January he had a major cerebral attack, which left him incapacitated. Within days it was clear that he would be unable to resume the premiership, and Ehud Olmert became acting prime minister. Israeli politics were entering uncharted waters.

With Israeli politics in a state of unprecedented turmoil, Palestinians prepared for their first Legislative Council elections in ten years. In 1996, they had overwhelmingly backed Fatah, electing 55 members to the 88-seat body. But with little to show for a decade in office, unemployment at record levels, and beset by insinuations of maladministration, Fatah no longer held the affections of large sections of the Palestinians. Above all, perhaps, it lacked the aura of Arafat, who, for all his shortcomings, had personified the Palestinian movement. By contrast, Hamas, campaigning under the name 'Change and Reform', was untainted by office, had built up a solid reputation for the provision of social services, enjoyed an unparalleled record of resistance to Israel, in the course of which it had seen its founder and his successor killed. It ought, therefore, to have come as no surprise that when they went to the polls on 25 January 2006, Palestinians endorsed Hamas by a massive margin, giving them 74 seats in the new 132-member assembly. Not only did the movement record success in its stronghold of Gaza, it also did extremely well in the West Bank. Fatah, for decades the voice of the Palestinians, could only manage 45 seats (Pina, 2006). Hamas's win placed President Mahmoud Abbas in an unenviable position. It horrified the Israelis and alarmed an American administration which had made such a feature of promoting democracy in the Middle East. Leading Israeli politicians, including Olmert, proclaimed they would have no links with a government which included Hamas. At issue were the movement's association with violence, and its 1988 pledge to reclaim the whole of Palestine for Islam. While fundamental concerns for Israelis, they also posed questions for secular and Christian Palestinians. How Fatah was to respond to the loss of its long-held position of authority remained to be determined. The prospect of a Palestinian state inspired by Islamic, rather than secular, principles and values added a new dimension to Middle Eastern affairs.

Whatever outsiders might think, a democratic vote had meant that a Hamas-led government for the Palestinian Authority was now inevitable. On 29 March 2006, therefore, Hamas's Ismail Haniya, a specialist in Arabic literature and former dean of Gaza's Islamic University, became prime minister. A Hamas government was not, it may safely be assumed, exactly what the Americans had hoped for when they had spoken of 'a new and different Palestinian leadership'. But Hamas, too, had to confront the realities of governing a polity already in the grip of an economic crisis. Both the United States and the European Union, between them prime financial supporters of the Palestinian Authority, quickly made it clear that continuing support depended upon both a renunciation of violence, recognition of Israel's right to exist and acceptance of existing Israeli–Palestinian agreements (Pina, 2006). Hamas's refusal to comply with these demands meant the withholding of funds. For its part, Israel refused to hand over tax revenues to the new government. As Palestinian government employees went without pay, the strategy seemed obvious; namely, to exert pressure on Hamas to join with President Abbas in the pursuit of a two-state solution, not something which the movement's highly dedicated supporters, accustomed to the rhetoric of confrontation, would find it easy to accept. Continuing economic hardship in the already impoverished Palestinian Authority was the inevitable result. Even so, Abbas's willingness to continue negotiations as Chairman of the PLO, and Haniyah's statement that Hamas would not object to this, seemed to offer a mechanism for progress (Migdalovitz, 2006).

Israel, too, was embarked upon the democratic process, but without the man who had been for so long a dominant force in her affairs, since Ariel Sharon's medical condition had not improved. When Israel went to the polls on 28 March 2006, Kadima, now led by Olmert, won 29 of the 120 Knesset seats, fewer, many felt, than if Sharon had been at the helm. It was, nonetheless, a creditable performance for the fledgling party, confirming Olmert's claim to the premiership. With 20 seats, Peretz's Labour party was the obvious partner in the inevitable coalition government. Reduced to 12 seats, Likud, led by Netanyahu, was the major voice of the right wing, though it was reinforced by some 20 other rightist members. When the new government was announced at the beginning of May 2006, Olmert was confirmed as Prime Minister, with Kadima's Tzipi Livni, who was also Minister of Foreign Affairs, and Shimon Peres as Vice Premiers, and Labour's Peretz as Deputy Prime Minister and Minister of Defence. This was the team who would have to confront the new reality of Hamas's dominating role in Palestinian affairs.

Olmert's government was not fated to have a long honeymoon period, however. Since security lay at the heart of the Israeli public concerns, any challenge on that front would be the major test of the new administration's credibility. It was not long in coming. On 25 June 2006, a young Israeli noncommissioned officer was kidnapped, and held prisoner in the Gaza Strip. As his captors proposed a prisoner exchange, three days later Israeli forces entered the southern part of the Gaza Strip, as the previous year's disengagement plan had always said they would, and then Israel began the detention of Hamas activists. On 4 and 5 July, rockets were fired at the Israeli town of Ashkelon, at which point Israeli tanks moved into the northern part of the Gaza Strip. Olmert's government and Hamas seemed bent on confrontation. In the early hours of 12 July 2006, Israeli aircraft attempted to kill a leading Hamas figure in Gaza; instead, another Hamas leader, Nabil al Salmiah, his wife and seven children were killed.

Hours later, Hizbollah fighters crossed Israel's northern border, killing eight Israelis, and seizing two soldiers as hostages. Olmert's government, now facing challenges on two fronts, castigated what had happened as an act of war. The Winograd committee on the conduct of the war, which submitted an interim report to the government on 30 April 2007, concluded that: 'Some of the declared goals of the war were not clear and could not be achieved, and in part were not achievable by the authorized modes of military action' (Israel, Ministry of Foreign Affairs, 2007). Air and artillery strikes, not just on Hizbollah strongholds in southern Lebanon, but on targets such as Beirut International Airport, were then reinforced by a substantial Israeli invasion. Hizbollah, long anticipating such a turn of events, was well dug-in, and knew the country intimately. Fighting was intense. Olmert's government was soon confronted by the sustained bombardment of northern Israel, including the key city port of Haifa, by Hizbollah's Katyusha rockets, some 4,000 in all. In 34 days of fighting, Israel signally failed to break the power of Hizbollah in southern Lebanon. After serious casualties on both sides, United Nations Resolution 1701 came into effect on 14 August 2006. Under its terms, Israeli forces were to withdraw from southern Lebanon, Hizbollah was to cease its attacks, units of the Lebanese army were to deploy in the south of the country, and the United Nations Interim Force in Lebanon was to be reinforced to oversee the ceasefire. By then, it is estimated that over 1,000 Lebanese and 144 Israelis, 104 of them soldiers, had been killed. It was a striking indication of the limitations of Israeli power, and on 22 September Hizbollah's leader, Sheikh Hassan Nasrallah, presided over what he called a victory rally in Beirut (Prados, 2006). Many also noted that the comparative ease with which his organisation had bombarded Israel with its relatively primitive missiles raised questions about the military effectiveness of the country's security fence. The crisis in Gaza proved more prolonged, with periodic rocket attacks being launched into southern Israel, which reponded with retaliatory strikes which left widespread casualties, and only came to an end with a cease-fire in November.

Events in Gaza were soon to take a different twist, but at the end of 2006 attention turned to two publications which, for rather different reasons, caught the headlines in the United States, where public attention was inevitably focussed upon the situation in Iraq. The first was a book by former President Jimmy Carter under the challenging title of *Palestine: Peace not Apartheid.* Architect of the 1978 Camp David Accords and the subsequent Egyptian–Israeli peace treaty, Carter had never given up on his hopes for peace between the Israelis and Palestinians. Pleading for all Arabs to acknowledge Israel's right to a peaceful existence, he nevertheless pointed to continuing Israeli occupation and annexation of Palestinian land as, in his view, the main obstacles to peace (Carter, 2006). Carter's concern that the United States must engage with the conflict found more than an echo in *The Iraq Study Group Report,* a bipartisan enquiry into the situation in that country, and chaired by the veteran politicians James A. Baker III and Lee H. Hamilton. While focussing on what they believed needed to be done in what they described as the grave and deteriorating situation in Iraq, the authors clearly pointed to the need to address the wider regional context, which included the Arab–Israeli conflict, without which, they argued, the United States could not succeed in the Middle East. The formula contained little that was new, but it was significant that the authors saw the need to state it. In a clear message to the Bush administration, it recommended negotiations to bring about a settlement based upon the president's two-state solution (Baker and Hamilton, 2006).

On the ground, however, matters were far from simple, since the worsening economic situation in the Palestinian Authority, especially in Gaza, brought to a head the simmering rivalries between Fatah and Hamas. Bitter internecine fighting was only brought to an end on 8 February 2007 when the Saudi Arabian government brokered a deal in the holy city of Mecca. President Abbas and Prime Minister Haniya agreed the principles of a government of national unity with portfolios shared amongst Hamas, Fatah and independents. On the critical question of recognition of Israel, it seemed that the most Hamas would agree to was that they would respect agreements made by the PLO. It fell short of what the Israelis, the Americans and other members of the Quartet needed, and formed a rather unpromising prelude to a visit by Secretary of State Condoleezza Rice to Jerusalem and Ramallah on 18–19 February 2007. Together with Abbas and Olmert, she discussed how progress could be made on moving forward the obligations set out under Phase I of the roadmap, the three reaffirming their commitment to a two-state solution. They also discussed the implications arising out of the proposed Palestinian unity government, including the 'position of the Quartet that any Palestinian Authority government must be committed to non-violence, recognition of Israel, and acceptance of previous agreements and obligations, including regarding the Roadmap' (Department of State, 2007).

Although the Palestinian coalition government formally came into existence on 17 March, conditions in the Gaza Strip continued to worsen. Symptomatic of the breakdown in law and order was the kidnapping, five days before, of BBC correspondent Alan Johnston. By mid-May serious clashes between Hamas and Fatah supporters resulted in over forty casualties. The situation deteriorated further when rocket attacks against the southern Israeli town of Sderot, which killed two, resulted in Israeli air strikes against Hamas targets in the Gaza Strip, in which over fifty died. In an attempt to maintain pressure, the Israelis detained over thirty officials in the West Bank, including two Hamas cabinet members.

Notwithstanding the growing tensions with Israel, the coalition government proved to be a feeble vehicle for Fatah–Hamas unity, and in June 2007 the tensions between them broke out into the bitter internecine conflict so long feared by Palestinians. Fighting between the two groups, which began in the Gaza Strip on 11 June, quickly became a major push by Hamas fighters for control of the territory. By 14 June, with an estimated 100-plus casualties, the Hamas men had taken the presidential compound and the Fatah security headquarters in Gaza city, and were fast gaining unfettered control of the Strip. It was a challenge President Abbas and Fatah could not ignore. Dismissing Prime Minister Haniya, Abbas brought the coalition government to an end, declaring a state of emergency which allowed him to government independently of the Hamas-dominated parliament. On the West Bank, Fatah fighters asserted their position in key cities like Nablus, and seized control of the parliament in Ramallah. On 17 June, Abbas appointed an emergency government, with the independent Salam Fayyad as Prime Minister. As the United States and the European Union expressed their support for the new government, the stark reality was that by June 2007 the

Palestinian Authority had fractured into a Fatah-dominated West Bank and a Hamas dominated Gaza Strip. The Israeli political map was changing, too, with the veteran Shimon Peres being elected President in the Knesset, and the replacement of Peretz as Labour leader and Defence Minister by Ehud Barak.

An early confirmation of Hamas's new authority in the Gaza Strip was its key role in the liberation of Alan Johnston from the group which had kidnapped him. On 4 July 2007, the well-respected BBC correspondent was freed. Even so, the fracturing of the Palestinian Authority made no easier the challenging mission of former British Prime Minister Tony Blair, who became the Quartet's representative, charged as he was with assisting the reconstruction of the Authority's institutions and economy. On 16 July 2007, a new statement by President Bush pointed the way towards an autumn meeting of the nations that, he said, supported a two-state solution, rejected violence, recognized Israel's right to exist, and were committed to previous agreements. Contrasting the visions of Hamas with those of President Abbas and Prime Minister Fayyad, he appealed for support for the latter, while signalling that the Israelis should end the expansion of settlements. The negotiations, he confirmed, must ensure the security of Israel, while guaranteeing a viable and contiguous Palestinian state (White House, 2007).

# Conclusion

While no one doubted the historic nature of the handshake between Arafat and Rabin in Washington on 13 September 1993, it proved to be but the tentative first phase of a period of reappraisal for both Israelis and Arabs. The Oslo peace process, rejected by many Israelis and Palestinians, did not survive the failure of the Camp David summit in 2000 and the subsequent second Intifada with its litany of casualties on both sides. Even so, each party was forced to confront not just the positions of their former enemies but also their own fundamental assumptions. Goodwill was of the essence but proved to be in short supply. It was, at best, the first hesitant sign of a possible accommodation between Arabs and Jews since the 1920 riots had revealed the strength of Palestinian opposition to Zionist aspirations. Neither side had a monopoly of virtue. The Arabs had always been an unwelcome presence for the Zionists, standing in the way of the ultimate redemption of the land. There was no master plan to expel the Arabs en masse, but if circumstances arose, as in 1948 and 1967, when their departure could be encouraged, then it was. Decades of homelessness for hundreds of thousands, later millions, of Palestinians followed, their refugee camps a symbol of the disaster that had befallen them. From the 1980s, Arab lands were regularly expropriated in the Occupied Territories to serve as the basis for future Jewish settlements. The feeling that this could not be allowed to proceed unchecked was a major reason for the outbreak of the 1987 Intifada. The seemingly relentless expansion of settlements in the 1990s undermined for Palestinians their faith in the peace process, especially as they threatened to thwart any prospect of a contiguous Palestinian state.

Nor had the Palestinians been able to adapt to the Jewish presence and creation of a state; from 1937 to 1988 they had publicly rejected the concept of the partition of Palestine. While their leaders tirelessly argued that they could not accept what they saw as an unjust division of their country, they consistently failed, or refused, to come to terms with the reality of the Jewish presence. Relying on their numbers, the support of the Arab world and the sympathy of the British, after 1945 they failed to grasp the strength of purpose that the Holocaust had given to the Jews, and the sympathy this had attracted, not least in the United States. Crushed by the events of 1948–49, by the time Palestinian political activism began to revive in the late 1950s and early 1960s Israel was an established member of the international community. Frustrated that the world seemed to have forgotten them, the Palestinians' resort to violence succeeded in putting them back at the centre of the political agenda, but in a manner that enabled the Israelis to castigate them as terrorists and Western governments to keep them at arm's length. Palestinian activities in the Middle East provoked the wrath of Jordan, and helped start the civil war in Lebanon. By the mid-1980s, the exiled PLO leadership seemed far removed from the daily concerns of the Palestinians of the West Bank and Gaza. The events of 11 September 2001, and the subsequent American 'war on terror', threatened the Palestinian position even further, not least because the Israeli Government was quick to grasp the rhetoric coming from Washington, realising that a campaign of suicide bombing would arouse little sympathy in a country where over 3,000 innocent civilians had just perished in a suicide attack. The 'war on terror', and its subsequent extension to the American campaign against Saddam Hussein, was a distraction from the core issues, but its significance was undeniable. The 'linkage' between the Arab–Israeli conflict, events in Iraq and violence in the

Middle East was spelled out in the 2006 *Iraq Study Group Report* (Baker and Hamilton, 2006).

The political developments of 1993 had, for a time, seemed to show a way forward from this sterile impasse. Quite apart from the dangers that everyone knew would accompany the way ahead, there were deep-seated social, economic and political problems in both Israeli and Palestinian societies which needed to be addressed. Zionism had aimed at the creation of a Jewish state, ideally a state to which all Jews would be attracted, but two-thirds of world Jewry still lived in the Diaspora. Uneasy fears over the country's demographic future, given a low Jewish birthrate and the attraction for many Israelis of life in New York and Paris, were certainly eased by the sudden arrival of some 800,000 Jews from the former Soviet Union (Bregman, 2003). How many of them would have preferred to have gone to the United States or Canada was a question no one wanted to probe too deeply. One important consequence of the 'Russian' immigration was to tip the balance back in favour of European as against oriental Jews. This carried the obvious danger that oriental Jews would see the gains of the previous 15 years receding from them as well-educated Russian Jews established themselves in society and the economy.

Problems of the nature of the Jewish state remained. Zionism always had a complex relationship with religion, since its early pioneers, while recognising the central place of Judaism in Jewish life and tradition, were overwhelmingly secular. The state they established in 1948 was in no sense a theocratic one, but it always contained a dedicated minority who believed that Israel should embody specifically Jewish values. The 1980s saw the growth of ultra-orthodox political parties prepared to articulate this belief. Their electoral support was enough to give them considerable influence when political leaders were building their coalition governments. The result was a noticeable tension between secular and religious Jewish traditions. Perhaps too much can be made of the various splits within Israeli society, for there remained an ultimate consensus around the nature of the state and its Jewish identity. This left an inevitable question mark against the Israeli Arabs, who formed over 20 per cent of the country's 6,426,679 inhabitants, and were a local majority in parts of the north of the country (CIA World Factbook, Israel, 2007). Israel was not unique in having to accommodate a sizeable minority population – witness, for example, Slovakia with its 600,000 Hungarians – but there is no doubt that the Arabs had been left behind in the process of building the Jewish state. They were determined to demand their rights as full citizens (Kyle and Peters, 1993). Israel had to confront the hard reality that while it aspired to be a Jewish state, it was by any definition binational. As such, it had to afford recognition and respect to its Arab citizens.

Israel's ambivalent relationship with its Arab minority ought to have brought into sharper focus the position of the Arabs of the West Bank and Gaza. From the start of the occupation in 1967, wise voices had advised that any long-term occupation would result in the de facto emergence of a binational state, and questioned whether this was what Zionism had hoped to achieve. Put more simply, annexation of the West Bank and Gaza would have produced a state in which by 2007 Arabs numbered some 2,535,927 and 1,482,405 respectively, raising for some Israelis uncomfortable comparisons with Lebanon, or with Northern Ireland, which had proved unable to accommodate its 42 per cent Roman Catholic minority, at least until the 1998 Good Friday Agreement offered Catholics the prospect of full equality and respect for their Irish sense of identity (CIA World Factbook, West Bank, 2007; CIA World Factbook, Gaza Strip 2007). These were not arguments that seemed to concern right-wing ideologues until the nature and extent of the Intifada in 1987, and then again in 2000, forced them to confront the hard political and financial realities of holding on to the Occupied Territories.

Simultaneously the PLO leadership was also having to reassess long-cherished positions. Acquiescence in a two-state solution meant abandoning the hopes of refugees to return to Haifa, Jaffa and other towns and villages inside the 1967 border, except in the event of Israel allowing a 'right of return', something Israeli opinion was unwilling to contemplate. The best that could be hoped for was that a Palestinian state on the West Bank and Gaza would act as a focus for pride and loyalty in the same way that Israel did for the Jews of the Diaspora. Such a state would depend on Israeli goodwill for contact between its two parts, and would have a much wider dependence on the stronger and more developed Israeli economy. The West Bank and Gaza had essentially a service economy, not in itself a disaster, but certainly in chronic need of diversification. American thinking had for some time looked to an economic confederation, linking Israel, Jordan and a Palestinian state, which would make best use of the markets, communications and the scarce water resources of the region. All of this required a constructive attitude from both the parties to the Arab–Israeli conflict, which seemed a distant prospect. Moreover, the two-state solution, only accepted by the PLO in 1988, had its critics. From its different perspective, Hamas, now in the seat of power since the January 2006 elections, had as its vision a single Islamic Palestinian state. For the Israelis, and many Palestinians, a two-state solution along the lines attempted by President Clinton in 2000 remained the only sustainable option, even given the future of the settlements and the hitherto intractable issues of the refugees and Jerusalem.

The accumulated legacy of almost half a century of conflict was there for all to see. The removal from the political scene of the venerable adversaries Yasser Arafat and Ariel Sharon opened the way for new personalities, but this did not alter the hard realities they had to deal with. The world had become used to dismissing the Arab–Israeli problem as a source of permanent hostility always likely to erupt into open warfare. The wars which broke out in 1948, 1956, 1967, 1973 and 1982 were all bloody and dramatic. They were triggered by different things. The Arab League invasion of 1948 arose out of Arab rejection of the new Israeli state. In 1956 both Israel and Egypt became caught in a wider game, which involved both Britain and France in the dying kicks of empire. The 1967 war was a classic example of miscalculation on the part of almost everyone involved, but which had far-reaching consequences. The Egyptian and Syrian attack of 1973 was essentially the result of frustrated diplomacy, a particularly bitter struggle fought for limited aims. Israel's invasion of Lebanon in 1982 was launched by an ideologically motivated government, which hoped to resolve a number of issues, not least the future of the PLO. If the circumstances were very different, the underlying cause of conflict, as with the Intifadas of 1987 and 2000, remained the same: the apparent incompatibility of Arab and Jewish claims to the one land.

For most Israelis the key issue was that of security. On the ground, there seemed no defence against the suicide bomber beyond eternal vigilance, the construction of security fences, and pre-emptive and retaliatory strikes against those identified as organisers of the campaign. Impressive though the fence was, it offered no defence against rocket attacks, as thousands of Israelis discovered in 2006 and 2007 when rockets were fired from Lebanon and Gaza. For over 30 years most Israelis had feared that the only logic of diplomatic negotiation was to push them into concession after concession until the very integrity of their state was in doubt (Kissinger, 1999). In that respect, they may be compared to those Northern Irish Protestants who held a similarly dismal view of their future, equally unrealistically it may be held. Israeli security was, after all, underpinned by the world's only superpower, the United States of America. American aid and loan guarantees were an important dimension to Israel's economic and financial stability. In July 2003, the House of Representatives voted by an overwhelming majority for an aid package to Israel totalling an overall $2.6 billion. The extent to which the United States might be prepared to push for the achievement of a Palestinian state remained to be resolved, but American support for Israel seemed set to remain one of the fixed points of the Arab–Israeli conflict. Not only did Israel command the loyalty of the American Jewish community, politically deployed in Washington through AIPAC, but it had an important constituency on the Christian right, an influential group within the Republican party.

For their part, Palestinians pointed to the reality of continuing occupation, the consolidation of Israeli settlements, frustrated hopes for statehood, and a bleak and uncertain future for the refugees. By June 2003, according to UNRWA figures, there were 4,082,330 refugees; 1,718,767 in Jordan, 409,662 in Syria, 391,679 in Lebanon, 907,221 in Gaza, and 654,971 in the West Bank (UNRWA, 2003). The violent events of 2002 left the political and economic infrastructure of the Palestinian Authority, fragile at the best of times, in ruins. Unemployment soared, while the curtailment of international funds after Hamas's electoral victory in 2006 compounded the problems facing ordinary Palestinians. Surrounding Arab states, while sympathetic, seemed to offer little by way of tangible support. While the elements of a settlement had seemingly been established in the closing weeks of the Clinton administration, peace remained elusive, as events in Gaza and Lebanon in the summer of 2006 confirmed all too graphically. By then, the hopes generated by the Oslo accords were but a distant memory for Israelis and Palestinians. President Bush's 'Roadmap for Peace' in 2003 promised a way forward, with two states coexisting side by side, but in the context of a Middle East unsettled by the war in Iraq. But the plan, like so many before, failed to attract momentum. The figures – over 2,000 Palestinians and 800 Israelis, as well as hundreds of Lebanese, killed since the collapse of the Camp David summit and the start of the new Intifada – spoke for themselves.

# BIBLIOGRAPHY

The Bibliography lists works which have been particularly useful in preparing this study. It does not claim to be exhaustive. The Arab–Israeli conflict has generated a vast literature, much of it highly partisan. Many of the protagonists maintain highly informative web sites, where key documents can be studied. These include the governments of Israel and the Palestinian Authority; the various branches of the American government, notably the White House, the Department of State, the Department of Defense and the Central Intelligence Agency; and the United Nations. Newspaper coverage of the conflict is extensive, with *The New York Times* and the *Guardian* particularly useful.


Anon. (Chatham House Research Staff), *Great Britain and Palestine 1915–1939* (London, 1939).

Arab Republic of Egypt, Ministry of Defence, Strategic Symposium. *The October War. 25 Years On*, 2 vols (Cairo, 1999).

Baker III, James A. and Hamilton, Lee H., *The Iraq Study Group Report* Washington (http://www.usip.org/iraq study group report/report/1206/index.html, 2006)

Begin, Menahem, *The Revolt* (London, 1979 edn).

Bein, Alex, *Theodore Herzl* (Philadelphia, PA, 1941).

Bell, J. Bowyer, *Terror out of Zion* (Dublin, 1979).

Benvenisti, Meron, *Jerusalem* (Jerusalem, 1976).

Bernadotte, Count Folke, *To Jerusalem* (London, 1951).

Bethell, Nicholas, *The Palestine Triangle* (London, 1979).

Black, Ian and Morris, Benny, *Israel's Secret Wars* (London, 1991).

Blumenthal, Sidney, *The Clinton Wars: An Insider's Account of the White House Years* (London, 2003).

Bregman, Ahron, *A History of Israel* (Basingstoke, 2003).

Bregman, Ahron, *Elusive Peace: How the Holy Land Defeated America* (London, 2005).

Brzezinski, Zbigniew, *Power and Principle* (New York, 1983).
Bromberger, Serge and Merry, S., *Secrets of Suez* (London, 1957).
Brooks, Robert, Khamais, Rassem, Nasrallah, Rami and Ghazaleh, Rana Abu, *The Wall of Annexation and Expansion: Its Impact on the Jerusalem Area* (Jerusalem, 2005).
Browning, Christopher, R., *The Origins of the Final Solution: The Evolution of Nazi Jewish Policy 1939–1942* (London, 2004).
Bullock, Alan, *Hitler and Stalin* (London, 1991).
Caradon, Lord, Goldberg, Arthur J., El-Zayyat, Mohammed H. and Eban, Abba, *UN Security Council Resolution 242: A Case Study in Diplomatic Ambiguity* (Washington, DC, 1981).
Carter, Jimmy, *Keeping Faith: Memoirs of a President* (New York, 1982).
Carter, Jimmy, *The Blood of Abraham* (Boston, MA, 1985).
Carter, Jimmy, *Palestine, Peace not Apartheid* (New York, 2006).
CIA, 2007, *Gaza Strip, CIA World Factbook, Gaza Strip* (https://CIA.gov/library/publications/the-world-factbook/geos/gz.htp).
CIA, 2007, *Israel, CIA World Factbook, Israel* (https://CIA.gov/library/publications/the-world-factbook/geos/is.htp).
CIA, 2007, *West Bank, CIA World Factbook, West Bank* (https://CIA.gov/library/publications/the -world-factbook/geos/wc.htp).
Clarke, Thurston, *By Blood and Fire: The Attack on the King David Hotel* (New York, 1981).
Clinton, Bill, *My Life* (New York, 2004).
Cmd. 1700, Statement of British Policy in Palestine, 3 June 1922.
Cmd. 5479, Palestine Royal Commission Report, 1937.
Cmd. 5957, Correspondence between Sir Henry McMahon and the Sherif Hussein of Mecca, July 1915–March 1916, 1939.
Cobban, Helena, *The Palestinian Liberation Organisation* (Cambridge, 1984).
Cohen, Michael J., *Palestine and the Great Powers, 1945–1948* (Princeton, NJ, 1982).
Copeland, Miles, *The Game of Nations* (London, 1969).
Dayan, Moshe, *Diary of the Sinai Campaign 1956* (London, 1966).
Dayan, Moshe, *Story of my Life* (London, 1976).
Dayan, Moshe, *Breakthrough* (London, 1981).
Department of State, 1978, *A Framework for Peace in the Middle East agreed at Camp David*, 17 September 1978, Department of State Bulletin, vol. 78, no. 2019, October 1978.
Department of State, 2002, Remarks at David Citadel Hotel, Secretary Colin L. Powell, Department of State, Washington,

DC, 17 April 2002 (http://www.state.gov/secretary/former/powell/remarks/2002/9478.htm.)

Department of State, 2003, *A Performance-Based Roadmap to a Permanent Two-State Solution to the Israeli–Palestinian Conflict*, Department of State, Washington, DC, 30 April 2003 (http://www.state.gov/r/pa/prs/ps2003/20062.htm.).

Department of State, 2007, Secretary Condoleeza Rice, Palestinian President Mahmoud Abbas and Israeli Prime Minister Ehud Olmert, Jerusalem, February 19 2007, Department of State, Washington, DC (http://www.state.gov/secretary/rm/2007/feb/80659.htm, 2007).

Dobroszycki, Lucjan (ed.), *The Chronicle of the Lodz Ghetto 1941–1944* (New Haven, CT, 1984).

Eban, Abba, *An Autobiography* (London, 1977).

Eden, Anthony, Full Circle (London, 1960).

Eisenhower, Dwight D., *Waging Peace* (New York, 1965).

Eitan, Raful, *A Soldier's Story* (New York, 1992).

Ennes, James M., *Assault on the Liberty* (New York, 1979).

Feldman, Shai and Rechnitz-Kijner, Heda, *Deception, Consensus and War: Israel in Lebanon* (Tel Aviv, 1984).

Findley, Paul, *They Dare to Speak Out* (Westport, CT, 1985).

Fisk, Robert, *Pity the Nation* (London, 1990).

Fisk, Robert, *The Great War for Civilisation: The Conquest of the Middle East* (London, 2005).

Fraser, T. G., *The Middle East, 1914–1979* (London, 1980).

Fraser, T. G., *Partition in Ireland, India and Palestine: Theory and Practice* (London, 1984).

Fraser, T. G., *The USA and the Middle East since World War 2* (London, 1989).

Fraser, T. G. and Murray, Donette, *America and the World since 1945* (Basingstoke, 2002).

Friedman, Thomas L., *From Beirut to Jerusalem* (New York, 1989).

Fromkin, David, *A Peace to End all Peace: Creating the Modern Middle East 1914–1922* (London, 1989).

Frum, David, *The Right Man. The Surprise Presidency of George W. Bush* (New York, 2003).

Ganin, Zvi, *Truman, American Jewry, and Israel, 1945–1948* (New York, 1979).

Gillessen, Guenther, 'Konrad Adenauer and Israel', The Konrad Adenauer Memorial Lecture (St Antony's College Oxford, n.d.).

Golan, Matti, *The Secret Conversations of Henry Kissinger* (New York, 1976).

Gowers, Andrew and Walker, Tony, *Yasser Arafat and the Palestinian Revolution* (London, rev. edn 1991).

Halevy, Efraim, *Man in the Shadows, Inside the Middle East Crisis with a Man who Led the Mossad* (London, 2006).

Harkabi, Yeshoshafat, *Israel's Fateful Decisions* (London, 1988).

Hart, Alan, *Arafat* (London, 1984).

Heikal, Mohamed, *The Road to Ramadan* (Glasgow, 1976).

Hersh, Seymour M., *The Samson Option: Israel, America and the Bomb* (New York, 1991).

Herzl, Theodor, *The Jewish State* (London, 1972 edn).

Insight Team, *The Yom Kippur War* (London, 1975).

Israel, Ministry of Foreign Affairs, 2007, Winograd Commission submits Interim Report, 30 April 2007 (http://www.mfa.gov.il/MFA/Government/Communiques/2007/Winograd+Inquiry+Commission+submits+Interim+Report+30-Apr-2007.htm).

Jansen, Michael, *The Battle of Beirut* (London, 1982).

Kamel, Mohamed Ibrahim, *The Camp David Accords* (London, 1986).

Katzmann, Kenneth, *Iran: U.S. Concerns and Policy Responses*, Congressional Research Service, The Library of Congress, Washington, DC (http://fpc.state.gov/c18185.htm, 2006).

Kenen, I. L., *Israel's Defense Line* (Buffalo, NY, 1981).

Kimche, David and Bawly, Dan, *The Sandstorm* (London, 1968).

Kirk, George, *The Middle East 1945–1950* (Oxford, 1954).

Kissinger, Henry, *Years of Upheaval* (London, 1982).

Kissinger, Henry, *Years of Renewal* (London, 1999).

Kollek, Teddy, with his son Amos Kollek, *For Jerusalem* (New York, 1978).

Kyle, Keith, *Suez* (London, 1991).

Kyle, Keith and Peters, Joel (eds), *Whither Israel?* (London, 1993).

Laqueur, Walter, *The Road to War* (London, 1968).

Laqueur, Walter, *A History of Zionism* (London, 1989 edn).

Lloyd, Selwyn, *Suez 1956* (London, 1978).

Louis, W. Roger, *The British Empire in the Middle East 1945–1951* (Oxford, 1984).

Louis, W. Roger and Owen, Roger (eds), *Suez 1956: The Crisis and its Consequences* (Oxford, 1989).

Makovsky, David, *Making Peace with the PLO: The Rabin Government's Road to the Oslo Accord* (Boulder, 1996).

Mark, Clyde R., *Israel's Proposal to Withdraw from Gaza*, Congressional Research Service, The Library of Congress, Washington, DC (http://fpc.state.gov/c18185.htm, 2005).

Mattar, Philip, *The Mufti of Jerusalem* (New York, 1988).

Meir, Golda, *My Life* (London, 1975).

Mendes-Flohr, R. Paul (ed.), *A Land of Two Peoples: Martin Buber on Jews and Arabs* (Oxford, 1983).

Migdalovitz, Carol, *The Middle East Peace Talks*, Congressional Research Service, The Library of Congress, Washington, DC (http://fpc.state.gov/c18185.htm, 2006).

Mitchell, George, 2001, Sharm El-Sheikh Fact-Finding Committee Report, Washington, DC, 30 April 2001 (http://www.state.gov/p/nea/rls/ppt/3060.htm).

Morris, Benny, *The Birth of the Palestinian Refugee Problem* (Cambridge, 1987).

Nachmani, A., *Great Power Discord in Palestine* (London, 1987).

Nutting, Anthony, *No End of a Lesson: The Story of Suez* (London, 1967).

Oren, Michael B., *Six Days of War: June 1967 and the Making of the Modern Middle East* (Oxford, 2002).

Oren, Michael B., *Power, Faith and Fantasy. America and the Middle East 1776 to the Present* (New York, 2007).

Palumbo, Michael, *The Palestinian Catastrophe* (London, 1987).

Palumbo, Michael, *Imperial Israel* (London, 1990).

Pappe, Ilan, *A History of Modern Palestine: One Land, Two Peoples* (Cambridge, 2004).

Parker, Richard B., 'The June War: Whose Conspiracy?', *Journal of Palestine Studies*, vol. XXI, no. 4 (1992).

Peretz, Don, *Intifada* (Boulder, CO, 1990).

Pina, Aaron D., *Fatah and Hamas: The New Palestinian Factional Reality*, Congressional Research Service, The Library of Congress, Washington, DC (http://fpc.state.gov/c18185.htm, 2006).

Pollack, Kenneth M., *Arabs at War: Military Effectiveness, 1948–1991* (Lincoln and London, 2002).

Prados, Alfred B., *Lebanon*, Congressional Research Service, The Library of Congress, Washington, DC (http://fpc.state.gov/c18185.htm, 2006).

Quandt, William B., *Decade of Decisions: American Policy Toward the Arab–Israeli Conflict 1967–1976* (Berkeley and Los Angeles, 1977).

Quandt, William B., *Camp David* (Washington, DC, 1986).

Quandt, William B, *Peace Process: American Diplomacy and the Arab–Israeli Conflict since 1967* (Washington, DC, 2005).

Rabin, Yitzhak, *The Rabin Memoirs* (Boston, MA, 1976).

Reagan, Ronald, *An American Life* (New York, 1990).

Reitlinger, Gerald, *The Final Solution* (London, 1953).

Rhodes James, Robert, *Anthony Eden* (London, 1986).

Rodinson, Maxime, *Israel and the Arabs* (London, 1968).

Rogan, Eugene L. and Shlaim, Avi (eds), *The War for Palestine: Rewriting the History of 1948* (Cambridge, 2001).

Roseman, Mark, *The Villa, The Lake, The Meeting: Wannsee and the Final Solution* (London, 2002).

Ross, Dennis, *The Missing Peace: The Inside Story of the Fight for Middle East Peace* (New York, 2004).

Sachar, Howard M., *A History of Israel* (Oxford, 1976).

Sadat, Anwar el-, *In Search of Identity* (London, 1978).

Said, Edward W., *The End of the Peace Process* (London, 2000).

Schiff, Ze'ev and Ya'ari, Ehud, *Israel's Lebanon War* (London, 1985).

Schiff, Ze'ev and Ya'ari, Ehud, *Intifada* (New York, 1989).

Schneiderman, Harry, and Fine, Morris T. (eds), *The American Jewish Year Book 5704*, vol. 48 (Philadelphia, 1943).

Sharon, Ariel, with David Chanoff, *Warrior* (New York, 2001).

Sheehan, Edward R. E., *The Arabs, Israelis, and Kissinger* (New York, 1976).

Shlaim, Avi, *The Iron Wall: Israel and the Arab World* (London, 2000).

Silver, Eric, *Begin* (London, 1984).

Siniora, Hanna, 'An Analysis of the Current Revolt', *Journal of Palestine Studies*, vol. XVII, no. 3 (1988).

Snetsinger, John, *Truman, the Jewish Vote and the Creation of Israel* (Stanford, CA, 1974).

Spiegel, Steven L., *The Other Arab–Israeli Conflict* (Chicago, 1985).

State of Israel, 2004 (http://www.knesset.gov.il/process/docs/DisengageSharon_eng_revised.htm).

Stein, Leonard, *The Balfour Declaration* (London, 1961).

Stephens, Robert, *Nasser* (London, 1971).

Tivnan, Edward, *The Lobby: Jewish Political Power and American Foreign Policy* (New York, 1987).

United Nations, Report of the Secretary-General pursuant to General Assembly Resolution ES-10/10 (Jenin Report), 2002).

Wasserstein, Bernard, *Divided Jerusalem: The Struggle for the Holy City* (London, 2001).

White House, 2002a, President to Send Secretary Powell to Middle East, 4 April 2002, The White House, Washington, DC (http://www.whitehouse.gov/news/releases/2002/0420020404-1.html).

White House, 2002b, President Bush Calls for New Palestinian Leadership, 24 June 2002, The White House, Washington, DC (http://www.whitehouse.gov/news/releases/2002/06/20020624-3.html).

White House, 2003a, President Discusses the Future of Iraq, 26 February 2003, The White House, Washington, DC (http://www.whitehouse.gov/news/releases/2003/02/20030226-11.html).

White House, 2003b, President Discusses Roadmap for Peace in the Middle East, 14 March 2003, The White House, Washington, DC (http://www.whitehouse.gov/news/releases/2003/03/20030314-4.html).

White House, 2007, President Bush discusses the Middle East, 16 July 2007, The White House, Washington, DC (http://www.whitehouse.gov/news/releases/2007/07/200701716-7.html).

www.un.org/unrwa/publications/statistics (2003).

# Index